Editorial

Chapman 100/1 was a huge success, including over 100 authors and many illustrators. A general invitation was issued to authors who had appeared previously and anyone else who cared to submit work. The result was a deluge, and so a double issue was necessary. The "party between two covers" has turned, in fact, into a party between six covers: this is part two of three, because the celebrations will run into *Chapman* 104 also.

But a magazine must change and develop. In recognition of this, we have successfully applied for Lottery funding to redesign the magazine, set up an interactive website and market it in ways hitherto impossible. We still have to raise about £5,000 in matching funding to realise our hopes. We also have successfully applied to the Writers Factory for an ambitious programme of publication, beginning soon with a new book, provisionally entitled *Lure*, by Dilys Rose, and featuring such *Chapman* regulars as Angus Calder, George Gunn, Stuart B Kelly and others.

Our *Chapman* New Writing Series has made a real difference to its writers. The Wild Women Series has put Magi Gibson on the map, her *Wild Women of a Certain Age* quickly sold out and is now reprinted. Janet Paisley's *Ye Cannae Win* has also sold out (to be reprinted soon). *Last Tango with Magritte* by Lydia Robb introduces a new author to a new constituency, establishing her in the line of Helen B Cruickshank, Violet Jacob and Marion Angus as an sensitive woman writing out of the heart of her experience, urban and rural. These poets do not fall dead from the presses, but instead achieve a new prominence, a recognition, always well-deserved.

The lottery award from the Audience Development Scheme, and commissioning writers via the Writers Factory will allow us to publish more better. While we cannot, given the general lack of funding, over-extend ourselves, we can use this money to make everything more self-coherent, more intrinsically effective, to the benefit both of our writers and our readers. The 'big' Scottish publishers have mostly stopped publishing poetry or drama, and it falls to Luath Press, Diehard and others such as ourselves to carry that function. Poetry does, I still believe after all these years, in a small way change the world, make our lives richer, better, which is why we will continue to do this – even in the most disadvantageous of circumstances.

Here we celebrate William Neill, 80 last year, one of the most underrated wordsmiths of the 20th century. Scots is his native tongue, but he excels in English also, and in Gaelic, becoming, after George Campbell Hay, a 'makar in thrie leids', learning Gaelic, both the language and the scholarship underlying it. Neill represents a continuous line from the great Greek dramatists to now and is truly international in range. His work includes his translations of Homer, Giuseppe Belli and many others. He has always raged in a good cause, and in this issue we reprint two important essays in which he has raged, not against the dying of any night, but against the extinguishing of the lights of the future. At first glance, his work may seem backward-looking, but his vision, perhaps too ruthlessly and dogmatically expressed at times, is unerring, true, and uncompromising. To go forward, we need that sense of continuum, of things bigger than ourselves. The alternative is the kind of limbo complained about by Hayden Murphy, in his important statement here about the Edinburgh Book Festival, that fame, celebrity, marketability, must not obscure that real, small, but potent light, that comes from a mind such as William Neill's.

One justification, if there needed one, for the *Chapman* New Writing Series was our publication of *Avoiding the Gods* by Ian Abbot. It was the second book we published, being inexperienced at the time, with very bad binding so that the pages had an alarming tendency to fall apart. Alexander Hutchison refers to a reading of Ian's at the National Museum, in which he over-ran his time dramatically, carried away with the joy of being published and at last having an audience. But, six months later, he was dead. Some unpublished poems appear here, and we will produce a definitive 'collected poems'. He was just getting into his stride when he hit 45 (he was always secretive about his age). But his presence still stalks the consciousness of all who knew him. And his poems are like the proverbial 'Thought-foxes' (*pace* Ted Hughes), exploding into the reader's mind.

The present and past double numbers have concentrated mainly on regular contributors to *Chapman* over the years. With 104 we look to the future, to the new, and subsequent issues will take us to a new place entirely. An important anchor of 104 will be a version of the lecture, 'Language and Freedom' by Alastair Reid at the Talbot Rice Gallery in February this year, and also new poems by Hugh MacDiarmid, recently unearthed by John Manson in an entirely unselfish, unfunded work of scholarship.

Yes, the literary world in this small country is beginning to look possible; that you can survive, survive, and still be a magazine- or small- publisher, that our authors will get an audience. In response to the positive feed-back to the articles republished from *Chapman* 16 in 100-1, we are here re-issuing articles from *Chapman* 35-6 – *The State of Scotland: A Predicament for the Scottish Writer?*. This issue was published in 1983; readers can judge for themselves how much has changed, or not.

Which brings me to the leading article by Donald Smith. We now have a brand new parliament, a new Scottish Executive. Literature has been the spring of so much in Scotland; it is now time for it to be properly funded. Printing presses can no longer be relegated to someone's spare bed-room; in this 'professionalised' world, we can't function at all if we don't do things well, but the money is still not forthcoming. The Scottish Arts Council has done its best – over to the politicians. Much has been done for 'the living writer', but little for the publishing and marketing infrastructure, in particular the magazines. It is time we were properly funded for what we do.

Meanwhile, we will continue with our work and, I must emphasise, how important the support of writers and readers is, in particular towards raising the money we need to implement our successful Lottery Award. Please help if you can. Small voices like ours, crying in whatever wilderness, have made a lot of rain. Small voices, in chorus, make a lot of noise.

Chapman 102 3

Centenary Double Issue Part 2 (of 3)

1.50

(15)

Subscribe to Chapman

Scotland's Quality Literary Magazine

Ensure you have all 3 parts of
the centenary celebration!

One year UK subscription only £18

Centenary package £20 (inc. p + p)

For existing subscribers,
free subscription for a friend!

See back page for contact details ...

Time for Literature?

Scottish Literature after the First Parliament

Donald Smith

Reading the letters of Henry James you wonder how he ever found time to write his copious novels. There were nights when James Boswell wept for tiredness as he sat up into the small hours keeping his Journal up-to-date and dreading the hangover to come. To have Virginia Woolf's novels without the Diaries and the Essays would be to miss out on the complex world of linguistic artifice and literary relationship from which the prose was created. Literature does not occur in a vacuum. Those background relationships were once quaintly acknowledged as the world of 'Letters', but behind that phrase is the full inheritance of European Humanism – learning and language, essays, literature and interpretation. Literary culture was seen as transcending political boundaries and uniting a community of understanding and human endeavour, although the relationships of European Humanism with non-Christian cultures remain problematic. Personal letters have all but disappeared in favour of the instant junk we call emails. To love language as much as life it is now almost essential to become a Thomas Merton-like recluse. The meanings of literary language need to be savoured on ear, mind and tongue but technology is increasingly circumscribing that space. Even as we draw illusory comfort from the celebrity status of some writers, the social contexts of literature are under pressure.

The savouring of language is the corollary of the many means by which associative language is formed – means of which technology is impatient. Stevenson said that he owed his style to 'the Covenanting writers'. What he meant is that, behind his supple prose and its dramatic psychology, were the Puritan divines, the authorised version of the Bible, and their interaction over generations with spoken Scots, oral poetry and storytelling. Stevenson was also the heir of the Scottish Enlightenment and its formal English prose. In short, it took centuries to create the linguistic conditions from which Stevenson fashioned his own ethos and literary style.

Linguistic globalisation puts that slow burn at risk, not just because apparent diversity is eroded, but because undertones are lost. If time and attention to language are constricted then there is a thinning of the web of words. The contexts of literature or conversation, storytelling, drama, film and television, provide the essential base for creative writing. I start with these obvious points to stress that any discussion of Scottish literature belongs in a global context. The vitality of our literary culture is tied to the scope available in the literature of a small nation in an era of rapid social and economic change. What freedoms are there and what possibility?

The positive answer is that small nations have a capacity to nourish continuity, sustain diversity and contribute to a world of shared difference, rather than imposed conformity. The small nation may constitute a community of speech and thought out of which literature can grow. Conversation may still have public and private dimensions, storytelling remains a distinctive seedbed, and readership is still an aspect of citizenship as well as a source of pleasure. Democracy and ideas, spoken and written language, writers and readers, can enjoy a robust interaction. Such conditions do not necessarily produce fine literature, but they are contributory factors. The key centres for Modernism were metropolitan, but the post-modern world enables different cultural geographies.

Scottish literature has long European tap-roots. It is a vigorous if turbulent relation of English literature, and profoundly international in scope, not least because Scots have scattered worldwide in pursuit of wealth, religion, adventure, or all three. The career of Robert Louis Stevenson is instructive here: Scots stylist, passionate Francophile, American adventurer, and native by adoption of Samoa, where he finally came to rest.

Scotland has its own linguistic and cultural tensions which perpetually possess or are possessed by a creative uncertainty that drives us outwards, open and curious as to others quests for identity and their creative refashioning of literary traditions. Enlightenment and vernacular, Scots and Gaelic, Edinburgh and Glasgow, rural and urban, indigenous and multicultural: Scottish literature and language are on the edge of international change, because, not in spite of these tensions. Such environments help distinguish between a true internationalism and deracinated globalisation.

One random example is the poetry of George Campbell Hay, recently emerged from the obscurity of this 20th century poet's fractured life in the superb *Collected Poems and Songs of George Campbell Hay/ Deòrsa Mac Iain Dheòrsa* edited by Michel Byrne. During World War II, Hay, already tri-lingual in Scots, English and Gaelic, learned Arabic. In his long war poem 'Mochtàr is Dúghall', the poet creates a deeply-felt fusion of traditional Gaelic and Arabic poetry in the crucible of modern warfare.

Turas Mhochtàir

Bu ghiorra an duan, a Mhochtàir, dhuit.
Cha do ghin do fhreumhach blàithean;
cha do bhàrc meas do shnodhaich air bàrrgheug;
do bhith, is gann gun do bhlàthaich
bean no clann, luchd gaoil no càirdean
aig lughad is aig luaths do làithean.

Treiseag dhuit ri uilinn Òmair,
treiseag sna raointean 's mu na cròithean,
treiseag an caidreabh do mhnà pòsta,
is dh'fhalbh thu, 's cha b'ann gu deònach,
air thuras gu craos a' mhòrtair.

Clach aoil a' sgagadh fon teas,
  sgreuthadh nan creag 'na ghathan duslaich;
an ùir bhruante suas 'na smùid
  fo chrùidhean aindeonach nam muileid.

An nathair adharcach 's gach gleann;

an dipeardan is srannraich chuileag;
druim mar sgian gun neul, gun deò
's na sgiathalain a' crònan uime.

Am Bàs grad am measg nam preas,
ri feallfhalach air slios gach tulaich,
a' faire o sgàil' an alltain chèir,
air Saghuàn fo ghrèin gun dubhar.

Mokhtârs Journey

Shorter was your song, Mokhtâr./ Your roots yielded no blossom;/ the fruit of your sap never burst forth on a topmost branch;/ hardly did your being give warmth / to wife or children, loved ones or friends,/ for the brevity and haste of your days.

A short while you had at Omar's elbow,/ a short while in the fields and at the folds,/ a short while in the intimate company of your spouse,/ and you left, not willingly, / on a journey that led you to the gaping maw of the mortar.

Limestone splintering in the heat,/ the shrivelling of rocks in its dust-speckled rays;/ pounded soil up in puffs/ under the recalcitrant hooves of the mules.

The horned viper in every defile;/ the shimmering heat and buzzing of flies;/ a knife-sharp ridge without cloud or breath of air,/ circled by the droning planes.

Nimble Death among the thickets,/ ready to ambush on the flank of every hill,/ keeping watch from the shade of the gloomy wee burn,/ on shadeless sunbaked Saghouan.

So Jebel Zaghouen, a mountain in Tunisia, becomes as powerful a symbol as the green hills of Campbell Hay's beloved Kintyre which are celebrated in the poet's deeply traditional Gaelic memorialisation of landscape. But the impulse is immediate and historic as the desert landscape is transformed from a nomadic and sometimes raiding backdrop to a theatre of technological conflict – North Africa then, Iraq now.

To a large extent global circumstances will shape what happens in Scotland, regardless of what we as a community do. The first Scottish Parliament and Executive have certainly presumed this, whether consciously or unconsciously. But communities, not least small nations, can create favourable or unfavourable conditions, and these have been clearly laid out in the *Literature Nation* strategy which the Scottish Arts Council Literature Committee and the Literature Forum for Scotland have distilled from extensive consultation and discussion with writers and literary organisations:

- to nurture writers
- to encourage readership, storytelling, poetry and drama
- to recognise and support Scottish literature as an international forum
- to increase public awareness and debate
- to sell ourselves more vigorously and effectively to publishers, the media and booksellers worldwide
- to exploit literature as an economic asset
- to be more informed about our achievements past and present
- to foster imaginative experience and intellectual curiosity through education, and in political discourse.

The emergence of a Literature Forum for Scotland is, in itself, a significant development. As the Scottish Arts Council's Literature Department faced the challenges of severe underfunding and benign neglect at governmental level, it commissioned a rigorous audit of the work and resources of literature organisations in Scotland. To make this exercise and any potential follow-up properly effective SAC needed the support and understanding of its own 'client' organisations. Under its quietly effective Chair, Ann Matheson, the Literature Committee of SAC appealed for such support and received it in a rare demonstration of consensus.

Even more remarkable was that the concensus achieved in 2001 continued with the formation of a sustainable Literature Forum to foster cooperation. More organisations representing writers and libraries were drawn in. The existence of the Forum facilitated wide consultation and agreement on a national literature strategy entitled *Literature Nation,* and a collective resolve to implement that strategy now endorsed and promulgated by the Scottish Arts Council. The Literature Forum is fully appreciative of the support demonstrated by SAC, albeit within its own limited means, yet the literature organisations remain unsure about their subordination to a generalised and sometimes confusing catch-all term 'the arts'.

As Chair of the Literature Forum I have been in personal contact with all Scotland's political parties and with every MSP. I am struck by the recognition of literature's role and the wide support for our objectives. Yet at the same time virtually no-one knew of the officially published and promoted Scottish Arts Council Literature Strategy. In fact, many seemed unaware that literature was subsumed within the arts, which may explain why literature was omitted from the Scottish Executive's arts strategy *Creating the Future; Minding the Past*. The wide public support for literature is to a large extent obscured rather than enhanced by, the generalised 'arts' labelling.

Another area of potential confusion lies in education. While SAC has vigorously promoted the arts in education over recent years, its effects have been concentrated on the notional 15% of 5-14 curriculum time devoted to the arts! However, 40% of curriculum time is devoted to language and literacy. The very focus on 'literacy' that may be frustrating to expressive arts is a gigantic opportunity for the literature, readership and creative language aims promoted by the Literature Forum. Schools are busy places and we cannot afford to be diverted by any confusions or mixed messages.

This paradox suggests that it is time for a devolution settlement for literature. Whether within the Scottish Arts Council or as an independent national institution, there is an urgent need for a 'Literature Council for Scotland' to relate, support and promote the outstanding work of Scotland's writers and literary organisations, locally, nationally and internationally. The period when Scotland's literature could be adequately served as a junior partner in SAC's funding line-up is over. What Scottish literature needs now is an infusion of hard cash and a ferment of creativity. A host of 20th century writers have imagined us into this place of opportunity. It is time for literature in Scotland to help make time for literature globally.

Literature Forum membership and details from Sophy Dale, Scottish Arts Council

Ken Cockburn

The Chief Executive, or The King of Jordan

The Chief Executive, or The King of Jordan
to his subordinates, and not to his face,
is on the road. He is planning a surprise
for whichever department is earmarked for today.

His car has been parked in the managers' car-park.
Its distinguishing features have been concealed.
Laid out like a corpse, his body is wound
in black drapes, his face framed

by flowers. The hidden cameras are running.
Provocative and ruthless yet also magnanimous,
not without interest does he await
the functionaries' reaction.

Judas I-IV

Some wine. Him and Peter, in deep. I'm sent with the reserves for supplies and meet a woman, vaguely familiar, pair of Rottweilers in tow. I'm reassured nothing unfortunate will happen if ... hardly a nod and it's done.

Not pleasant. What have I done? They're bluffing. And He's too resourceful.

*

Relatively painless. They were asleep, no lookout - then panic, some of them lashing out but He cancelled their arms. I kissed Him and imagined I belonged again but He was weak and they marched him away unresisting.

He's run out of time. I clocked Peter, following at a safe distance.

*

The world reduced to this: a misshapen field full of rubbish; cornelian; a sturdy elder, about to flower; a length of strong rope. My words dealt with repentance, Peter's with denial: his rock, my tree.

There is no-one now who can offer me forgiveness. Don't think about it any more.

*

Here comes in Judas,
Judas is ma name,
If ye pit no siller in ma bag,
For guidsake mind oor wame!

Hogmanay. To the glamour of the treble zero – a toast!

Hungry birds, dormant seeds, the way these numbers are spun. I'll take everything – or whatever you can see us.

Converse

It's policemen who listen to Radio Tay I believe so they tell me
something rhythmic with recognisable pattern and form

delightful bluntness
to those of us from the boonies

that's just humanity and what have you
an awful scrambled egg of a building.

And Only the Snow

by Tina Stroheker, translated from the German

Look at the wall
the white wall
it's an ironed sheet
an iceberg
a sheet of paper
it is a bare wall.
It's snowing and snowing
look at the snow
it's a curtain of snow.
Listen, how quiet it became
outside and inside
it is quiet now.
Take the paper
and write at last
the words for white
in white crayon.

Football Haiku

by Arne Rautenberg, translated from the German

Like an away game:
Losing again, the records
Show only the 'nil'.

Hey, you, arsehole! Get
In goal! screamed the wee-est one
The first time I played.

A kick-out soaring
Way over the centre-line:
That's how good I feel

Football Haiku

by René Schoemakers, translated from the German

This is how it starts
Kick-off The action Full-time
This is how it ends

Descended from the
Pufferfish: team coach Dietmar's
Bulging corduroy

Me, once a goalie
Dietmar: like a barricade
put up just too late

The football father's
Metaphysical insult:
To be caught offside

Lord above bring it
Pissing down for United
Will just take the crap

Offside hard to tell
Video replays follow
The foot's good fortune

On the terraces
The flags burn: a quarrel with
God and the woodwork

Supporters fired up
By the ball's flight: in judgement
With God and the posts

Completely over
The line: thus providing proof
Of God's existence

Grown into the knee
Cinders from the pitches of
An opposing world.

Chant on going up:
We'll support you ever more:
Chant on going down

Alec Finlay

"Yes Haiku" – "No Fanku"

silent office
fax paper
unfurls

soft trees
still
beside us

Koi
doing their thing –
vague radio

Winter Session –
the Parliament of the Birds
silent

burnished
among branches
a blinding orb

The yellow plant
has eaten
its name

the squirrels behave
exactly
as they should

the wind blows
straight through
our little house

up close
all the bubbles
trapped in the ice

high in anti-
oxidants
the poet's tea

pools
on the swings
a flitting

loving the dirt
under her nails

scolding the kids
holding back
a smile

sleeping apart
sharing
a bug

Renga

The Little Coldsfoot

by Gerry Loose, Colin Will, Alec Finlay, Elspeth Murray and David Sandreuter

Rhododendron blossom
already dropping –
spring arrives unseen

the first mowing –
a scent of oil

a hooded girl
in moonlight blue
walks on the grass

soft trees
still beside us

speak to the magpie
listen to the dove
sing to yourself

the heat on my head
long days

in a glass –
blue sky
sunk in the wine.

she dances on a bridge
until led away

10,000 leaves
he sees
only her eyes

the wind blows straight through
our little house

chaff scatters –
soon we'll bake
new loaves

the woodstack creaks, settles –
it will hold

moon is not an option –
every bloody night
the same stupid mask

glass after glass
the laughter comes more often

in the cold
the winter verse
comes easy

buttered parsnips –
warm and filling

satisfying –
a sharp knife
through fresh fruit

the best time
to plant dreams

up before the prize blooms
the little coltsfoot
's yellow

the old man knows spring
moves hand to heart.

a nijuin renga *in Spring:*

Royal Botanic Garden Edinburgh
April 6, 2002

Participants:
Master poet, Gerry Loose; Host poet, Colin Will; Coordinator, Alec Finlay; Elspeth Murray, David Sandreuter

Verse Attributions:
1-GL; 2-CW; 3-EM; 4-AF; 5-AF; 6-GL; 7-EM; 8-CW; 9-GL; 10-AF; 11-CW; 12-DS; 13-CW; l4-GL; l5-AF; 16-CW; 17-EM; 18-CW; 19-GL; 20-comp.

A Year from Now

a selection of football haiku from Croatia, Germany and Scotland

first snowflakes –
amongst them flying
a football.
Zoran Doderovic

goaless match –
only the birds
singing.
Alenka Zorman

gooooaaaalll!
No-one notices
the rain.
Dragan J Ristic

Kantrida!
Sing me a song
of the gulls & the sea.
Borivoj Bukva

the first goal –
fireworks and birds
take to the sky.
Alenka Zorman

beneath the floodlights –
a winger's shadow darts
in four directions.
Matthew Paul

Alan Spence

Four Haiku

spring snow
trying its best
not to fall

it's just the wind
in my eyes, she says,
explaining the tears

high summer –
strawberry birthmark
on the old man's face

one small dog –
two hundred geese
panicked into flight

W Gordon Smith

Haiku

Glasgow is a place
For driving, whoring, swearing,
Glasgow is a place.

By noticing your
Idiosyncracies I
Lend them distinction

Caledonia
Mediterranean skies
And arctic friendships

Survivors of War
Are not specially adept at
Surviving the peace

Suicide won't do
Because there is nobody
To leave a note to...

Two black candles, we
Send shadows dancing in the
Most private places

A special kind of
Optimist believes that tears
Can wash the slate clean

Spring's clear promise is
Sullied by the decadent
Stench of hyacinth

Writing with oblique
Nibs gives an interesting
Slant to my thinking

History is how
We think it happened, we don't
Have to believe it

Summer is best for
Roses and rheumatism
And looking at breasts

Standing alone on
The meridian I feel
Neither here nor there

Recognising love
In another is maybe
Only reflection

Alan Spence calls his
Book of haiku "ah!" – I think
I should call mine "so!"

The sick man's body
Is at rest but his eyes look
Over his shoulder

I ask no special
Favour of the world, but it
Should ask one of me

You don't know your own
Strength, he complained, so she
Got off him, and left.

I long for your hands
These white winter nights to put
A torch to my fire

W Gordon Smith, courtesy of Jay Gordon Smith

One early day the
Sun will come and claim
Its inheritance

The jiggling tit is
Not part of an erotic
Mirage; it is real

This small stream of words
Without tributaries flows
Sluggishly, but flows

The sun climbs so high
Above me today that I
Become my shadow

Hugh MacDiarmid at
Eighty five – a volcano
Still belching brimstone

Time was when time passed;
Now, alas, watch it take to
Its heels and gallop

Logic is fine, till
It assassinates ideas
And murders my dreams

The squirrel seems too
Aristocratic to be
Rat with bushy bum

Equanimity
Is the capacity to
Shut out silent screams

I long for winter
When I can pee my private
Haiku in the snow

Even if we were
Struck dumb we could speak to
each
Other with Mozart

These lines are written
For you out there because
I think them in here

I am moved to write
And use indelible ink
In case it is good

In the house of the
New widow destiny has
Unfinished business

America, land
of the free, listen to your
Children rattling chains

I don't care who tells
Me that you are dead, I shall
Ask for you – in case ...

A haiku is not
An elevated Scottish
Milk-making machine

Some haiku I write
In waterproof ink so that
Tears cannot smudge them

White mice descend on
Paper-napkin parachutes;
Should we surrender

The band plays – it is
Sad so many people march,
So few sing and dance

It is too trusting
To believe that a road must
Always lead somewhere

The Somme, July 1, 1916
Mud, bayonets, and
Lily-white boys staining the
Earth a poppy red

Even my ashes
Should stay gritty enough to
Be irritating

Drumming syllables
With my fingertips I send
You secret haiku

Conker boys swagger
Home, jerseys stuffed,
pockets full, Capitalists all

If I could buy
A packet of stars I would
Sow the sky for you

When I'm in Venice
Can I order you a glass
Staircase to the stars

Stars you were, and are,
Gordon, and Jay still sings
to the stars. (JH)

John Murray

Tree Haiku

Oak

Maker of galls
Maker of joists and masts
Ant armies on the move

Beech

Vaulted canopy rising
From muscular gothic,
Sandals pace the brown leaves

Sloe

White flower on thornwood
Makes the walking stick,
Bears black and bitter fruit

Rowan

Bumpers of spring wine
Bitter jelly for deer meat
Ghosts at bay

Birch

Supple twigs in a soft breeze
Bundled to chastise,
White paper bark peels

Elder

Hollow stemmed
Musky and purple mouthed
Pea shooter and flute

Aspen

Music in the wind top
Martyrs pinned to your wood
Suckers from underground

Ash

Black buds slow to leaf
And slow to shed
Hammer wood, hard as frost

Haw

Drops of blood in the hedge
Scent of the cowshed
The old homestead

Yew

Pinned to the grave
Arrow across millennia,
Green in your own season

Willow

Wood too wet to burn
Weaves baskets
Sends balls over boundaries

Box

Chessmen moves
Confined to the board
Parterre to bigger visions

Reservoir

1 *There is nothing to say*
because there is nothing more to be said.

There is nothing to see
because there is nothing more to be seen.

There is nothing to hear
because there is nothing more to be heard.

There is nothing to feel
because there is nothing more to be felt.

There is nothing to reach
because there is nothing more to be reached.

There is no sliver of hope
between passive night and active light.

How can something so replete
become so bereft?

How can windows
collapse so complete?

in the fingers and thumbs
of keyboard error,

in the swordsman's feint,
in the cardsharper's slight,

in the twinkling of an eye.
in the batting of an eyelid.

Peerless eyes
that held worlds beyond measure,

dulled by the deceit of surface detail
beneath a soul's shifting flux,

are shoals of silver darlings
gone from inland shores.

Oases of enchantment
are deserts of disenchantment,

The spring of our enlightenment
is the winter of our disaffection.

2 I walk the length of the loch
scooped from the hills,
proud above the plain

and its fossil city, blunt headed,
fish tailed and vertebral,

beached as an ark.

Summer's zenith,
and the city streets have flushed
the upland pools away.

And in the dry margins
revealed by the downdraw
of drought.

Broken the pipe that drained the land.
Broken the road that sought the town.
Broken the bell that called the mass.
Broken the fence that held the beast.
Broken the stem that bore the birch.

And in those dry margins
revealed by the downdraw
of drought.

A tiny bead, an oyster pearl
a gem clasped in a rood mass of lava

an immaculate refracting sphere
of water pure, perfect and complete.

Perfect reflection
of imperfect world

borne between
epidermal layers of clay,

forming in its plenitude
as like multitudes cohere

a ribbon of silk
from a string of jewels.

Tiny pebbles tumble down
among the finer grains.

Here lies the whole of life
in all its effluvial joy and joylessness.

3 I roll a ball of clay
in the palm of my hand.

This is how it must have been
all those undreamt of years ago.

I could contain the water's
virginity in this.

I could make a pot of this
and mark its surface, whilst still soft,

with my thumbnail,

first one way, and then another,

ringwise around
its yet uncertain flesh,

then put it aside to harden
by the heat of my hearth.

4 And as I walk barefoot
across the sands and gravels

peat and rock, marbled substrates
of forgotten worlds, but new revealed,

I feel the curve of the globe
within the mould of my instep

and I know that
I must make myself whole,

make myself
in my own image again.

Replenish the absence
your presence has left.

Uplift my beaker
with both hands

stretch up to the sky
and drink deep the blessed draft

drink deep the philtre of my being,
commune with myself anew.

Touch the clay with the tip of my tongue
See beads of water winking there
Hear tiny bubbles singing there
Smell the long trek out of rock
Taste the fountain breath.

Lover-Diver

I gather wildflowers from the meadows of your eyebrow.
I brush through the bamboo groves of your eyelid.

I glissade down the curve of your cornea.
I dangle my feet over the rim of your iris.

I dip my heels into your aqueous humour
and dive into your vitreous interior.

Distant flares sparkle and sputter
from the upturned bowl of your retina.

I cannot escape the gravity of your orbit.
I'm trapped in the amber of your eye.

Diessenhofen Bridge

Regi Claire

Leon slumped into the nearest chair in the function suite, ignoring his niece's stare. His shirt felt damp after the heat outside. His tie hung like a cut-off noose. He gave it a few half-hearted tugs, then glanced round the rest of the audience – mostly relatives several decades younger than himself.

The birthday concert for his cousin Anna had already begun. Some ensemble he had never heard of. The violinist and cellist looked in danger of dislocating their shoulders, and the pianist kept tossing his head like a prophet in ecstasy. Leon blushed with embarrassment at their histrionics.

As the Mozart piece approached its climax, he wiped his brow with a handkerchief. There was a *föhn* again and the air sultry beyond relief. Through the wide-open French windows the Alps seemed etched into the sky, almost within reach. For a moment, he fancied he could smell the scent of apple blossom from the hotel's small orchard. His palms still felt prickly after pressing against the roughness of its chest-high wall. On the other side the waiter he'd spoken to at lunch, a young man from Greece, had been lying spread-eagled in the grass, fast asleep.

Leon cocked his head at the woman seated next to him. Katja was strikingly ugly, skeleton thin, with a Gothic flourish for a nose. But she had produced two nice little daughters. "The state," he used to tell Lilou, "would collapse if everyone behaved with *your* kind of irresponsibility. Families are the backbone of any social order." That was why, as a teacher, he had always exhorted the parents of his pupils to stay together at all cost, for the children's sake. Lilou being Lilou, of course, used to laugh in his face. "You try it some time, Uncle," she'd taunt.

The Mozart had finished and everyone started clapping. Leon winced when Katja flashed one of her brusque smiles. He could feel the red wine scouring his insides. Not that he had drunk much, the Bordeaux clearly wasn't one of the better years and he'd left his second glass half full. Lilou and some of the younger people must have been rather less discerning, judging by the cluster of empty bottles on their table.

Someone touched him on the shoulder. "Enjoyed that, Leon? You're the art expert here." Marcel, Katja's husband, was leaning towards him.

It was Marcel who had engaged the trio for his mother's 80th birthday party so Leon nodded and, gazing into his eyes, said, "A vigorous interpretation, yes. Full of youthful passion." Another nod, then a frown for emphasis. "Thank you for the treat, Marcel."

He wasn't going to mention the wrong notes in the middle movement, nor the violinist's slurry ornamentation. Marcel wouldn't have heard them anyway. He was a furniture dealer who bought books by the metre for the shelf units he sold, chose pictures to go with the colours of the various sofas and curtain fabrics on display, and appraised music by the money it made. And yet, Leon had always admired him. He still owned a black-

and-white studio photograph of Marcel as a twenty-year-old, which Cousin Anna had given him in a moment of motherly pride.

After the concert Leon complimented his cousin on her girlish appearance and thanked her for inviting him. Unfortunately, he'd have to leave soon to catch his train. Lilou would be going with him, to make sure he was OK. And to himself he added, Not that I really need a nursemaid. Least of all my niece.

"Oh yes, lovely little Lilou," Anna murmured, with a pointed glance to where Katja was standing, face in profile, laughing and gesticulating. Leon guessed she still dreamed of Lilou and Marcel as a couple. The perfect couple that didn't exist except in her imagination.

"Anyway," he said to change the subject, "it'll be my turn before long, remember?"

His cousin patted his hand absent-mindedly. Then she seemed to pull herself together and asked, "Where will you be this Christmas? You're welcome to –"

"Greece," Leon interrupted, naming the first place that came into his mind – a family Christmas was the last thing he wanted. Year after year Anna had sent him parcels of home-made Christmas cookies shaped like angels, stars, birds and hearts, which he would receive (and consign to the dustbin) weeks later, on returning home from some exotic holiday. "You're very kind," he said now. "Thanks for thinking of me." He smoothed down his tie and leant closer for a farewell kiss. Her complexion had that peculiar, soft-skinned ruddiness he'd only ever observed in old women who had lost their husbands and found new life.

A bit later Lilou minced up on her high-heeled sandals. Thanks to the extra few centimetres, the top of her head nearly reached his shirt collar. Even in middle age she was still rather pretty, Leon had to admit to himself, with her doll's face, the saffron-red hair down to her waist and the wraithlike figure that made most men instinctively bend over and talk to her in softened voices – until they realised her size was deceptive.

You used to be such a stickler for punctuality, Uncle. What made you late for the concert?" She ran a hand through her hair and the broad silver torque on her wrist gave an accusing glint.

Leon shrugged and smiled down into her eyes, cornflower blue like his brother's, dead for more than 20 years. Lilou didn't smile back. Instead she swung her head round sharply, her excessive hair flicking at him, and steered off towards a group of younger relatives whom Leon had no desire to meet.

"Please, Lilou, we'll have to go shortly," he called after her, trying not to sound too pleading.

As he walked towards the French windows for a view from the balcony, perhaps even a glimpse of the spread-eagled waiter, it occurred to him that in certain ways he'd grown more like Lilou, and she more like him. She used to hate bourgeois values. "Rules are there to be broken," she'd say and blow cigarette smoke into his face. But now that her own daughter had produced three grandchildren by as many fathers, at the age of only 24 his niece seemed to have unexpectedly opted for the rut of accepted behaviour.

Slowly, they teetered and ambled through the noise of the central station. Leon was glad his hearing had blunted slightly with age, which made the incessant shrieks of train brakes, the booming loudspeakers and the high-pitched squeals of the motorised luggage carts more bearable.

"So you enjoyed yourself, Uncle?" Lilou was looking up at him.

"Oh yes, very civilised. Good food, pleasant company." It was muggy under the station's glass roof, nothing like the warm freshness he'd felt near the apple orchard, and he passed a hand over his forehead. "The music was a nice surprise too, considering."

His niece blinked innocently, "Considering what?" He could tell she was resentful at having to escort him back before the party had broken up.

"Good God, Lilou. You know how much I like Marcel." He loosened his tie to ease his breathing; the *föhn* weather was getting to him. "Classical music just isn't his line, is it?"

"Trust you, Uncle, to always find the fly in the ointment." She pouted, then gave a laugh and shook out her saffron hair.

Leon remained silent. He was shocked at her flippancy. Humiliated. And acknowledged with a pang that he'd misjudged her. She hadn't changed. Not one bit.

When he looked up again, he saw a group of skinheads approaching. The starkness of their features attracted him, and filled him with dread. He tried not to gaze too obtrusively, pretending to study the departures board behind them. But they weren't interested in him. He was thin air. They were all ogling Lilou.

Doubly annoyed, Leon glared until he caught the eye of the tallest one, a fellow in his late twenties with razor-sharp cheekbones, a flaccid mouth and a cheetah tattoo below his left ear. The skinhead smiled and spread his hands in what Leon took for a gesture of surrender, then said something that made the others guffaw and move closer to form a wall. Now, still smiling at Leon, Cheetah Man stepped forward and picked up a strand of Lilou's hair. His friends clicked their tongues approvingly. Lilou didn't budge, just stood and looked down at her feet. If Leon hadn't been so confused with anger and fear, he might have been proud of her.

"Now listen, you," was all he managed to say, in a quavering old man's voice that was drowned out by the loudspeakers. Then he backed away from the wall of male bodies. He knew there were security guards and police officers patrolling the station. Maybe he could alert them. He gestured to several passers-by: someone with a rucksack, a young couple, a family, another family. But they all swerved to avoid the skinheads. Leon suddenly felt each year of his life pulling and tugging at him, dragging him to the ground.

Just when he thought he couldn't hold out any longer and would have to sit down, Lilou spoke. "Excuse me," she said pointedly. Then, with a flick of the wrist that made her silver torque flash, she lifted her hair free, grabbed him by the elbow and led the way straight into the wall. And the wall parted as Cheetah Man and his friends turned to stare in silence.

Leon felt awful. Here had been his chance to protect his niece and he had failed. Had most likely caused the problem in the first place, with his stupid vanity. "I'm sorry, Lilou. So sorry." One of the luggage carts whizzed past, its trailers piled high with suitcases.

Lilou glanced up at him and smiled, "It's not your fault, Uncle. There was nothing you could do." Her face was as round and pretty as ever, showing no sign that she'd just won a battle of wills. Except perhaps her eyes. They were darker, and fiercely soft.

"But he was rather good-looking, wasn't he?"

Leon knew who she meant and didn't answer.

She wouldn't let go of him and slipped her arm through his. As they carried on walking, her hair floated behind them like a flag of victory.

They found an empty non-smoking compartment in one of the old express carriages that made up the rear of their train. Lilou sighed as she shut the sliding door, drew the corridor curtains and pulled the sunscreen down over the half-open window.

Leon said, "Why not leave the door ajar?" They were still stationary, probably waiting for a connection, and the air in the *coupé* was so sluggish it seemed to get trapped in his lungs.

"It'll be all right once we start moving." Lilou slid into a seat, drooping visibly. She had the damp, squashed look of a flower clutched in a child's hand for too long and Leon felt obscurely vindicated. He smiled.

She never noticed; her eyes had closed and her head was lolling against her shoulder. Leon peered out to check on the skinheads, but his view was abruptly cut off by the arrival of a new train. All he could see now was the sausage-and-burger bar further along, with its motley clientele of drunks, dropouts, weary and frantic travellers crowded round the high tables. Through the black mesh of the sunscreen the scene had the melancholy gayness of a Van Gogh painting without the colours.

Next thing the picture was blotted out by several soldiers with heavy-looking backpacks clattering past their carriage. Leon quickly adjusted his tie, then pushed up the screen and beckoned, indicating the free seats within. Some of the men saluted and glanced at Lilou, who was rubbing her neck, eyes wide – like a doll someone had suddenly shaken awake.

"Why did you have to do that?" she complained. "It'll only make the place hotter. Stickier." To demonstrate how uncomfortable she was, she picked ineffectually at her black dress, whose silky material clung to her chest and thighs in damp ruffles.

"They would have come in here anyway," Leon retorted. "Better to make them welcome."

He was in charge again. Still an old man, of course, but a force to be reckoned with. Sitting down had restored him to himself. He now gazed at Lilou with a tight-lipped smile, then shrugged, irritation mixed with disappointment, the way he used to when he took her to the museum as a child – a twice-monthly occurrence to educate her beyond mere school level – and she'd baulk at some exhibit or other. He still remembered explaining to her the workings of the iron maiden. How on being shut, the various spikes in its door would pierce the eyes and heart of the victim within. By then, of course, Lilou was sixteen and no longer a child. Quite ready to be confronted with the horrors of humankind.

Shouts and heavy boots were sounding in the corridor.

Then a soldier stood in the door, smiling. "Are these seats free, please?"

"Oh, yes." Leon nodded. Lilou waved a languid hand and crossed her legs.

Leon watched as the men hoisted their backpacks into the luggage racks. There were three of them. Burly specimens. Officers by the look of their epaulettes. The youngest one, with a flat pumpkin face, settled down in the seat by the sliding door, stretched out his legs and yawned from ear to ear. "Sorry, busy weekend," he muttered, half asleep already. His companions grinned and Leon saw the man opposite him wink.

The train had pulled out of the station and the sunscreen was flapping feebly, creating the sheerest whiff of wind.

The officer next to Leon turned his head and said, conversationally, "No AC in these old carriages."

Leon, who didn't understand the phrase 'AC', mumbled something. Lilou gave one of her light-hearted giggles and joked: "Well, how about getting the army to install it then? Wouldn't that go under 'humanitarian aid' – protecting the poor, suffering civilians from heatstroke?"

The two officers laughed.

Leon cleared his throat. This was his chance. "Actually, when I was in the army we were engaged in quite a lot of civil work. *After* the war, that was."

The officers nodded politely and said nothing.

Leon hoped Lilou wouldn't remind him that he had also served during the war. He'd been a private in a militia unit dispatched to secure the Rhine border, but ended up watching Diessenhofen Bridge bombed into flames.

For a moment Leon closed his eyes. He did feel rather tired. Yet the body of the officer beside him kept him alert. He'd inspected the man's hands. Not a worker's hands, quite definitely. Fine-skinned and covered in golden hairs, with strong, long fingers and smooth, neat nails. At one point the soldier had fumbled some sweets out of his trouser pocket; his elbow had touched Leon and he had apologised profusely.

There was a jolt and Leon realised he must have dropped off. His neighbour was now leaning forward, perched almost on the edge of his seat, and talking with Lilou. Discussing action films. The officer next to her was wearing headphones and tapping a foot, a rather silly expression on his face.

When the train slowed for their destination, Leon stood up. His neighbour started fussing with a flap on his backpack, then brought out pen and paper. Leon squinted to read the message before the slip was passed to his niece.

"Just give me a ring if you fancy meeting up for a drink some time."

"Thanks," Lilou smiled a dopey smile. "I might do that."

Leon managed a terse goodbye all round. The man with the headphones blinked and Pumpkin Face sleepily moved his legs out of the way.

The train stopped. Leon looked back to see whether Lilou was following. And caught the officer who'd been sitting beside him kissing her adieu. He could barely contain himself, stumbled down the corridor and out on to the platform, ignoring Lilou who had come up from behind and was extending an arm to support him.

Once they were out of earshot, he exploded, "Really, Lilou, what a way to behave! You didn't even know him! Disgraceful!"

Her blue eyes suddenly froze over. "You'd better be quiet now, Uncle." Her voice, too, was icy. "Don't think I didn't notice. You could hardly keep your hands off him. What if he'd given *you* his number? Would you have flung it back in his face?"

Leon walked on, feeling a little shaky. Shaky and old and tired. The *föhn* heat had finally beaten him. He avoided Lilou's eyes. So these were the thanks you got for looking after your own, cultivating their sensibilities for the beauties of this world. Classical music. Paintings by the old masters. Frescoes restored to their original glory.

Helen *by John Bellany (1985)*

D M Black

January 2003

After 60 years my gums are not so good.
I dental-floss them in the one-sex toilet.
Returning, clamber over wife and daughter
And look down five miles to the Hindu Kush.
You can see how India thrusts into Eurasia:
Flat plates and frills of mountain rear and crumble
Far as the eye sees through this luminous ocean
On which our plane is riding, almost motionless,
Almost without a tremble, as it eats
The abstract kilometres. In front of me,
A computer geek in glasses has not raised
His blind since Kuala Lumpur. On the monitors
The arrow pointing to Mecca has rotated
To almost along the wing. Two countries away
Across this lion-coloured world a war
Is brewing. I imagine
Our air-conditioned bubble dropping bombs
On the tiny square of village far below us,
Less than a camel's foot-print. I get dizzy,
Peering directly down. No bombs are dropped.
Nor would they be if I were captain here
Over this fragile, integrated planet,
Spinning unscripted. Our bubble carries us,
Deep in computer solitaire or sleeping,
Safe, I can hardly say that, but for this moment
Warm in the thin air and the killing cold.

Goethe: Translations

When Goethe was 37, he escaped from his courtly life in Weimar to spend two years in Italy, mostly in Rome. This was the turning-point of his life, during which he discovered the brilliance and rationality of classical art, and also, probably for the first time, entered into a full sexual relationship. On his return to Weimar in 1788, he almost immediately embarked on another sexual relationship, with Christiane Vulpius, whom many years later he married.

In celebration, he wrote the Roman Elegies*. These are a series of 22 or 24 poems in elegiac couplets, making up a sort of loose-knit narrative account of a love-affair, ostensibly set in Rome but in fact expressing the delight and happiness of his new relationship with Christiane. I have translated them as best I can to capture Goethe's tone, and into Goethe's classical metre. Below are Numbers II and III. The sarcastic references in*

No. II are to Goethe's early novel, The Sorrows of Young Werther, *which had been a runaway best-seller and which Goethe had never been allowed to forget. 'Malbrouk' is the French popular song, Malbrouk* s'en va t'en guerre, *supposedly a reference to the Duke of Marlborough. In No. III Goethe is very self-consciously classicising.*

At this wretched time in the world's history, it is a relief to turn back to sensible, playful Goethe.

Roman Elegy II

Now you may ask whom you like, you fine society ladies,
  Excellent men of the world, I am not to be caught!
"Did Werther really exist?" "Did all those things really happen?"
  "In the streets of which town did unique Lotte belong?"
Ah, believe me! how often I've cursed those fatuous pages
  Which once paraded my youth's grief to the public gaze.
Were poor Werther my brother, and I his assassin, his ghost could
  Not have more vengefully stalked after my wandering track.
Thus the ditty *Malbrouk* pursued the travelling Briton
  Out of France to Milan, then from Milano to Rome,
On down from Rome to Naples, and were he to sail to Calcutta,
  Still in the harbour he'd hear Malbrouk was off to the wars.
Praise to the Gods I've escaped! When it comes to Werther and Lotte,
  She scarcely knows their names, nor has she heard of this man
Whom she is meeting: to her, he is one of those vigorous strangers,
  At home in mountains and snow, building their houses of wood.

Roman Elegy III

Do not, my dearest, regret that you gave yourself to me so quickly.
  Truly, it shows nothing base, nothing immodest in you.
The arrows of Amor are diverse: some seem barely to scratch us,
  Yet their slow venom invades: years-long the heart will be sick.
Others, mightily feathered, with arrowheads flashing and sharpened,
  Pierce to the marrow at once, turning the blood to fire.
In those heroic days, when God and Goddess were the lovers,
  Merely a glance would excite, ecstasy follow, desire.
Do you think the Goddess of Love, when she fancied Anchises
  In the Idaean wood, spent time counting to ten?
Or had the Moon delayed before kissing her beautiful dreamer –
  O, then, envious Dawn would have soon wakened him up!
Hardly had banqueting Hero made eyes at Leander, when hotly,
  Eager for love, he plunged into the night-bound sea.
Down to the Tiber for water Rhea Sylvia ventured,
  Queenly, and virgin, and there! – there she was grabbed by the God.
Thus Mars came by his sons: those forceful twins whom the she-wolf
  Suckled and raised and by whom Rome became Queen of the world.

The Doors

Moira Burgess

"Out! Get out!" the bastard yelled above the music, and threw her out of the car. Should have known, the look in his eyes, blue eyes like china plates, nothing there. She hit her head on the road.

He'd taken her somewhere way in the country so she'd never be found, but still she was in the lane, on the cobbles, in the pigeon shit, dog shit, human shit. The smell of it, the taste in her mouth. Taste of blood and that other sick salty taste. There was a door in front of her and she crawled in.

That door opened into the hospital and she didn't want to be there. He's a lovely boy, but it's looking after him, you see. They carried him away, loaded with the stuff already though you couldn't tell. Another door and she crawled through.

Picked another bastard and I should have known, she apologised to Sam.

Not your fault, he said, come on, let's sort you out. As he always did. So good to her. Too good to live, she heard her mother caw. He sorely needed sorting out himself, but looking after her seemed to help him too. She lost the scrapes and bruises and that pain she'd never had before. She was going to tell him about the baby but he fell asleep. Anyway he wouldn't see the baby. Wasn't going to see that day.

He opened his big blue eyes. Hers were blue too, though her mother's were brown. Her dad's must have been blue. Why do I pick them, Sam? she said.

Through that door, he drowsily said.

They were both there and getting edgy. I'm not late, she cried before he could hammer her, it's not my fault! She hoped the stuff was what he wanted or it would be bad. She hated him so much, lumped all over the sofa with his arm round her mum. Still hated him, always would. Because of the night thing. And he wasn't even her dad. Her blue-eyed dad, she wanted and needed him.

This one's not important, said her mum, and her stepdad faded out of sight. Who was he, she begged, my dad? And because she was desperate, Bet you don't even know who he was.

Her mother didn't hammer her. The strength wasn't there. Oh, I know who he was. Who he is, her mother said. You don't want to. Leave him to rot, that bastard. You don't want to know.

But she did. If he was there it would be different. She heard footsteps at the close mouth, on the stair, in the lobby. He was coming and it would be all right. Her daddy that she longed to see.

Shouting and a sick smell. Her mother getting hammered. "Out! Get out!" the bastard roared, and his blue eyes stared like mad stones. She was on her face in frozen waves of shit and slime. "Come in, hen," he said, and his china-blue eyes smiled, and she opened the car door.

W N Herbert

The Wee Yang

They pit thi Wee Yang tae thi Test
that sorts oot which Scots ur thi best –
and foond he couldnae sing:
he'd stert wan verse, furget thi rest;
and he widna wear his stringy vest,
and his oxters didnae ming.
He left thi hohos til his brither,
thon big bahookie Billy;
he left thi drinkin til his mither
and didnae flash his willy.
They'd invite him tae write things
aboot thi wurkin class,
and keep it grim, they'd bleat at him,
or else you shall not pass.

He didnae gae ti thi clubs they'd listed,
or pley up links wi thi mony-mistit
Pissheids o the Isles;
thi Wee Yang wiznae that quick-fistit;
ye kicked a baa at him he missed it –
and sae he flunked thir Trials.
He tramped nae machairs, nor climmed Munros,
he niver sailed a yaat;
he fucked nae Farquhars, wrote nae prose,
pleyed pipes or strangilt cats –
but this hero of a zero,
whas soul wiz oan thi dole,
he had not got plans for Some Like It Hotland
sae kept oot that own goal.

Thi Jockstar Test thi Wee Yang failed
huz left oor culture sair impaled
upon St Andrae's Cross;
thi types of Scot wi which we're nailed
are: London Licklips, Kilt n Kailed,
and Buckies actin Boss –
that's anely three, fur hingin free,
tho mebbe no fur lang,
's a pen in a haund that still can dree
belangs tae thon Wee Yang.
There's roisters and oysters
and shysters fuhl o stink:
North Britain gets written
wi pearlies in uts ink.

The Cargo of Light

Bidin in an auld
guidin licht
hoose Eh'm
keepin up wi aa
thi licht gone loose.

Ablow us juttin
frum thi sheds
aroon thi Gut
stauns wur marra
thi auld laich licht.

Twa hunnert years back
sails flappin lyk
sark tails, shups
werr aimed at us
tae jink thi Midden's hack.

Eh'm pleyin keepie
up wi aa
thae blinders that
thi sun keeps scorin in
uts net o gless an waves.

Thi cargo comin hame
still sillery as herrin
prime as an ashet
still needin us baith
lined up an able.

Grandparents Kabitika

When you meet them in dreams
as though they hadn't died
your comfort still feels wrenched.
It's like they continued to grow
as you grew: twenty, thirty feet
tall, too big for home, standing
like lampposts, horses, telegraph poles,
gathered into forests of dead relatives,
redwood ancestors, where you run
to clutch their legs in the dream's distress
while they attempt to
bend and reach you with
their careful huge caress.

White Armour

shelled now of their little
noble occupants
they stand around in cases
in case of curiosity's
unfired missile

their empty resolve
effete and combative at once
in their pointy armadillo shoes,
their sabatons, the faulds and tassets of
portcullis girdles,
their shoulder plates or spaulders
arced like society eyebrows
disdaining all blades

stylish in stainless in steel
in
emphatically that,
within, all that
ingenuity of Missiglia and Gratz
engineered to contain,
their interiors
crabby with doubt

is there anywhere an aperture a besagew forgot
a loosened lames
a slit or grille or occularia
where anything
thin
could search out, pin and skewer?
to be in
is to be housed in hedged in hopelessness
coddled cast in aketon
encroached

they make us enemy
with their eyeless gaze
whereas
their long shanks and bubble breasts
show exactly
how we shaped up once
to the pike the mace the battleaxe the bolt

exactly how
we shape up still
to being bare

The Rest on the Flight into Egypt

(after Carravaggio)

The naked angel that appeared to play
scores of miles from the sacrifice of babies
was unaffected by the desert cold.
We were pursued by unrevealed night clouds.

I felt my face go soft and sag, as though
rotting with weariness, an apple in
the grass of my beard, but I held the song-book
and listened to it play its violin.

Mary had folded over the infant, gone
from balancing her draining flux of love
with our eroding dune-jarred flit. And He
slept on, returned to where He'd always been,

since we'd accepted that small head held Heaven,
continuous home. No cot from me yet, just this
panicked rush, gums raw pink with trapped sand grains,
lids twitching at His own created darkness.

I'd looked to Egypt like a line to cross
and found the blank-skinned book of staves instead.
I'd looked for safety, or a mothering bed,
instead we got some staggered brief oases.

Our only armour was this freezing music
which wouldn't halt the clouds' advance through gloom.
Our only sword the angel's pliant bow
which couldn't saw our future from a tune.

Facts about Things

Things are tired.
Things like to lie down.
Things are happiest when,
for no reason, they collapse.

That French plastic bottle, still half-full,
that soft-back book, just leaning on
another book, drowsily:
soon they will want to go outside,

soon you will find them in the grass
with the empty bleaching cans and that part
of an estate agent's sign
that's covered in a fine grime like mascara.

That plastic bag you've folded up
feels constrained by you and wants
to hang from bushes, looking like
a spirit, sprawled and thumbing a lift.

Things are bums, tramps, transitories:
they prefer it when it's raining.
Lightbulbs like to lie in that same
long, uncut, casual grass

and watch the funnel effect: the way
on looking up the rain all seems
to bend towards you,
the way the rain seems to like you.

Things which do not decay
like it best in shrubbery, they like
to be partly buried.
They like the coolness of the grass.

Most of all, they like it
when it rains.

A Dead Porpoise Washed up on the Beach at St Ives

Scrubbed to the cooked salmon blush of the sunset,
scraped by the surf and the scuff of the sand
it's landed, raw and birled, pointed into the fall
of light, its tail still curled up slightly, as though
one flick were left in it and would be enough
to free it back into the snap of night-fishing,
that compulsive tapping and clicking at
the furniture of currents that has always loosed
those netted shoals for which it's now been drowned.

Eyeless, brittling at the tips of fins like iron –
and there is a gleam as it decays: a sense
of greaves about the shank and plates to shield
the cheekbones: it looks dusty and dung down
as any Trojan, any Greek we'd like to lament
as equally as Homer. Its sonar shield has dropped,
it's chopped of psyche, fallen, and we hear no soul
chivvied from its flesh to Hades or the rivers which
surround that place, to bewail its loss of youth.

Moira Burgess

Said the Lord

And the Lord said:
I shall send my child to earth
to be a teacher and a comforter
and my child shall have wisdom
and shall love and nurture and save the children of men.
So shall it be, said the Lord.

And down came the Holy Spirit
and a virgin bore a daughter
who was the daughter of God.

A girl? people said.
Better luck next time.

And the child grew and ran about in Galilee
and told her cousins stories about God. For a while.

Bring in the goats!
Mix the porridge! Sew on that sandal strap!
What's the matter with you? people said.

And the day of her womanhood came upon her
and she rejoiced. Life ahead,
and her family rejoiced –
soon she'd be off their hands.

But I want to put people right about God, she said.
Nobody likes a lippy girl, they replied.

The spirit of the Lord is upon me, she said.

You're odd enough already, her family said,
don't you want a husband or what?
as they beat her
and married her off rather quickly
to a nice young fellow with his own flock of goats
so that was all right.

And she lay with her husband, of course.

And she bore him a son so everybody was pleased
and a daughter, well, can't be helped
and two more sons and another daughter,
and another son
(not counting those who died)
the spirit of the Lord on a back burner
for fifteen years and more.

Wouldn't have been without them. Heavens, no.

And when the children were grown
she said to her husband:
The spirit of the Lord is upon me.

Who's going to make my supper?
her husband enquired.

He didn't beat her. Didn't need to
begot another son instead, who died.

So she went to milk the goats
and make the porridge
and the Lord came to her in the tent.

Why don't you begin your mission, my daughter,
said the Lord, rise and go about Galilee
with twelve disciples
as my spirit may command?

I have tried, you know,
said the daughter of God.

And the Lord looked at her, at her stretch-marks,
her dishpan hands, the snaggly teeth
the place where the goat bit her
and he knew that it was so.

They are a stiff-necked people,
the children of men, said the Lord.

That's one way of putting it,
said the daughter of God.

And the Lord sighed.

You are an idea, my daughter, said the Lord,
whose time has not yet come.
A thousand years from now
still no chance.
Two thousand years? Not really.
How are you on flower-arranging? said the Lord.

It's never been my forte,
said the daughter of God.

And being weary she closed her eyes
and was gathered to Abraham's bosom,
or Sarah's bosom, perhaps, let's hope,
a bit more empathy there.

I think I'll try again next year,
said the Lord,
but this time I'll make it a boy.

And it was even so.

God's New Frock

John Clifford

Hello. Hello ladies, hello gentlemen. Hello those of you who are not ladies and are not gentlemen, but maybe something in between or maybe something that's a bit of both or something or somebody that has never been thought of or imagined yet.

Somebody or something this evening may even bring into being.

Welcome. Welcome to this precious time, this precious hour we're going to spend together, this hour that has never happened before like this and will never happen quite like this again.

I thought of doing something very simple and perhaps something a little corny. I thought I'd tell you a story. An important story. An important story because we're all important people, we all of us matter, though the world puts a lot of effort into telling us the opposite.

An important story because I've been told it explains who we are and how we came into this world. And I expect some of you were told the same.

When I first heard it I really believed it. I believed it because I was told to and because I was told it was one of the most sacred stories in the whole wide world and because I was told it was a story about God and what he did when he made the world.

So it's a story about me. About me and about you when we were all boys or maybe girls or maybe something in between, or maybe a bit of both or maybe something or somebody that has never been thought of or imagined yet. And you may think that fanciful, but let me tell you, ladies or gentlemen or maybe something in between, that part of us is divine and does live up high in the sky, or maybe deep down below in the pits of hell, or maybe in both places at once, and that part of us just like the god of the story does create the world every day, every day we get out of bed.

Every day we get out of bed and open our eyes, we create the world. We create the world we're going to inhabit for the whole of the day to come and we do it again and again. Every time we open our mouths, every time we say even a single word, we create the world.

Only because we're a little old or a little tired and certainly have no confidence in ourselves every single day it's usually just the bloody same. It's the office or the school or the hospital or whatever and then the telly. Every day the same. Except for tonight. Tonight is different.

So why can't it all be different? Why shouldn't it be different? Why shouldn't it be different? So today, ladies and gentlemen and everyone outrageous in between, today at this moment that has never happened before quite like this and will never ever happen quite like this again, today I am going to tell you of a time when it really was, it really was different.

An old story. A very old story. A story that may be one of the oldest stories in the whole wide world. You may have heard it before. When you were still a boy, or maybe a girl, or maybe something in between. And you may have lived it, too. When you were a god and lived up high in the sky or maybe down in the deepest pits of hell or maybe both places at the same time.

And then maybe again like me a time came when you forgot the story, forgot you'd ever lived it, forgot you'd ever believed it, and tried to believe in evolution instead. Or the big bang or something, and you thought the old story had just withered away.

The trouble is that it didn't. Wither away. This story. It's still there deep deep in the heart of us. The story is in us and we are in the story. We are its heroines, or maybe its heroes, or maybe something in between. And we live through it, and it will live through us. And until we somehow discover a new story to understand ourselves, we'll never escape it. We will go on and on living inside it for ever and ever. So. I hope you're sitting comfortably. And then I'll begin.

Now once upon a time, a long long time ago in a far far distant country ... And it really was a long long time ago, because it was all so amazingly long ago it all happened before time had even been invented. Before time ever was: or anything else for that matter. It was a time and it was a space where there was nothing at all. Absolutely nothing at all except for this one being, apparently, this one being who thought he was very big, but who actually, in the middle of this great big nothing, was really very small. And this being, who liked to think of himself as big, this very big being has many different names, and important names too. I mean they must have been important because many people have killed each other over them. Killed each other over which was the right name to use. Burnt each other to death and tortured each other with red hot pincers or electric shocks. And still do.

There are people who line a street on the way to a primary school, brave, upright, manly people who line the street and yell SCUM! and FILTH! at four year old children because even though they use the same name for this being 'God', they seem to understand it differently. So you see we're entering really dangerous territory here. And we've hardly begun. I'm not sure I know what to do for the best.

But I'll tell you what I'll do: just for the moment, and to get the story going, what I'll do is call this being God. And then we'll see.

Because that's what he likes, and although he says he's all powerful he's actually very easily hurt. So we'll call him God for now, and keep him happy. But I want you to do something: I want you to promise me that deep in the secretest corner, the secretest corner of your innermost hearts, you'll keep for yourselves the right to call this Being anything you want.

And you do really have the right to do this because you are the heroes of this story, or maybe its heroines, or maybe something in between, and so you can call this being anything you secretly choose. You might want to call him Terry. Or possibly Jim. Or Malcolm or Edith or Elizabeth or Jane. Only that might get us into even worse trouble because he tended ferociously to insist on the fact that he was male. Very ferociously. Very very very ferociously, and also (and this is important because you'll get in the most terrible trouble if you ignore this one), he used to insist he was all alone in the world and there was no-one like him. Anywhere. And that's kind of sad, when you think about it, because he must have been so lonely.

Besides there are Gods everywhere if you think about it. Under that chair. In the eaves of the roof. In the secretest corner of your own deep hearts. Which is another reason why you can call this being, this him, or this her, or this something in between, absolutely anything you like. But he wouldn't have that. He'd rather be lonely he said, and he used to threaten the most terrible torments on anyone who dared suggest otherwise. And not just on them, who said it, or who even thought it, but on their children too. Even on the children of their children. He's like a drunk in a bar that'll pick a fight with anyone who dares to hint that's he not a real man. And like any drunk in any bar the chances are he's talking absolute shite.

But you still have to be careful. So where were we? We were a long long way away. A long long long time ago. So long it was before the beginning of time when there was this being all on his own, apparently, and apparently most emphatically male, floating on the waters ... And when I think waters, when I think waters ... I think womb.

And I get the strangest feeling, I get the strangest feeling that that's where he is. In the womb. And that means when he says all that bit about being all alone and all male and all that – that means he's lying. And me a little wolf cub too. Because that's what I was, ladies, gentlemen and something in betweens, that's what I was when I first heard this story, a wolf cub. All young and trusting with my little woggle. Hearing about god being all male and all powerful and all alone, floating on the waters.

And he'd been in the womb all along.

But let's not be like him, let's not get all vindictive, let's be calm and reasonable and just try to see it through his eyes and imagine what it felt like, what it felt like floating in the womb. Not imagine so much as try to remember, because we've all been there, even if we've forgotten how it was. But even if we can't remember, we all know somewhere, and even if it feels impossible to go back there, we can at least begin to try.

So what we have to do, heroes and heroines and possibly either or both, what we have to do is this: close our eyes, close our eyes very tight and shut out the noise of the world – close our eyes and remember: floating on the water, floating in the water and the warm water all around. No light no dark, and no up and no down and no before no after, and no left and no right, no right no wrong, and absolutely no need to do anything at all.

Bliss. Pure bliss. And if this was a sensible story this would be the end of it. Only it would have no beginning and it would have no end. Only this. This bliss. But then this is not a sensible story.

This is our story. This is about us. This is about us being born. And about God being born too. And no-one knows how it happened or why or what started it because actually no-one ever does. In spite of everything doctors and scientists know, or think they know. No-one has ever been able to figure out exactly what triggers us being born. Not even God. And that's why none of this ever turns up in the story. And also because he'd forgotten it. God. Forgotten all about it. Couldn't bear to remember it. None of us can. Remember being born. Too painful.

But if you watch a baby god being born, if you watch a baby – and I won't call them human because we're not, really, when we first came into the world, it's only later that humanness settles upon us and shuts us in. But when we're born, these beings, us, these amazing beings, born into chaos and confusion, into the bright naked lights into the naked place where we have to gulp for air. What do we do? The minute we can, the minute we've stopped yelling and sucking and doing little green poos, we try to make sense of it. We divide light from dark, day from night. We create the world. Create the world every day of our lives.

So listen. Listen to how he does it: like us. He starts with light. Let there be light, he says, and blam, there it is, and he likes it. And so he goes on. He goes on by dividing. Light from dark, upper from lower, water from dry land, sun from moon, good from evil, masculine from feminine, yin from yang, on from off, one from zero. And this produces day and night and the ocean and the dry land and the animals and the fish and bricks and mortar, concrete and clay, aluminium and steel, and those fighter planes that circle above our heads. And where were we?

We were with God, going on and on, making big creatures and little creature, creatures that moved on land and creatures that moved on the sea and creatures that flew in the air, on and on, elephants and goats and humming birds. On and on. Leopards and fig-trees and mushrooms and diamonds and strange little creatures whose names have been forgotten, or not even thought up yet, on and on, and if we were to list everything, everything he made in his passionate creation, we'd be here until the end of time, or possibly next Tuesday. On and on. Butterflies and buffaloes, and the possibility of orange marmalade and coffee beans and tobacco plants and hash plants and headlice.

And because he had never had to remove lice from anyone's hair, or perhaps because he'd sat down and had a smoke from one of the new hash plants on the sly, before anybody else even knew they were there, and so no-one had even begun to try to ban them, or perhaps just because it was all so beautiful and so amazing and all fitted together in such utterly absolute beauty, it was like a crossword in forty-five dimensions he'd thought up and put together and solved all at once, and perhaps also because he was still so caught up in the joy of his creation, he looked again at everything, again and again, at everything he had made and he had created and said how good it all was, how very very good.

As you do, at moments like these, then he had a rest, and invented Sunday. And apparently he invented church services too.

There's me when I heard this, just a boy, sitting in a church pew and wriggling, all scratchy in my wolf cub uniform and I believed every word of it, as you do at moments like these, when you're very young and grown-ups tell you things, even grown-ups in a church wearing odd white frocks. "Only it's not a frock, Johnny you naughty boy. Men don't wear frocks. It's a surplice. And that's different." I didn't understand that really and felt a bit silly because that's something else, something else that people tell you: and if you don't understand what they're telling you it must be your fault.

But according to the book God created human beings twice over. Once before he went to sleep and invented Sunday and then again afterwards.

And he told us we could have dominion over the fish of the sea and the fowl of the air and every living thing that moveth over the earth. We like that bit, because it means we can eat pork sausages and cut down the rain forest and feed dead cow to other cows and still feel self-righteous. He also told us he made us in his own image, which may be puzzling if you happen have breasts and a womb but which is still on the whole quite flattering. So we remember those bits. But what we forget is the bit where he says: Male and female created he them. Or possibly him. Or possibly singular of dual gender, the authorities differ, and an obscure rabbinical school has speculated on the androgynous nature of the first human being.

What is implied is the androgynous nature of God, too, which is highly embarrassing for everybody, and so has also been forgotten. But we will remember. We will remember in spite of the version of the story everybody knows. Adam and God and the finger (It Could Be You!) and God creating man. And when we say man, we mean man. I must apologise to those of you who identify yourselves as heroines, but at this point in time, apparently, you do not exist.

The universe is a kind of gigantic old-fashioned golf club from which women are definitely barred. That's one reason why this version has been remembered and the other one forgotten. Because this one is so much more convenient. For priests and patriarchs and golfers. See the story goes that he made men from dust. And he made women from a bone. But only as an afterthought. And for a certain type of mentality, that is the story's main attraction. They like the fact he made men from dust and from earth and from mud and I suppose at least a little spit. Like you'd make a pot or maybe a saucer or a cup. Only more complicated, because of the insides and all. And when he had finished making men, inside as well as out, he breathed on you, and by you I mean you who out there identify yourselves as men and so are made out of earth and mud and dust and a little bit of god's spit, or maybe a lot, he breathed on you and you became alive. That's why the word for wind, roooookh, in Semitic languages is the same for breath and the same for soul, and I like that.

At that time he was still proud and happy and he made you the most beautiful garden that could ever be imagined. And he planted it. He was his own seed catalogue, and he planted it with his hand. And there were beautiful trees that gave sweet fruit, and beautiful flowers that gave sweet scent, and hot and cold running water, and gorgeous butterflies, and the most delightful singing birds. That's where you lived, you and Adam, you the heroes of this story, you lived in this beautiful garden. And were utterly miserable. God saw this, because he wasn't altogether daft, and God said: "It is not good for Man to live alone."

And he was right. It's not good for anyone to live alone, not alone alone. Not alone without anyone to see even at the supermarket, and so of course you were miserable. Poor thing. But you see God, God's supposed to be all wise, so couldn't he have foreseen this? Isn't it strange that he's so good at getting the material circumstances right – birds bees butterflies flowers hot and cold running water – but screws up when it comes to making people happy? Aren't we entitled to a Being with a little more insight?

Anyway, there he was, man should not live alone, sounding magisterial, but actually making it all up as he went along. Because he gathered together all the hundreds and hundreds of creatures he had made and paraded them in front of Adam. And he had to give them all names, must have been exhausting, and also have a good look at them and see if any of them would make a suitable companion.

The thing is, and I'm really sorry to tell you this, you who identify yourselves as women and so are the heroines of this story, that you were obviously an afterthought, because it was only after Adam had looked at all the animals, and turned them all down: turned down the pet dog and the pet cat and the pet gerbil, the pet tiger and the pet warthog and the pet bunny rabbit, the pet donkey and the pet elephant and the pet dung beetle, only after he had turned down all these beautiful creatures as his companions that God invented anaesthetic, whether gas, or injection, or just a single look from his terrible eye, and Adam was fast asleep.

When he woke up there was a woman beside him. And also a strange hollow space just underneath his heart. Now the first woman was Lilith, though we've been told she was Eve. But Lilith, apparently, quarrelled with Adam, and left him. God sent three angels after her to try to force her to return, but she was stronger than all of them, and never came back. And so she was consigned to hatred and oblivion.

But I remember her. I remember her well. And were I the woman I once so desperately wanted to be, I think I might tell her story. But I am not.

I am who I am, like the bush that is always burning. Isn't it strange the way this story says that woman came from man, and how often have we believed it, when if you think about it for a moment, it's so perfectly obvious that men come out of woman. Yet the whole world's organised as if the opposite were true. As if men were the centre of things and women really were only an afterthought. So what's the moral of this? What's the moral of this holy wise and sacred story? That if you're going to tell a lie make it a big one. And the bigger the lie, the more people will want to believe it. And they'll never change their minds, because to change their minds they'll have to accept what idiots they all were in the first place.

You see, there's me, as a boy, listening to it. Listening to the man who's wearing a white frock that isn't a frock telling me all about it. I'm sitting in a pew in my wolf cub uniform, in my scratchy shorts and my neckerchief, and I'm not happy at all because I hate my woggle, I don't want to be with Akela and dib dib dib and do my best and climb trees and be brave and learn to tie knots. I want to wear a nice brown frock and be with brown owl and the brownies and learn how to be nice and bake cakes. And that puzzles me. I mean, there's men and there's women but who am I? I don't seem to figure anywhere in this story. It's like God didn't create me at all, yet here I am, feeling utterly alone.

We know it's not good to be alone. If only I'd known it, there was almost certainly another little wolf cub in the same room, somewhere, feeling just like I did, just as I know there'll be at least one here in this room, somewhere. There always is one. We just had to hide, that's all. And again if I'd known there was almost certainly in another room somewhere in the same town at least one girl who hated her silly frock and would have gladly swapped it for my scratchy shorts and run off to climb trees and be happy.

And if ... if only we'd known ... Where was I? In the garden. Adam and Eve were in the beautiful garden. And they were happy, as we all were happy, once. Eating and sleeping and looking around, looking at the beautiful world. At our beautiful world. Being. Just being in the beautiful world.

The deal was they could go anywhere they liked, and eat anything they liked, and have any number of hot baths, and any number of cold baths, and listen to any number of beautiful singing birds, and just be happy, be happy for ever and ever just so long as they didn't eat the fruit of one particular tree, the tree of the knowledge of good and evil. That one over there. That one over there with the gorgeous red fruit. The red fruit hanging from its branches. The red fruit ripe and ready to eat.

You don't need a degree in psychology to tell what happens next, nor the wisdom of hindsight either, it was all so obvious to everybody, except the people involved in it, and except to God too, apparently. And this is another of those moments when it's impossible to believe in the supposed all-wisdom of God. In his all-seeing knowledge of the mysteries of his creation. The man was obviously a fool. A demiurge. A bungler. And there's no need to invent the story of the serpent and the temptation of Eve to explain. It's just a cover-up that is, a diversionary tactic, to draw everyone's attention away from the real culprit: the incompetence of God himself.

But where was I? They're eating, look, they're eating the fruit for the very first time, and it tastes delicious, and they're looking at each other. Looking at each other as if for the very first time. And then she sees he's got a prick. And he sees she's got a cunt. And for some reason that makes them both intensely ashamed. And that was how he knew. That was how he knew what they had done.

He was walking in the garden, the story goes, walking in the garden in the cool of the day. And he was happy, perhaps. And they heard his voice. Perhaps he was singing. This is the last time he walks the earth. From now on he absents himself: he thunders from mountains, he sends down angels. He inspires prophets and sends down his own son. He is a raging wind, he is a dove, a light in the heaven, a burning bush. And sometimes he is a still small voice. But this is him, this is himself, walking down simply on the earth among us. Walking down simply among us for the very last time. And we hid from him. We were terribly terribly ashamed.

That's how he knew. He was furiously uncontrollably angry. He was like a spoilt child who has never been contradicted, like a child who destroys a toy because he doesn't know how to work it. Like a child who doesn't know how to work it or make it do what he wants. And so destroys it. Like a being quite incredibly insecure, a being who, because he is so insecure, is also astonishingly vindictive. He threw them out of the garden. Threw them out of the beautiful garden he had laboured so hard to create. He told the woman: you will always be frightened of snakes, and in childbirth you will suffer great agony and hate it. And he told the man: you will have to work for your living, labour with the sweat of your brow, and hate that too.

And then he posted a particularly malevolent and officious being at the entrance to the garden armed with a flaming and particularly sharp sword. For he didn't want them coming back to the garden, and didn't want them eating the tree of life. He wanted them to stay ignorant; and if he couldn't have that, at least he could make sure they both died. For he wasn't all-wise, and he wasn't all-powerful. He was frightened. And he left behind him the division of labour, and an infinity of unhappiness. And was never seen again. Adam and Eve, weeping bitterly, turned their backs on paradise and never returned. As we have never returned.

And I'm left trying to remember, trying to remember as we all must. All must try to remember when it was I first ate of that fruit. When was it? We all must remember, otherwise this vague deep down feeling of somehow always being in the wrong, of always being in the wrong somehow and things never ever going to be right, if we don't remember that feeling will never leave us, and things never will be right. Never will be right at all.

It wasn't when I went to school wearing my mother's knickers, because that didn't feel wrong. That just felt peculiar. It wasn't the primary school play when they asked us what did we want to be, gnomes or flowers. I said a flower please, and was very surprised to see I was the only boy. And it wasn't in the battles in the school playgrounds when the boys were warriors and the girls were nurses who looked after the wounded. I always got myself wounded early on because I knew I would rather be one of the nurses. That just seemed sensible.

It wasn't even when I was a wolf cub and detested my woggle, because that just felt like a kind of blank. It was later, when my voice should have been breaking – only it didn't and I felt ashamed to be heard speaking.

About then I discovered I was an abomination. I discovered that God loathed me. That I was an offence in his nostrils. I discovered God despised me, and that the world would despise me too. Would despise me and reject me and loathe me and detest me, if ever the world discovered who I really was. I don't know, ladies and gentlemen, ladies and gentlemen and something in between. I don't know if you've ever had the experience – ever had the experience of being an abomination.

I expect you have. According to the book, you're an abomination if you shave your face. You're an abomination if you wear clothes that mix fabrics. And you're also an abomination if you do something with a goat.

Something so terribly technical I'm not even going to begin to explain it.

You just live with it, don't you. And it's not that bad. I tell you it's better to be mocked; it's better to be laughed at and spat upon for being whoever you are. Better than being a nothing – better than being a blank – better than being someone who cannot be who they truly are. Where was I?

I was with Adam and Eve, weeping as they left behind the garden. I was with Jehovah thundering on the desert plain, thundering at the Israelites at the foot of the mountain, hurling abuse at me in his book of Leviticus. And what didn't I understand? I didn't understand when I was first terrified by the thought of who I was. I didn't understand that he was terrified too. He was waging a war with the Mother Goddess. That's who Baal was, and the golden calf, probably, and all the other abominations he darkly hints at.

Sometimes her priests wore drag and looked simply gorgeous. That's why God gets so angry in Deuteronomy. And Numbers and Leviticus. And Judges I. And Judges II. And Kings I and Kings II. And Micah and Hosea and Isaiah and Jeremiah. And Macabees I and Macabees II and Macabees III. And Habakuk. It's because he's struggling with the Goddess. Struggling with his other half. Hunting her with nets, piercing her with sharp spears, setting traps for her in dark places and hacking her to pieces with knives.

And he's never stopped. And nor have we. Those rare fleeting intervals in which we are not at war with each other, those occasional moments we are not engaged in wounding or maiming or killing or torturing our fellow human beings, we are still, always and for ever mining, gouging, poisoning: making war on our mother. Making war on our mother the earth.

But the God of our story uses stronger weapons still. Of course he used his spear, his net, his lightning bolt, and the horrid sharpness of his knife. Of course he did. But stronger still were the weapons he used last of all. Last of all and all the time: oblivion and silence. So he passes over in silence the titanic struggle he waged to secure his existence; he ignores the fact that he came from the womb. He pretends not to notice that even his name Elohim: even his name is female.

It's feminine plural. And all the male theologians do their best to help him get over his embarrassment by saying that although feminine and plural in form his name is masculine and singular in intention. God is like a middle aged man with a wardrobe full of frocks. A closet he keeps firmly locked because he dare not open the door.

And Adam is labouring in a field. And Eve is screaming in the agony of childbirth. And Adam would really like to help but hasn't a notion of what to do. And I'm listening to these stories, these stories being told me by the man in the white frock, the white frock which isn't a frock, really, but a vestment, and I'm not a wolf cub any more, I'm a bit older and I got defeated by the mustard and cress, and also by the clove hitch, and I'm quite excited because I'm going to get to be a girl in the school play and wear a yellow dress. This dress. But what's seeping in, seeping in all soft and insidious is the moral of the story, this holy vile story.

And all of a sudden there's this lawyer friend, this lawyer friend just beside me. Hello lawyer friend. She says she's conducting a judicial inquiry that may lead to a criminal prosecution. An inquiry into the nature of God and the story of the book of Genesis. So she puts God in the dock, and she says: "God I warn you anything you say may be taken down and used in evidence against you." And God doesn't dare say a word (she's dead scary, my lawyer friend) Before I know what's happening she's citing me as a witness. And there I am in the witness-box, about 10 years old, wearing the yellow frock, this yellow frock, with the flowers on it, the yellow frock I used to be so proud of and which now makes me so horribly ashamed.

Observe, she says, ladies and gentlemen of the jury, ladies and gentlemen and something in between. Observe this boy. He knows what is right and what is wrong. His innocent but truthful knowledge has been corrupted by this wicked story, purporting to represent genesis but in fact perverting both the end and the beginning of all things. He knows in the uncorrupted part of his self that the god of this story is unjust and vindictive.

But what they keep telling him, the men in the frocks they claim are not frocks but vestments, allegedly, the accomplices in this vile crime, is that the God of this story is supremely just and wise. So the first lesson he has learnt was not to trust his own perceptions. We have all learnt it, ladies and gentlemen of the jury and whoever between: we have all been corrupted. But that is only the beginning, ladies and gentlemen of the jury and everything in between, that is only the beginning of the wickedness

Observe the boy. He knows the story is unjust and unfair and so the second lesson he has been taught is that injustice is woven into the very fabric of the world. That injustice is part of the natural order of things. And there is nothing anyone can ever do to change it. But even that is still only the beginning, that is still only the beginning of God's wickedness. For the third lesson taught to this innocent boy is that the division into genders is something fundamental. Fixed and immutable. And that there is shame and there is guilt attached to it. And worse still: for the fourth lesson is that the female is inferior to the male and must be subjugated. Because she is somehow responsible for all the evil in the world.

And so this story we are taught is one of the most ancient stories we possess. This story is fundamental, one of the first and best attempts to understand our world, and give it shape and meaning. This story we are taught is one of the most profound and sacred texts we shall ever know or read. This story is full of lies and does us the most profound harm.

This boy, this innocent boy in the beautiful yellow dress, has already stopped feeling his body as part of the beautiful world. This boy feels instead as something separate and tainted. And this is all, ladies and gentlemen of the jury, all the work of this vile book. This vile book that teaches its victims that women are inferior and dangerous, and to want to be one is utterly disgusting.

Look what has happened to this boy. He doesn't know now when it was he first ate the apple. He can't remember when he first opened his eyes, when he looked in the mirror and detested what he saw there.

Detested what he saw because he saw a man, or a boy turning into a man and didn't want to be a man. Didn't want to be a man at all.

So what did he do, ladies and gentlemen of the jury, ladies and gentlemen and something in between? He did the same as the God in the wicked story. He did the same as every young boy and every young man who has been exposed to it, every young boy and young man who thought he didn't measure up and who was made to be ashamed of his own tears.

He split himself in two. He took out his rib, the part of him closest to his heart, and he tried to cauterise it, cauterise his own heart. And make it numb. He took out his rib and he split himself in two. And became divided into male and female. And the female half he tried to lock up inside himself and trample and forget. But he could not forget, ladies and gentlemen and something in between. He could never forget. Because none of us can.

And then when he looked, and now when we look, ladies and gentlemen and everything in between, when we look and when we see, we see that both are bad. Both are very bad. And as for the boy, there was the man his body was, and hated. And there was the woman he thought he really wanted to be. He hated the man for being manly, and he hated the woman for making him feel ashamed. And now see him, ladies, gentlemen, something in between: see him now:

And I grew older and spottier I developed the most shockingly awkward stoop. See the effects of pornography, she says. He's wearing check shirts and Y fronts and never ever wears feminine clothes.

But it's useless, his desires are just getting stronger, compulsive and twisted and bitter. He feels perverted and monstrous; sick and repulsive and utterly alone. And that, members, of the jury, is the classic effect of the pornography of the bible.

And she pointed behind me to the witness box that had grown quite incredibly large. No-one knows, she said, how many victims there are, for they are countless. How many people, hiding their secret selves, as if they were criminals. Hiding their secret selves or else lamenting their loss, the loss of all their dreams. How many men spending their days in suits pretending to be normal men, and their nights in dresses, pretending to be normal women? How many hiding feminine selves in closets, lock-up garages or garden sheds, post office boxes or safe addresses, suitcases hidden under beds or anonymous packages at the back of chests of drawers? How many closets, would you say? How many secret cross-dressed places?

I'd say millions. How many others out on the streets taking endless precautions not to be read, not to be noticed, not to be observed. How many breast implants, how much vocal retraining, how many testicles removed with pincers, how many penises cut off with sharp knives? And how many still imprisoned in deep anxiety of their secret being revealed, of their being discovered to have committed the so-called crime of wanting to be female? And how many men afraid of their tenderness? How many men afraid of being hurt? How many men in the cockpits of fighter planes, the fighter planes circling slowly above our heads? And I looked at the witness box overflowing with unhappiness.

And this, said my lawyer friend, all this shocking damage is only a tiny fraction of the shame and anger and guilt that's been caused by the infinite pornographer going under the name of God. For this book, this so-called holy book, is pornography. *Prima facie.* Pornography.

I base my case, ladies and gentlemen and everybody in between, on the classic definition as established in Regina vs. Hicklin, (1868): not the common and incorrect definition of it being a text, picture or moving image that incites us to lust, but the wider, deeper, truer sense that it demeans and it degrades. It degrades our capacity to think, degrades our capacity to judge, degrades our sense of what is right. Above all, it corrupts and degrades those whose minds are open to such immoral influences.

As yours are, ladies and gentlemen of the jury, ladies and gentlemen and in betweens. And as was this boy, this boy in the beautiful yellow dress.

My friend won her case, of course.

God ran away from the courtroom. And before I knew what was happening all the bishops went to sewing classes and made real frocks out of all their gorgeous vestments, and allowed all the priests to enjoy them. Churches became temples of sexual delight, and the mullahs were laughing as they filled their beards with flowers. And all the stealth bombers turned into gorgeous butterflies.

Where was I? With Adam. With Adam and Eve. And Eve left Adam and ran away with Lilith her new best friend. And so there's Adam, poor Adam all lonely. And he's built himself a bunker, a bunker where he lives alone, with God on his side, a castle-cum-locker-room, club-house and gentleman's convenience, built of damp concrete with graffiti on the walls, a decaying fortress where he sulks in aggressive self-pity, without his role as breadwinner and useless in the home.

Adam and Jehovah, in there together, smelly feet, huge beer bellies, no good at cooking, useless at cleaning, with the football on the telly, yelling insults at the ref, lashing out at poofs and at women, at war with his self, at war with the world. And the young men, the young men in their cockpits, for whom we are just blips on a computer, and flesh and blood, feeling and tenderness, compassion and love. Just blips, blips on the computer screen. The young men, the young men in the fighter planes, circling above our heads, circling closer now, circling ever closer

Where was I? Look. Look there in the corner, in the corner of God's bunker, in a tiny corner is a tiny door. He would love to open it, but he's too afraid. Oh go on, God, open the door. Take a peek inside. It won't kill you. Open the door, God open it wide. It's all right really. There's a tweed jacket in there, and the most gorgeous green silk sequinned frock. And they're both yours, both yours for the taking. And there's stilettos and walking boots and terribly sensible shoes.

Open the door, God. Open the door Adam. Open the door heroines, heroines and heroes of this story. Bless the timid and the shy, for they shall be shameless. Bless the lonely and misunderstood, for she shall have everyone she wants. Bless the poor. For she shall be rich. Bless the chairman of the board, for she shall lose everything!

Bless the boy in the closet in the silk wedding gown, for he shall come out. Bless the prostitute, for she shall be honoured. Bless the frigid and the impotent, for they shall have sex for ever and ever! Amen! Amen!

Bless the fathers who don't care because they've never been cared for, for they shall be loved. Bless the mothers who hit because they cannot still their children's tears, for they shall be comforted. Bless the bully and the criminal, for they shall lose all fear. Bless the inadequates in government, for they shall lose their power. Bless the gangster who boasts of the women he's raped and victims he's robbed and the enemies he's killed, for he is them. And they are him. And shall be for ever and ever. Amen amen.

And bless this boy who's been frozen in terror. Remind him he is not alone. Don't let him ever forget. And don't let us, don't let us ever forget. For he is she. And she is he. And we are they. And they are we. And ever shall be. For ever and for ever and for ever.

Graphic courtesy of John Clifford

Ian Crockatt

Self Portrait

The background is blank, suggesting this artist saw
nothing but himself. Whatever the medium is
it is unstable as steam on glass –
it gives the impression the artist could scarcely draw
breath, has the feel of a failing man's kiss.
But to assume he was picturing his own death is as
fanciful as photographing ghosts.

History calls him the 'Lord of Hosts',
and his biography reads like fiction –
a big, tortured character, but somehow never
complete; a hand, a beard, a voice, all diction
and bossiness and given to words like *forever* ...
No other likeness is known, or allowed.
Illusion is given substance by his use of the shroud.

Giving Blood

Of all the crazy tricks
our water-to-wine crowd-pleaser
was the cheapest; vulgar
as mooning at nuns from the back of a bus.

Lazarus was the riskiest –
and my best. That felt like giving
blood, simultaneously draining
and ennobling; who'd have believed it?

You said I'd gone too far,
but I needed to test our plans.
If one dead man can be raised,
I thought, I can.

Right now the crowd's turned moody
and it's thundering. I'm jittery
as Houdini when snare-drums roll. Of all
our tricks this has to be the trickiest

– and Father it hurts. How many times
will Mother have to endure it?
I love her, her and the sweating extras
we roped in to heighten the drama,

I even love the hecklers in the crowd;
but where are you? You make me feel
like a poster glued to a hoarding.
What am I saying? Who am I speaking to?

I wish I was back by the lake
with loaves and fishes up my sleeves,
or taking that stroll on the water.
How I longed to believe

in myself, the legitimate arts
of prophecy and love – but *Love me*
above all others you had me roar.
Is this what you saved me for?

I've stopped believing in fathers –
they're tricks of the mind. Mother,
unfasten these hands; carry me
bleeding to that Promised Land.

The Idealist

In those blonde moments when
sun and silk marry
he imprisons himself in her hair.

He loves the way intelligence
lends its witty gloss to her skin;
those eyes miniaturised explosions

of atomic-fission blue. Could he not
have spent a lifetime ex-
ploring her strawberry mouths, all

the blind alleys of experience?
Truly this earth has proved innocent
of pity, learning, justice, intent,

all meaning; her beauties incidental.
And desire in its visceral cage contracting, exploding, contracting, exploding ...

He is like the man waiting to die
for her rape; shall he fight for the right
to endure more dawns like this?

Christine De Luca

Afghan Madonna

The photo has a title
'Mère afghane, Kaboul '98'
This one of many mothers,
this Madonna, is of all time
of each and every place.
In each line, the curve of fear,
uncertainty. There is no blasphemy
in such a title for a Moslem girl.
From her veiled *burkha*
her child's small head protrudes.
He is asleep, swaddled on her lap.
With her hidden hand she keeps him close,
the other rests upon his little head.
This hand, her one uncovered part,
could be of alabaster. It draws the eye,
glimpsed this way by chance. So still

she could have sat there for a day
or for two thousand years. The pair
are one in outline, ancient in their
presence, their significance.
One hand protecting, one hand blessing

Any God that ever listened
to the poor's entreaty,
bear them safely.

Yarbent

You took time ta mak sure I'd gotten
ivery tirl, ivery whenk o da wird
you'd used: dat een I'd aksed aboot.
Sic an owld wird hit soonded: 'yarbent'.

I can still see you luik ta Mousa, say
"Weel, hit's a boo o wadder fae da sooth-aest,
laid on herd an dry, no lik ta shift,
maybe roond voar, or eftir hairst."

Der's a yarbent settled apön me fae you gud:
sic a peerie wird, but nirse. A'll varg
i da face o him, an keep i da mind's eye,
is you wir wint tae, da bigger pictir.

Easter Past

Fae ivery croft, paes eggs,
plunkit peerie-wyes athin
bairns' wirsit socks

Easter Present

Tree windmills on a hill
a techno-Calvary
at da Brig o Fitch

Water Mirror

Drumsö Fiord, Helsinki

Above the harbour, swifts flit
in the still of a bright morning.

By afternoon, a slight breeze
choreographs a ballet of sails.

In the evening, tip-toeing cranes
lay down their burdens, lightly.

In the water's mirror I recollect
an early paradise, its dizzy freedom
reflected perfectly; and life's dance,
elemental and unrehearsed,
gracing its several worlds,
towards all receding Edens.

Winter Break

Nothing in Nice is as it was an hour ago.
The city's Cleansing team has swept
and hosed away the carnival.
Only the occasional child still dressed
as princess or pirate gives the game away,
or a monstrous *papier-mâché* head
still lolling on a bollard.
Even the flower stalls have vanished
and their thousand fragrances.
In their place, a flea market,
a temporary re-housing of clutter.
We observe this action from the safety
of a street café; let it wash over us.
We may take this city to our hearts

but our hold on it is slight. We are
merely a credit card away from selling

knick-knacks from a pavement patch
or plucking banjo strings as decent beggars.
Stripped of all reference points, we balance
on a fulcrum of fear and freedom.
The big things can be scary –
like who we truly are, and all the whys.
So we attend instead to little things:
the sheen on heaped olives, the headiness
of mimosa. We live merely by a map
and the sun's path across the sky.

Balance of Improbabilities

I will not read all Shakespeare's tragedies again,
nor the books of the bible end to end,
from thundering poetry to meditative prose.
I may not even re-read *Middlemarch*.

I will not bag the friendliest Munro
nor ride bareback through canyons' tilt of time.
I will accept I light up eyes no more,
and have become invisible to most.

I may not make that slow train *hadj* through France
with serendipity of stopping places;
swirls of wine in old plane-shaded squares,
a pilgrim to the subtlest taste of difference.

I'll learn to cope with table-turning love,
become the cherished child again myself,
try not to show I worry just as much
about their future, especially those they trust.

I'll settle for the almost midnight sun,
give up the battle with non-native plants,
savour the late flush on my clematis: transient
as sun sinks and the season turns its back.

But if a favourable alignment should occur,
a kind coincidence of planets or the stars,
I may surprise myself, backpack through canyons
and in the evening, re-read *Middlemarch*.

Essays from Chapman 35-6:

Scotland: a Predicament for the Scottish Writer

Dotted through this issue are essays, by aonghas macneacail, Joyce McMillan, George Byatt, first appearing Chapman 35-6, 1983, which considered whether 'Scottishness' was any sort of prediment for Scottish writers, and Scotland. The stimulus was the reprint of Edwin Muir's Scott and Scotland (1936) which enraged MacDairmid who thought it a betrayal of everything he was fighting for. The issue provoked a controversial and vociferous debate, polarising the writing community into those for whom Scottish identity was a real issue, and those who thought it irrelevant as we sail into the post-modern age. Despite coming from vastly different stand-points, all contributors agreed that greater political autonomy was essential for Scotland's cultural survival. In a real sense, the controversy marked a watershed, an upward surge, turning the tide on post-1979 referendum depression and the blight of the Thatcher years towards something better. The litmus text is for us all to guage how far we have moved from then ...

Rage Against the Dying of ...

aonghas macneacail

My first weeks at school were devoted exclusively to learning a foreign language. Once my classmates and I had attained sufficient fluency in the imposed tongue our own language was discarded from the learning process.

The transition must have been effective and, superficially at least, painless, for no Gael I know can recollect the process. I certainly cannot. Our experience could not have been without trauma, however. Just when we were most alert for the naming of things, including the common place which surrounded us, the language which should have been our natural tool, was undermined by school. I quickly took it for granted that a little white flower which abounds in pasture and meadow is the daisy. I have to remind myself that it is also, and for me primarily, *neòinean.*

It was only when I began to write that naming became important and, in the case of my native language, a source of frustration. If I have to think twice before identifying a common flower, there are more complex subjects, for which a rich vocabulary was once available, that are now, for my generation of Gaels, a burden to articulate. The necessary words have to be searched for in a range of inadequate, frequently antiquated, dictionaries. Often, the word stays unfound. It is accepted that the years of schooling, through to diplomas, degrees and doctorates, are the 'formative' years, when the basic adult vocabulary is developed. For the Gael, as Gael, they prove to be the 'deformative' years. There is an entire lexical geography between the exotic and everyday, a whole range of concepts which are first named through the language of our schooling. In large areas of awareness, our native language has become, in effect, our second language.

My experience is that of a generation of Gaels (the last) whose infancy predated the transistor age. With no television and little radio available to influence our pre-literate minds, the impact of other languages was minimal: until school sucked us in to suck the Gaelic out of us. It's much worse now, given that television is available to every Gaelic household at the flick of a switch: and TV only speaks Gaelic on rare occasions. As the parents of today's infants belong to the very generation that school did so much to degaelicise, it's small wonder if they should lack the will or confidence to assert their native tongue in the face of such a persuasive influence.

The tragedy of the Gaelic experience this century is that what should have enriched our lives – the acquisition of a second language – was actually a means of alienation and impoverishment. It is essential to consider such facts in any assessment of the role, or place, of the Gaelic writer in contemporary society. On reflection, I am surprised that I, or any of my generation, should have chosen to write in our native language at all.

Gaelic authors of earlier generations were less beset by such dilemmas. Those whose childhood predated the 1872 Education Act (establishing compulsory education throughout Scotland yet omitted to acknowledge the existence of Gaelic) lived their lives relatively untouched by any other language. As often as not they were non-literate – a very different thing from being illiterate except in the specific sense of being unable to read. For them the mind was word-store as well as word-mill. In their relatively self contained world they could happily be, and frequently were, monoglot. Even those who moved out of their native territories, into the lowland cities, could submerge themselves in communities of their own people. As early as the 1790's, the noted bard Duncan Ban MacIntyre served in an Edinburgh City Guard that was almost entirely composed of Highlanders.

Mary MacPherson, 19th century Skye-born laureate of the Highland Land Law Reform movement, spent ten years in Glasgow. As she trained, and worked, as a midwife and district nurse on Clydeside, she could hardly have been monoglot. We may safely assume, however, that the essential world for her and her generation, as for many Highlanders after them, was the world of their fellow expatriate Gaels. There were Gaelic churches and Gaelic concert-houses which nourished, in very different ways, the spirit of the urban Gaelic communities. The commitment of 'Great Mary of the Songs' to the land campaign was also an essentially Gaelic matter. The society most threatened by lawless landlordism was that of her own people, the predominantly Gaelic crofters in the North and West. Whatever problems they may have had to overcome, both Donnchadh Bàn and Màiri Mhor would have remained innocent of the dilemma which confronts their twentieth century counterparts. Both were steeped in their own culture. Each had a virtuosic command of the language. They knew, without presumption, that an audience existed which could comprehend their work.

We, their literary descendants, enjoy no such luxury. We cannot put words to metre or pen to paper without having made a choice. Having resolved our first dilemma – whether Gaelic is any longer a legitimate vehicle – we still have to assess the particular circumstances and ask, *which language do I use?* It's not simply a matter of mood, style or etiquette like *what suit should I wear?* Even if we 'are what we eat' I don't believe that substituting the subtleties of French or Indian cuisine for the homelier bannocks, beef stew or brose would have a profound effect on our psyche. With language there is something much deeper at stake. The language I elect, or am required, to use is not only a means of self-expression, it is the elemental medium through which I connect with the society I inhabit.

Assuming I have a need to make contact with that society, a number of issues must be resolved. They include

(1) Which layer of the demographic onion do I mean when I say 'the society I inhabit'? Am I referring to the relatively homogeneous parish or to the gallimaufrous nation?
(2) Will my message be intelligible to that society?
(3) Is that society likely to be interested in what I have to say?

One answer to question 1) is that, even without aspiring to the universal, I can, and do inhabit more than one society, or subculture. If, within Scotland, I am addressing the community of writers, I will adopt a different register from the one I use with my fellow Gael. Not only will the register be different, it will also be necessary to use a different language, as only a tiny proportion of my fellow-writers share the Gaelic language with me.

But supposing Gaelic is the only language I want to use? It is, after all, my first language and mother tongue: the language of my first expressions of elemental feelings, love, hunger, fear. Why not also the language of the more sophisticated concerns of my maturity? Why not that if I see writing as being my primary occupation, not just a preoccupation – I have to recognise that I live in a materialistic world. The work I produce, be it poetry, prose or drama, has to command a market.

What audience, then, am I likely to have? According to the 1981 census, less than 80,000 Gaelic-speakers remain in Scotland. There may be a scattering elsewhere, with concentrations like the ageing Gaelic community in Cape Breton Island, but the essential Gaelic society is represented by that four score thousand who inhabit the traditional homeland. Of their number, the great majority will be, for reasons already alluded to, illiterate in their own language. The remaining minority, which is not in the strictest sense illiterate, must itself be further subdivided. There is every reason to believe that a large proportion of Gaels who can read would regard themselves as only partially literate. These would certainly be unable to write in their own language. Many acquired what reading skills they do have not at school but from the churches. Sunday schools, Bible-classes and particularly the parallel-text New Testament have helped many Gaels toward literacy in their native tongue. Nevertheless, many who can read substantial chapters of the Bible with confidence will baulk at a short piece written in their own colloquial speech patterns. (Biblical Gaelic, a synthetic form dating from the 18th Century, is the nearest we have to a 'Standard Gaelic'. It is not, however, normally heard outwith the devotional environment.)

We still have to find our competent, confident Gaelic general reader. Those who fit the description will probably have studied Gaelic throughout secondary schooling and probably beyond. As a proportion of the 80,000, they represent only fragment. Even if we isolate this fragment, numbering no more than a couple of thousand *at most*, as the total potential readership a Gaelic writer may expect to command, we must accept that such a readership will be no more homogeneous than any other reading public. Gaelic literary tastes like those of other societies, run the gamut from *Peoples' Friend* to Pound or Pliny. So the most popular Gaelic author will quickly recognise that writing solely in the native language is not a commercially viable venture. It's as well that Gaelic writers are not primarily motivated by the size of the potential audience, nor by the likelihood of any significant financial benefit accruing from their labours.

It is, though, a cause for anger that such a situation should exist, not so much from the point of view of the writer but that of the reader. If, say, only ten out of 80,000, or 80 million for that matter, should want to read my work, then I must look to its quality or relevance. But if only a small multiple of tens out of the 80,000 *can* read the work of any Gaelic writer, it is clear that something is seriously amiss, particularly as we inhabit a culture that takes pride in its level of adult literacy. There are historical causes, of course. I've already made passing reference to the Education Act of 1872, which achieved in Law what successive regimes since that of the most foolish sage Jamie the Saxt had sought to obtain through legislation – the extirpation of the 'savage Irishe tongue'. Fortunately, *de facto* ignored *de jure*, and the language survives, if debilitated by its long struggle to stage a successful educational resurrection. The struggle continues. It is essentially the struggle for the survival of the language itself.

In the days when the world of the Gael was a Gaelic world and education – the acquisition of knowledge – an osmotic part of being, the survival of the language and its rich literary treasury could be taken for granted. There have been many changes since then. For a long time now, Gaelic in the Gaelic community has been peripheral to the educational process. It has been squeezed into an equally marginal role in other fields where the larger world impinges on that of the Gael. There are powerful and malign influences that begrudge it even that precarious peripheral existence. Such influences are powerful because of the positions they occupy, either as 'elected representatives' or as high-ranking operatives within the bureaucracies, both national and local. They are malign not so much because of what they do but because of what they contrive to avoid doing. For them, the continuing survival of Gaelic is an irritant. God knows why, but it is. The concept of a Gaelic Revival is, to them, an idea charged with negative energy as welcome as an unprotected radioactive isotope. It has to be contained, neutralised, isolated, so that it cannot energise others. If kept dormant for long enough, it will turn to lead. It will have lost its disseminative potency while still retaining the capacity to poison.

The black militia engaged in this campaign operates at various levels of the body politick. Sometimes they act clandestinely. Often they are quite brazen. Their ranks include Ordinance Survey cartographers who for perfectly logical reasons find it impossible to restore Gaelic placenames to their proper form and status. These deprive us of a geography. They include Government stationers who are unable to provide us with official forms or documents in our own language. (This saying that Government does not recognise our right, as a community, to exist, however platitudinously politicians may plead the contrary.) They include broadcasting administrators, some of whom have acquired our language. They may wish us well, but do not feel they can promise ever to be able to provide is with a comprehensive broadcasting service in Gaelic. This makes them also tacit conspirators in the scheme to eliminate us. They will also be found running schools, colleges, universities and departments of education.

They may and, frequently do, overflow with goodwill, but each has an excuse. No matter how much they wish to help, there will be convincing reasons why they cannot do anything to further the development of the language or culture of the Gaels. Even when the expression 'further the development' means no more than 'attempt to sustain the existence', these bland cultural assassins will use the force of their own inaction to tighten the noose around the already-emaciated neck of our Gaelic heritage. It is as well for the British Establishment that such people are its allies, not its enemies. They may seem the least probable candidates for membership of a guerilla force, but there is no denying their effectiveness. Almost without exception, they present themselves as pillars of society, the class of people who most eminently qualify for the designation 'reasonable'. There could be no better cover for a hit-squad. And how ineffably reasonable they appear to be when they deploy the most shattering weapon in their armoury. This projectile, small but significant, is the verbal equivalent to a nuclear hand-grenade. It is the innocuously disjunctive conjunction *but.*

"We'd like to, *but*... " How often have we heard, the sympathy disarming – then the devastation. In a recent superb example of the genre, a spokesman for the Consultative Committee on the Curriculum pronounced the CCC in "sympathy with the aspirations of" its own Committee on Gaelic, "so far as these are commensurate with the availability of resources". The absence of a naked 'but' does not prove me wrong: the quotation is suffused with the essence of 'butness'. Of course, the 'butlers' of destruction have been with us for a long time. They will probably always be with us.

This essay set out to explore the place of a Gaelic writer in the community. It's worth acknowledging that Willie Neill, in the last issue of *Chapman*, correctly identified yet another cell of destroyers: the analysts and anthologists of Scottish Literature who glibly excuse themselves for omitting anything on, or in, Gaelic, while continuing to serve up their product as a legitimate representation of *Scottish* writing. Gaelic writers, like all fellow Gaels, inhabit a precarious, inconstant, intrinsically hostile world. Sometimes there is good earth underneath their feet, sometimes hard stone. Then when they least expect it, there is vacancy. All the landmarks they might expect to recognise spin out of focus, and out of sight. Successive generations who suffered the same dislocation as I aged five will be familiar with the experience. And still we continue to ride such storms. And still, somehow, we survive. We survived James the Sixth, for all his Bills and Statutes. We survived the educational exterminators of 1872. We expect, and receive, no support from their successors, but we endure.

20th Century Gaeldom may seem to be teetering on the brink. It has, nevertheless, produced, in Sorley MacLean, arguably the greatest Gaelic poet of all time, and a figure of richly-deserved international standing in our own. During his career as a schoolmaster, MacLean felt compelled to engage much precious time and energy in resisting the tides of cultural genocide. He became particularly involved during his headship of Plockton Secondary School. Each annual intake of pupils was further evidence that Gaelic was dying on its feet in one of its heartlands, Wester Ross. MacLean chose to campaign for the introduction of a *Learners* Higher Grade paper in Gaelic. Inevitably, they met stiff resistance from the cohorts of crassness, but they fought on, and won. They won that crucial battle, but MacLean would be first to recognise that the struggle for Gaelic in education is far from over. Despite the bilingual programmes and projects that have followed in its wake, the struggle is far from over.

In retrospect, it seems more than ridiculous that MacLean and friends should have had to fight at all. What they were asking for was no more than equal status for Gaelic with other modern languages such as French, German or Russian. Till then, it had existed in a kind of educational ghetto, taught as if it *were* a foreign language, yet at such a standard as to be accessible only to the most academically able native speakers. Now we have a syllabus for learners. In theory it should be possible for any secondary pupil in Scotland to study Gaelic. The 'butlers' make damn sure it won't be.

For almost two decades, Sorley MacLean published virtually nothing. During that time he wrote no poetry. Teaching, particularly the teaching of his own language and culture, concerned him deeply. At the end of his working day, there would have been precious little energy left for poetry. We may regret the limitation this imposed on the corpus of MacLean's poetry. He cannot be regarded as any the less a poet for it. MacLean himself would consider it imperative that the poet should be involved in the issues of the day, particularly as they affect the society he belongs to. Those of us who are Gaels and writers are unlikely to forget that we are Gaels first and that the society we, primarily, belong to is that remnant of Gaeldom which, by some peculiar miracle, survives.

We cannot take for granted that the language we use in any given circumstances will be our own. As writers we have to make a conscious choice to use Gaelic. Such a decision may exclude the great majority of our fellow Gaels from immediate access to our work. It also excludes us, the writers, from the responses of that portion of fellow Gaels. These awarenesses, paradoxically, strengthen my conviction that choosing our native language to express our deepest thoughts is a necessary, political, act.

Angus Peter Campbell

A' Ghàidhealtachd

Acair os dèidh acair dheth bàn falamh,
mar nach robh na milleanan a' bàsachadh
gun òrlich talmhainn ann am Bombay.

Mar as fhaide tuath a thèid thu
tha an fhàsach nas brèagha buileach,
mar gun robh thu suirghe le Snow White
gun fhios gun robh i marbh.

Air làithean soilleir samhraidh
tha a' Ghàidhealtachd a' tasgadh bòidhchead
mar nach robh adhbhar eile bhith ann
ach teas is crith is cuileag is fois shìorraidh.

An t-uamhas *mirages* ri fhaicinn san teas bhrùiteach seo.
Nuair chì thu Beinn Shuileabhain san Lùnastal
tha e mar gun robh MacCaoig fhèin beò a rithist
dram na làimh air *Rose Street*, an Fhèill na làn teis.

Ach tha bràighean Ghlinn Eilg
agus stiopalan àrda Chinn t-Sàile
agus ceòl-mòr na Cuilthionn
mar lèintean-sìoda a' bhàis,
cuibhrigean a còmhdachadh an uamhais,
oir chan eil an saoghal falamh gun adhbar.

Oir dh'fhuadaich fir fir
agus dh'èignich fir mnathan
agus mhurt fir clan
mar ùrlar airson an t-sàmchais shòlamaichte,
mar chladh air Sàbaid buan.

The Highlands

Acre after acre of it vacant and empty,/ as if the millions weren't dying without an inch of earth in Bombay.

The further north you go/ the wilderness grows ever more beautiful,/ as if you were wooing Snow White/ without realising she was dead.

On bright summer days/ the Highlands collect beauty/ as if there was no reason for being/ except heat and shimmer and fly-buzz and eternal peace.

A remarkable number of mirages to be seen in this opressive heat./ When you see Ben Suilven in August/ it's as if MacCaig himself were alive again/ dram in hand on Rose Street, the Festival in full swing.

But the braes of Glenelg/ and the high peaks of Kintail/ and the big music of the Cuillin/ are like the shrouds of death,/ blankets covering the terror,/ for the world is not empty without reason.

For men evicted men/ men raped women/ and men murdered children as a foundation to this solemn silence,/ like a graveyard on an eternal Sabbath.

Cnòideart

Cluinnidh tu an t-shàmhchair an-seo:
chaidh an Gàidheal mu dheireadh
a thiodhlagadh o chionn dà mhìos, ann an Inbhirnis.

Tha fichead taigh an-seo,
cuid cho bòidheach le feasgar samhraidh,
's tu coimhead criogaid gu ciùin aig an Oval.

Tha cuid falamh,
ach làn bhogsaichean bhriosgaidean
airson na làithean-saora;

aig fear dhe na taighean
tha brat-ùrlar beag aig an doras
airson Rover, 'ic Rover.

Tha e mar taobh thall na gealaich,
far an do leum Niall Armstrong gu talamh
an latha thionndaich e càise gu dusd.

A-nis, on tha Rèis an Fhànais seachad,
's dòcha gum faodadh sinn soitheach a chur a Chnòideart.

Tha dusd an sin cuideachd,
a dearbhadh gun robh – uair – beatha air talamh.

Knoydart

You can hear the silence hear/ the last native Gaelic speaker was buried/ two months ago, in Inverness.

There are twenty houses here,/ any as bonny as a summer's eve,/ as you sit watching cricket at the Oval.

Some are empty,/ except full of tins of biscuits/ for the holidays;

at one of the houses/ there's a small door-mat/ for Rover MacRover.

It's like the far side of the moon/ where Neil Armstrong jumped to earth/ the day he turned cheese into swirling dust.

Now, since the Space Race is at end,/ perhaps we can send a rocket to Knoydart.

Dust also swirls there/ to prove that – once – there was life on earth.

Stafainn

Cha b'urrainn fiùs ministear seasamh an-seo
le cheann maol an aghaidh nan clachan-meallain.

Ge brith dè 'n taobh a sheallas tu
tha àite gu leòr airson nam marbh. Gu siar,
mar eisimpleir, dhan chuan far an do thuit
bràthar m' athair is iomadh luchd-adhar dhan bheinn
air madnaidhean ceòthach cogaidh.

Gu tuath
chan eil dad ach fairge gun truas
a' breabadh gu cruaidh suas na stallan
far do leum na h-eich àlainn
sìos
air las le eagal is iongnadh –
am t-iongnadh an uairsin, an t-eagal a-nis –
gu bàs
an latha thàinig a' chiad chàr a Stafainn,
a dèanamh air an taigh-òsd', airson tì is bonnaich.

Staffin

Not even a minister could stand here/ bareheaded against the hailstones.

Whichever way you look/ there's plenty room for the dead. Westwards, for example, into the ocean where fell/ my uncle and scores of other airmen headfirst into the mountains/ on foggy war mornings.

Northwards/ there is nothing but merciless sea/ kicking hard against the cliffs/ over which the beautiful wild horses/ leapt/ ablaze with fear and wonder –/ the wonder then, the terror now –/ to their deaths/ the day the first car came to Staffin,/ puffing towards the hotel, for tea and scones.

Deireadh an t-Saoghail

Bha e dol a thighinn gu ceann:
An Leth Meadhanach agus Gearradh na Mònadh air an losgadh gu luaithr',
Dòmhnall Iain agus Donaidh agus Iain agus Mòrag air chall
ann am priobadh na sùla bhon t-seada staoin aig ceann na sgoile,
bhon bhus a' dol gu tuath,
bhon treasamh treasta-cùil aig an aifreann,
bhon tràigh air madainn Shatharna.

Mu dheas,
mu Ghlaschu,
bha nèamh uaine
na bhreug na mhiann:
Simpson, Craig is Gemmell,
Murdoch, Macneil is Clark,

Johnstone Chalmers Wallace Auld is Hughes,
far an do choinnich dà shaoghal,
crois no dealachadh an rathaid,
dachaigh is bruadar, faoin.

'S Bàgh nam Mucan –
an rud a bha dol a chur crìoch air Kruschev,
no Castro, 's air Alasdair Fhionnlaigh aig ceann an taighe –
cha b'e deireadh an t-saoghail a bh'ann idir
ach dìreach raoidhteireachd rùisgte nam fir
nan seasamh mar àigich air leabaidh-shìoda Mharilyn.

The End of the World

It was all going to end:/ South Boisdale and Garrynamonie burnt to ashes, Donald John and Iain and Morag removed/ in the twinkling of an eye from the tin shed at the back of the school,/ from the north-going bus/ from the third-back pew at Mass,/ from the shore on the Saturday morning.

Southwards,/ about Glasgow,/ there was a green heaven/ like a lie, like a promise:/ Simpson, Craig and Gemmell,/ Murdoch, MacNeil and Clark, Johnstone Chalmers Wallace Auld and Hughes,/ where two worlds collided,/ the meeting or separation of the roads,/ home and vain exile.

And the Bay of Pigs –/ the event that was going to eliminate Kruschev,/ or Castro, and Alasdair Finlay at the end of his thatched house –/ wasn't the end of the world at all/ but just the naked ridings of men/ standing erect like lusty stallions over Marilyn's silken bed.

'S fheàirrd' thu Guinness

Am measg nam breugan
a chaidh a thàirnigeadh
gu cinnteach a-steach
do chiste Sheonaidh MhicAonghais
's e na laighe sin an t-seachdain sa chaidh
bha an tè mhòr:
Guinness is Good for You.

Aon turas chunnaic mi an saor ud
a dòrtadh dusan pinnt dheth sìos amhaich,
an t-uachdar mar bhruadar
feise
air a bhilean thiugh.

An t-seachdain mus do bhàsaich e –
a' chlaigeann air a phronnadh le bara-cuibhle –
bha e dìreach air crìoch
a chur air togalach ùr do Bhanca na h-Eirinn.

An-dè, 's mi giùilean
aon sreang air a' chiste cardboard,
chaidh sinn seachad air aon phub agus air aon bhanc'.
Agus an sin,
anns an dìle dhèarrsach,
chuir sinn san talamh e,
Dia eadar dà mhèirleach.

Guinness is Good for You

Among the lies/ which were nailed/ with finality into/ Johnny MacInnes's coffin/ as he lay there last week/ was the big one:/ Guiness is Good for You.

One time I saw that joiner/ pouring a dosen of these black pints down his throat,/ the white froth like a dream/ of sex/ on his thick lips.

The week before he died –/ his skull crushed by a falling wheel-barrow –/ he'd just finished erecting/ a new building for the Bank of Ireland.

Yesterday, as I carried/ one string on his cardboard coffin,/ we passed one pub and one bank./ And there,/ in the pouring rain,/ we lowered him into the earth,/ God between two thieves.

Aig an Fhèill

Ghluais iad uile, mar nancaidh nan cìochan,
a' giùlan ròsan cho dearg leis an tè
a choinnich mi uair le a fionnadh air a dhathadh
mar a Union Jack – dearg is geal is gorm.

Bha i dèanamh *phonetics* agus radacal
dìreach ann am polataigs na feise. B'e a leannan
fear dom b'ainm Uisdean, mac bancair. Tha iad a-nis
sgaraichte, sgaoilt' an àiteigin an Siorrachd Adhar.

Sin iadsan.

Thàinig iad as gach ceàrn chun an fhèill:
na teuchtars fhalaichte mar mi fhèin,
feadhainn a bha falach beartas,
feadhainn a bha falach creideamh,
feadhainn a bha falach polataigs,
feadhainn a bha falach a h-uile dad:
thàinig sinn uile chun an fhèill.

Bha stàl aig Einstein ann an oisean,
an ath dhoras do Chris Smout
agus Feddie Ayer
(agus Dr Drucker agus Gordon Brown).
Roinn na diathachd a reic BDs,
luchd-saidheans PhDs. Gheibheadh tu bogadh
agus/no drugaichean no/agus spòrs nan lìonadh

tu foirm. Dh'inns misgeir do bhàrd dhuinn
gun robh sinn òg is saor is farasda
mar ùbhlan fo chraoibh ann an Ceàrnag Sheòrais.

('S tric a chuimhnicheas mi caileag bhachlach chualach
a bhiodh air an saoghal a riaghladh
mura be gun dh'eug i air *amphetamines* an oidhche
bha i fichead, 's i coimhead – marbh –
mar eòintean air machaire Bhòirnis).

Tha fhiosam a-nis gun robh sinn mar isbeanan
air truinnsearan luchd-teagais, zeros ann an cunntasan-banca.
'S na h-igheanan òga, gu h-àraid, air an ith
mar *chipolatas* air latha Nollaig. Mar a shil
an saill air na forcan biorach, a' brùthadh a' chraicinn shùghach.

Àrsairean.

Le dùil gun toireadh sinne an *revolution* air adhart!
Airson libearalaich a bha radacal gu leòr airson feise
ach chan ann airson stailc no fòirneirt.

Dìreach foighnich dha na meinnearan.

Dh'fhàg foghlam mu shluagh gun chumhachd,
mar dh'fhag gach cogadh eile.

Tha òr an amadain air dèarsadh air mìle mìle ceum.

At the Fair

They all moved, like busty Nancy,/ carrying roses as red as the one/ I once met who'd dyed her pubic hair/ in the shape of the Union Jack – all read and white and blue.

She was studying phonetics and was radical/ only in sexual politics. Her boyfriend/ was called Hugh, the son of a banker. They are now/ divorced, scattered somewhere in Ayrshire.

So much for them.

We came from every part to the fair:/ the hidden teuchters like masel',/ those who hid wealth,/ those who hid religion,/ those who hid politics,/ those who hid (behind) everything:/ we all came to the fair.

Einstein had a stall in the corner,/ next door to Chris Smout/ and Freddie Ayer/ (and Dr Drucker and Gordon Brown)./ The theology department selling BDs,/ scientists' PhDs. You could have sex/ and/or drugs or/and sports at the filling in/ of a form. A drunkard of a poet told us/ that we were young and free and easy/ like apples under a tree in George Square.

(I often remember a golden-ringletted girl/ who would have ruled the world/ had she not died from an overdose of amphetamines/ the night of her 20th birthday. She looked – dead –/ like daisy on the long Bornish machair).

I now know we were sausages/ on the lecturers' plates, zeros in several bank accounts./ And the young girls, in particular, consumed/ like chipolatas *on Christmas day. How the fat/ dripped on the sharp forks, piercing the juicy skins./ You bastards.*

And expecting that we would carry the revolution forward!/ For liberals radical enough to fuck/ but not to strike or die on the picket lines.

Just ask the miners./ Education has left my people powerless,/ just like every other war.

The fool's gold has shone on a million graduations.

Eilean an Ionmhais

A dèarrsadh,
mar ghuth Alvar Liddell air oidhcheanan geamhraidh an Uibhist
ann an litrichean òr Gallda, a' dèalradh eadar *Black Beauty*
agus *Kidnapped.*

Bha iad gu lèir lainnearach, annasach:
gillean tapaidh le *flannels*, gun can nam beathaichean mun glùin,
gun ifrinn no locha-theine, no Beurla, gan tàladh, gan dìteadh.

Oir b'iadsan balaich na h-Ìmpireachd,
caileagan nan each,
nach robh leibideach no lag.

Ach b'e mo dhaoine-sa am maighstir-sgoile, salach geal le cailc,
agus an sagart àrd, a' spaidsearachd air ais
a dh'àm far nach robh aon duine slac.

Curaidhean coilionta: thug na ciùrramaich orm an trom-laighe –
mo chànan mabach fhìn,
Più Dall a dol tap-tap-tap.

B'e Long John Silver Dia le cas fiodh.
Am paids mo chreud, a' phitheid m' fhoghlam,
's na buinn Gaidhlig air an deagh thiodhlagadh fo map òir na Beurla.

X marks the spot,
ged nach robh *x* san aibideil ann.

Treasure Island

Glittering,/ like Alvar Liddell's voice on winter nights in Uist/ in golden English letters, shining between Black Beauty*/ and* Kidnapped.

These strangers all shone, marvellously:/ handsome boys in flannels, without cow-shit at the knees,/ without hell or the lake of fire, or English, tempting/ or condemning them.

For they were the boys of Empire,/ the girls of swift ponies,/ who were neither clumsy nor weak.

But my people were the school-master, dirty white with chalk,/ and the tall priest, marching backwards/ into a time where no one ever lapsed.

Perfect heroes: the disabled gave me nightmares –/ my own stuttering tongue,/ Blind Pew going tap-tap-tap.

Long John Silver was God with a wooden leg./ The patch my religion, the parrot my education,/ and the Gaelic coins well buried beneath the golden map of English.

X marks the spot,/ even though x doesn't exist in the Gaelic alphabet.

Nam Dheugaire

Innsidh mi dhut cò mu dheidhinn a bha Ghàidhlig:
can nam beathaichean 's oisglinnean,
buachar nam bò 's an dubh-chosnadh,
Sàbaidean sìorraidh buan is dìteadh
airson na cànan deireannach.

Air an làimh eile,
bha na fir
dhachaigh à Singers,
Fair Ghlaschu agus Geamachan Aisgeirnis,
Tom Paxton agus Woody Guthrie,
Jimi Hendrix agus Mick Jagger,
agus – eadar an ceòl dùthchail – Lulu
a' dol boom
bang-a-bang-bang
fad na h-ùin'.

Cha robh an roghainn
eadar na bòtannan fliuch dubh
agua ns sliasaidean fada lom aig Dusty
Springfield
doirbh sam bith,
fiùs ann an Gàidhlig.

As a Teenager

I'll tell you what Gaelic was about:/ cow-shit and oilskins, manure and hard labour,/ long eternal Sabbaths and condemnation/ for a dying tongue.

On the other hand,/ the men/ came home from Singers,/ for the Glasgow Fair and the Askernish Games,/ Tom Paxton and Woody Guthrie,/ Jimi Hendrix and Mick Jagger,/ and – in between the country and western – Lulu/ going boom/ bang-a-bang-bang/ all the time.

The choice/ between the soaking black wellies/ and Dusty Springfield's long bare/ thighs/ wasn't that difficult,/ even in Gaelic.

History Will Say

Jeff A Talarigo

Fiddling with the Strings of Fate

My balls are pushed tight, sometimes swallowed inside me. Winter and summer. Fear and cold. Day and night. That's what the Alleghenies do to me.

From east to west. Stony; Broad; Mahantango; Hooflander; Shamokin; Chestnut Ridge; Catawisa; Nescopeck; Shade; Big Poe; Tussy; Nittany; Bald Eagle. Ridges of the Alleghenies. Long and low. Fog or slouching clouds or even a clear night really makes no difference. Difficult to judge the distance from above. Rapid changes in the weather. Very few level places to make emergency landings. A graveyard for pilots.

Each of the ridges I have registered in my mind. I know them like past lovers. Each with its own distinctive scent. Some you need to get very close to, others from far away their scent reaches and lingers on my scarf, on my tongue. Cedars iced in winter, drenched maples in spring, fallen oak leaves crispy, summer's spruces. And like a lover, the Alleghenies can lift you to the highest of heights or plunge you to the deepest of depths.

We are told to follow the roads and railroads, but I've always preferred rivers and streams. Something about their uneasiness, their unpredictability that I love. How they can change course, forming small branches, how too much rain can overflow their sides, how too little can bring them to a trickle or stop them altogether.

The streams and rivers should have been given their names from above. Only from up here can their true form, their true path be seen. Susquehanna, Lehigh, Juniata, Allegheny. Beautiful named rivers all over the state. Names left behind as a remembrance, or guilt perhaps, to those we chased off the land. Why didn't we leave behind the people and change the names of the rivers?

To the children we were like gods, to the others who knew better, mere heroes. It really must have been quite a sight from down on the ground. To me it was what I did. I never really paid much attention to details like how thrilling it was for the children, everybody really. A doubled winged bird appearing, swaying out of the sky, getting bigger, hop-hopping to a landing in a field. We are so astonished by new things. Cars, radio, and now television. We have embraced them all.

Quite a long time it took for me to begin to enjoy the adulation; the landing, stepping out of the cockpit surrounded by children tugging at me, men shaking my hand, rapping me on the back, women giving me the eye. I did, I must admit, always enjoy the women who gave me the eye. It was all the other stuff that made me uncomfortable. Just a few minutes before I had been up there all alone. Most days, I couldn't wait to get back up. Many times I just wanted to fly away and never land. I think that one of the few times that I was like the other pilots was when I was above the ground. Many of them – Slim, Charlie, Wild Bill – thrived on the dramatic landings, swooping close enough to make the weather vanes twirl, near enough to spit into the eye of a bull, dropping letters of love with bolts in the envelopes to weigh them down. Over time I became more used to it, started to enjoy life on the ground a little more.

But, I was never like those guys. Not only great pilots, but also wonderful performers; they knew how to entertain. What we all did share was the passion for flying. It was much too dangerous a job to do only for what awaited you once you landed. All three of them – Slim, Charlie, Wild Bill – died in those early years of flying the mail. All three of them died on the ground. They were the lucky ones. I was left behind to fiddle with the strings of fate, left behind to die far above the ground.

Life on the Ground

She brought me to life on the ground. Clarisa. Her name rolls off my tongue like the smoothest of scotch. Clarisa. Makes me drunk just saying it. Clarisa. We met in the candy apple line at the Centre County Fair in 1928. The second daughter of a Greek goat farmer just outside Bellfonte. I spent a lot of time in Bellfonte, as did many of the pilots, the first refuelling stop on the New York to Chicago airmail run. A town of several thousand cuddled between Nitanny and Bald Eagle Mountains.

Before I had met Clarisa the ground was only a waiting place for going back up into the air. A place for me to refuel with sleep and food and perhaps a little snuggle with a woman. But with Clarisa I began noticing the trees and how tall they were when you lay beneath one, the beauty of the baaah of a sheep, the sharp angles of barn roofs.

Guided by a farm light, I would land the plane on one of the small roads outside of town and walk the mile or so to the farm. If the plane came too close, the goats woke her father, and although I think he had no ill feelings towards me, he certainly wouldn't have taken too kindly to me and his daughter going out to the plane and doing what we did.

What we did. Clarisa. Makes me tremble when I think of it. The wings swaying side to side with our inebriated loving, the beautifully crude jokes she made about the cockpit, wearing only my leather pilot's hat keeping her always cold love-making ears warm, the goggles I sometimes kept on steaming up, her fingers, like wipers, allowing me to see how the grids on the wings left imprints on my knees and elbows and how we laughed after she called me Waffle Knees.

Magical nights. But they always ended with her silence. A silence I knew was coming. The silence of worry. A worry that gripped her. I knew of it, but didn't understand, didn't, couldn't allow myself to think of it. Don't know of a pilot who really thought that their next flight may be their last.

Then she had to go, when I didn't understand such things, she had to go and ask me to do the one thing I couldn't.

So many dark days after Clarisa. So many times my plane dove towards a mountain top or face to face with a barn silo. But something, at the last minute, something that I don't know where it ever came from, something that made me pull the plane up, arch its back, soar and save me. It wasn't that I wanted to die, only that I didn't care if I did.

So many dark days. So difficult avoiding something from up in the air. On the ground a road or two away was enough to separate me from seeing Clarisa's house, but up in the plane I had to go miles out of my way to get away from it. Twenty miles is nothing in a plane, but it's like a thousand on foot when you're trying to escape. Escape every little thing that reminded me of her.

Bottom sides of leaves.

Bleating goats.

Candy apples.

Three gruelling years trudged by and it wasn't until the airmail refuelling stop was moved northwest to Kylertown that I was saved. Only then those memories of her started to slink away from hatred and back to fondness. So much I loved those times with her that I hated thinking of them.

They bore into me, scars they have left behind.

But those scars are nothing compared to those that I carry with me now. Impossible as it might have seemed, it is only those memories of Clarisa that can now give me any glimmer of peace with myself.

Stay on the ground she told me. How right she was. The one thing that if I had done it would have saved me from the taunting which has been following me every day, minute, microsecond. Only these thoughts of Clarisa – if ever so briefly – nurse from me my bitterness, my anger, my deep regret that I didn't die on the ground years ago like Slim and Charlie and Wild Bill. A spectacular crash, flames gobbling the plane, as it flips on the ground, the myths swirling, swelling, well before the chisel has left its first mark on the tombstone.

The Heaviest Pregnancy the World Has Ever Known

History will say it was cloudy. I know differently.

Dark skies, streaks of lightening over the Pacific. Maps, detailed aerial photos, weather reports, emergency landing areas. Talk is in low voices though we're thousands of miles from anyone.

We eat an early breakfast, a chaplain alongside. Stand huddled in groups of two or three. Waiting. The chaplain relays God's blessings to us. His premeditated absolution.

2:56 am in Saipan.

Dinner time in Italy.

Lunch in Pennsylvania.

Northwest over Anatahan, Guguan, Pagan, Agrihan, Maug. Only the Pacific. We dip and bump in heavy storms. I worry about the plane's belly – the heaviest pregnancy the world has ever known.

The weather clears. Smooth flying for Number Seventy-Seven. 5:00 am whispers of morning.

5:50 am the rising sun.

Italians kiss their children goodnight.

Pennsylvanians eye the clocks for quitting time.

9:00 am Japanese waters. No bluer or any less than all the rest. Seventy-seven begins to climb. Strap on my parachute, Yakushima is in sight. We are joined by two other planes, head north to Kokura. Kokura. Thirty-one thousand feet above. Kokura. Circle a first time. Kokura.

Looking through the rubber eyepiece. Technically you could say it is cloudy. History will say so. Most clouds, nothing more than pollution spilling from steel and blimp factories. It could be dropped – pretty sure of it.

"No drop!" I shout, as ordered back in Tinian.

A second circling, definitely no drop site. Certain of it.

"No drop!" Artillery fire is coming our way. We are still too high for them. One more circling. The third.

What do or don't I see? I see the river, our guide point. I see a child, waving. I see the blimp factory. I see a child, waving. I see steel factories. I don't see the child. Only a shadow on a crumbled wall.

"No drop!"

"No drop!"

In Italy they are deep asleep.

Pennsylvanians have Danny Kaye on the radio.

They go about their mornings in Nagasaki.

Illustration by Simon Kidd

Angus Calder

Politics, etc:

'The Trees are in their Autumn Beauty"

Bush versus Gore on the box –
impertinence and insolence
confront each other in consuming time.
The exquisite autumn descends to grime.
The passionate austerity of Knox
commands me a moment as delicious leaves
are consumed within their annual paradox --
'Time passing, beloved'. There is no innocence.
The essence of all experience is Fall,
and how could Americans choose a worthy man?
Yet because aerial gold is truly fine
I can revert to believe that the bottom line
is in fact this – because there is bliss,
we should be as young as we were for as long as we can.

"Ye are na Mary Morrison!"

There wis a kinda plainness
(and, tae be frank, plookiness) tae Mary.
She stood short and square
like the dream of a nation
in which truths wid happen – not scary,
not altogether ruled by vainness –
and very definitely there.
I appreciated the whiff of her knickers
wafting towards me above the heather
eftir we'd done the business thegither.
Her fingernails were strong, but nae vicious.
There wis a tang of parsley in her hair.
When she peed and flushed it wis like an avalanche,
and somehow her every utterance was seditious.

"My Heart's in Hiding ..."

Somewhere at the bottom of the grand
canyon where the child labourers scrabble
there is maybe a wee fountain could transform
people into deities from rabble.
Perhaps amid the saharan sand
of our desperation, an oasis will shed
sweet dates upon us. The laidly worm
is not perhaps finally master. Can the windhover
truly command the skies? I am led

somehow to hope because the dearness
of much is apparent from the occasional nearness
our hiding hearts eschew. Dead leaves cover
the bulbs of spring. There is the true
'we' we are usually missing, some clearness?

Fax for Armenia: Christmas to New Year 2001-2

to Ara Edoyan

When the sun rises, Embro streets
will no longer be empty.
Even now, before dawn in midwinter
darkness, industrious
pigeons forage in our festive rubbish.

Next sun scintillates on grey stone
and a headachey people
pace back to whatever daily business keeps them,
briefly, industrious
in a handsome city long spared war.

Elsewhere that dawn has filtered
through Polish forests
to sites stripped of death's machinery
once so industrious,
mute terraines of redundant railways.

In high skies over mountains, alien eagles
stare down into wrecked kitchens
while in waterless camps children are starving,
aid is industrious
in a cause which it seems can never succeed.

Where once there was massacre,
long abandoned churches in square cross style
are frequented by the ghosts of painted saints
cheerful, industrious
in good for woman, man and dumbest beast.

Whether gilt or blue sky framed
their frank, large-eyed heads,
they were reminders of how courageous
Noah, industrious,
brought us to rest on saving Ararat

where the bright pigeon returned at last
with the branch of hope.
In my streets once flooded with blood
by menyies industrious
in murder, a fragrance of rainbows persists.

Watching a Photograph of Robert Mitchum in the Cameo Cinema Bar

(for Miles, the barman, named after Miles)

Old men forever young in celluloid
stars not quite yet extinguished in their sky,
those presences which left us overjoyed
with notions that we'd never die –
reels of mooning country and western
thread through mid-afternoon
in late January, coming on June:
then a taped jazzman stabs with his trumpet –
oh blues, true blues, time is a strumpet.

two

The secret of jazz improvisation –
of art, indeed – is always going too far,
as if, at the risk of burglary
you leave the front door wide ajar.

three

Parker coming from all places at once:
Ornithology.
If you cannot fly with this bird you're a dunce,
which we all are and possibly always will be.
But we dwell with Icarus at Storyville
in legends which create us,
tales which kill.

The gunslinging heavy needs only one bullet,
the cavalry rides too late over the hill,
yet we need a destiny or we can't fulfill it.
Enlightened and befogged by art's afflatus
we prosper in the fiction of our will.

Outer Suburban Epiphany

On an overcast July morning
in what once claimed to be Surrey
but is now more London than ever,
a smart cricket-ball's throw from
the school which in my fraught
teens I grimly attended – a grey
heron, stupendously, stoopingly
stands by a pool of the Wandle
(John Ruskin's favourite river
when all its purlieux were rural)
in Beddington Park. Hard by

the busy main road, for several
rapt minutes, I watch this distinguished
creature, stock still, not to be fussed
by me, till it flaps with brooding
majestic-ness off towards Hackbridge
commuter Station.
Occasional visitor
now to this territory where under grey
sky, the heavy trees are soaked in grey
smirr, nettles are greyed, and aspirant
blackberries poking through slats
in the fence seem doomed to be dust –
grey, petrol-fume grey, I am grateful
that Heron with its particular grey
thisness has pointed with expectancy
and appetite my foreboded London day.

For Joy Hendry

At the time of the year
when the clocks go back
amid fierce winds and delicious skylight
as for a long blink no clouds lower,
so that death becomes a more serious fear,
imagining the sunshine we will lack
when we have passed through Hades' portal,
my aptly-named friend Joy
announces that the gift of an extra hour
convinces her that she is immortal,
as if time will give back what time destroys –
the golden leaves and the lasses, the doted boys,
the elixir of this extremely bright
Sunday, between dark and dark.

I Met a Man Who Saw Charlie Chaplin Taking a Family Holiday in Nairn ...

Inspiring me to suggest these titles for new strathspeys, reels and pipe tunes

Boris Karloff's Reel
The Mighty Sparrow's Descent on Wigtown
John Wayne's Retreat from Cowdenbeath
Lady Day's Farewell to Troon
Humphrey Bogart's Scrabster Fancy
Marilyn Monroe's Welcome to Achiltibuie
(And Madonna's Wedding in Skibo ...)

Everything is Fine

Rhoda Dunbar

Maudie counts out the money again, the two £2 coins, the three £1s and the fifty, the same total as before. She puts them back in her purse. She draws the coppers into her hand and puts them in too. Then she drops the fives, tens and twenties into their separate tins. She touches the £10 note, her safety note, out of sight in the thin slip-pocket. Alan would have laughed, "You can't take it with you, Maudie."

Maybe he couldn't take it with him, but he didn't leave much behind. He must have known. But if she asked it was, "Don't worry Maudie, everything is fine." And it was. Such fine times they had. And such fine things he liked to give her. Like this wrap she has on, so soft and warm, black mohair for going out at night. Now she wears it in the afternoons, sits in it listening to the radio. She doesn't need the heating till five or six o'clock.

She writes her list, tea, eggs, potatoes, two carrots, a leek. What a way to buy vegetables. Alan was so proud of his garden, "Maudie," he'd call, "come and see." She'd go, on bright summer mornings, to choose from the new-raked rows. She adds up the prices. She'll maybe manage washing-powder too. She folds away the mohair, buttons on her old Burberry coat. All these clothes, they'll last as long as she will. The lawyers let her keep things like that. She puts her purse and her list in the right-hand pocket. Then, from the shelf above the radio, she takes a separate set of coins, four fifties and seven tens. She puts them into the left-hand pocket. Such a deep safe pocket. She taps it with the flat of her palm. Riches, her morning routine, the pot of tea and the toast on the laid-out tray. Then the pillows propped, and her reading glasses and the paper.

She'd kept their bed. It fills the room, one side of it tight against the wall; on the other side, just enough space to squeeze along. She starts with the crossword, reading out the clues as she sips her tea and crunchies. Again, no need for the heating to go on, with the big down duvet. No need to smooth out crumpled pages – she used to smile at that – for a man who kept such a lovely ordered garden, so many things left crumpled.

"You must have known," they'd said as they pointed to her signature alongside his on the documents. But Alan had assured her, "There will always be enough." And there was, just enough to rent the tight little flat, and to buy the bare essentials in the shabby little shop on this drab edge of the town. It's cold as she walks along. The sun is bright but the wind whisks up sharp snaps of gravel that sting round her legs.

The shop is quiet, no other customer. At first, only the man. She usually tries to say something conversational. Today she says, "The wind is sharp." She doesn't know if he hears her but she doesn't try again. The sell-by date on the eggs gives only three days. The carrots are rubbery and the leeks have started to rot.

She goes to pay. It's a high glass counter with those shelves they have in bakers' shops to let you see the cakes. Except he has no cakes, only boxes of the penny sweets that children buy. His till is behind this and so is the computer that shows what you owe for your papers.

He tells her what the groceries come to. He has this way of not looking at you, looking somewhere over your shoulder while he waits for you to put your money up. The total cleans her out. That can't be right. She asks the price of the leek. It's too dear. Fresh and firm it would have been too dear. And she has a smear of green from its slimy outer layers on her fingers. She says, "I need a tissue, to wipe this green snot off." She thinks, I've said 'snot', I must be careful.

He points to the shelf where packets of tissue stand for sale. She opens the smallest size and wipes her fingers dry. She thanks him as she hands him back the packet. "Forty-two pence," he says, "for the tissues."

Forty-two, for cleaning up his mess! "That leek is rotting," she hears herself shout, "take the rotting leaves off before you weigh it."

He thumps it on the counter. She can see bright green splashes on his overall. A wet speck of it lands on her face.

"It's not for sale," he shouts back. He stuffs what she has bought into a crumpled plastic bag and pushes it at her. She still has to pay for the papers. She puts up her coins.

"Two weeks," he says, glancing at her coins, staring at the screen of the computer. Cold seeps around her body.

"But I pay every . . ."

"It's on the computer. See it for yourself." She can't see at that distance, not even with her glasses, just terrifying question marks scrolling through her head. Her coins are for one week, they're all she has. The coins in her tins aren't enough. Her safety note? She has no choice. She asks for a receipt, something to hold on to. He scuffles among bags and bits of paper on the counter.

"You'll have to wait," he says. "You're holding up the queue." A man's voice behind her says, "A receipt only takes a minute. I'd prefer to wait." She can't look round, she doesn't want to see the man's face.

Inside the stairway to the flat she leans against the breeze block wall. It smells clean, like rain on wet cement. As she searches for her key the street door opens. She's seen this young man before, in the shop on his way home from work, or pulling off his tie as he bounds up the stair. She's seen his girlfriend too, that's why he bounds.

"You all right?" he asks. It's the first time they've spoken but she knows his voice already, the one that said so firmly, "I'd prefer to wait."

"Not my day," she says. "Now I've lost my key."

"That man," he grins, "I think he's lost his marbles. Have you tried your pocket?" She checks again. It's there, among the change from her ten pound note. "Take care now," he calls as he bounds on up the stair.

She's shivering. When she turns on the water for the kettle it glitters, like coins swirling down the drain. She concentrates on taking her shopping from the bag. He's pushed the soap powder in among the food; the eggs are at the bottom underneath it. That hurts her. That man wanted to hurt her. Alan! It shouldn't be like this.

She doesn't let herself cry. She rinses her face and blows her nose with a tissue from the packet. She needs the tea strong. She sorts away the shopping while it brews. The carrots will have that sweet decaying taste. And there isn't any leek. She pours the tea. There's just a trickle of milk in the jug. And the bread's at the last two slices. She'd forgotten to put them on the list. But she did not forget to pay the papers.

How could he, she whispers when she creeps into bed. Then the cold softens out of her as comfort reaches her from Alan. "It will be all right," he says, and then she feels his smile.

In the morning when the paper clatters through the letter-box she stays still. She doesn't want to waken while she still feels Alan's smile. Then she hears another clatter. Usually she gets nothing in the post. She makes herself get out of bed and go to pick up the folded sheet of paper.

"Should you ever," it begins, "want an escort when you go to that shop..." He'd signed it, 'Galahad', and then, in brackets, 'Bob and Cath upstairs'. Making her smile. Just like Alan.

She knows she will have to face the shop. She needs the bread and milk. She puts it off till late afternoon. Only one ahead of her when she goes up to pay. He's young and thin, his T-shirt is so thin it seems to shiver. He asks for ten cigarettes, hands up a note and gets change.

He keeps his hand open on the counter. "And the rest . . ." he says.

"Here's what you gave me." The man holds up a fiver.

"I gave you a ten. It's all I had. It's all I've got. I want my change."

His voice is gruff. Maudie thinks he's trying not to cry. The way that man treated her, he's doing it again, to this thin boy. She won't let him.

"It was a ten. I saw it in his hand."

The shopman looks at her, "You! You don't know what week it is!"

That's it, now she is absolutely sure. She's not got her glasses but she doesn't let that stop her. "I know a ten pound note when I see one."

"This fiver," he holds it up again, "that's what he gave me."

A voice says, "Why would the woman tell a lie?" Galahad, Bob on his way home from work. A *frisson* runs along the queue, people wanting to get on. The boy reaches over and snatches the note, No-one tries to stop him.

The man shouts, "You're banned! Don't show your face back here!" But even he doesn't try to stop him.

Maudie is desperate to escape. She puts her money up. The man ignores it and says, "next", looking over her head.

Bob says, "The lady's next". Again, the *frisson* in the queue.

The man doesn't look at her or offer her a bag, and as he lays her scrap of change on the glass the coins roll over on the floor. She rushes to get out but someone picks them up and comes after her.

Inside the flat she leans back against the door. Her lungs won't inflate. She finds enough saliva to swallow. By the time her door-bell rings she can speak, "Bob?"

"Yes. Cath says come up for a coffee."

"Not tonight..."

"You sure...? Well you know where we are."

Now she can go to the kitchen. She lays the bread and milk on the work-top. There are crumbs in the bread-box. They'll mould if she doesn't clean it out. And the milk-rack in the fridge has those dry crusty marks. But she doesn't have the strength. It's dark when she opens her eyes. There's too much cloth wrapped about her. Her fingers grope to unfasten the buttons of her coat. She finds the thin metal handle of the door, And the next metal handle. Then she edges her way along the length of the bed and crawls underneath the quilt. She doesn't tell Alan, not yet. She won't let him say it's all right. Because it isn't. That man in the shop and the leeks that he sells, oh Alan, none of it is right. Tears slide out from underneath her eyelids and the warm pearly liquid flows down her face. She must have been asleep. The tears soothe her at first but then she feels them sting, that man saying she owed for the papers, wanting her to grovel for her money on the floor.

Alan wrote a letter to the papers once, some complaint about the rubbish collection. He even thought of having leaflets printed. Leaflets!

*That long harled wall of the shop, not a window all along it, nowhere to put leaflets, just those awful words sprayed on. Fuck the papers, fuck your rotten leeks!*She's awake again. Tears are scalding her face, strings of snivel blocking her nose. And fuck you, Alan, she shouts as she blows the snivel into his pillow-case. You must have seen it, Alan, the writing on the wall.

Spray-cans, they could start a fire. Or petrol – Alan keeps petrol in the shed There's the red plastic can, matches in the Xmas candle box. And newspaper, her hands wring it into kindling-sized spirals. Alan at the garden bonfire, the petrol smell, the hollow whoosh – then the flames. That man's face in the flames, at the glass counter counting out his money. She can see the coins through the glass. He's counting them over and over again, little heaps of fives and tens and twenties, flaming off the tips of his fingers.

She startles wide awake. What has she done? She pushes off the duvet and springs out of bed. She's still wearing yesterday's clothes. One shoe is kicked beneath a chair, her coat is in a heap on the floor. She knows there is no shed, no red plastic can. The papers are still in their pile beside her chair, weeks of them intact, the Xmas-candle box on a shelf out of reach in the cupboard. But that man's face in the flames, it was just like Alan's. Desperate. Coins dribbling down the drain, notes going up in smoke. Trying to hide it, trying to keep things going. Oh Alan, till you couldn't ... I should have seen, I should have tried to help.

The letter-box clatters. The paper, even after yesterday he still sends the paper. He's much more desperate than she is. She showers, puts on a skirt and jumper. She cleans out the bread-box and the fridge and fills the kettle. Then she puts fresh slips, their very nicest ones, on Alan's pillows.

"It's like you said," she whispers, "everything is fine."

And when she's had her tea and toast she puts on the Burberry and makes her way over to the shop.

Bashabi Fraser

My Initiation to Racing Pigeons

I was allowed to fill the narrow corn troughs
by this hulking, reticent neighbour of ours
who had the absurd Biblical name of Barnabus.

My full initiation came on one long warm July
when Barnabus called me aside and said he could rely
on me to take charge of his brood – to check their supply

Of food and water, of their flights and returns.
In that amazing, idyllic summer, I was able to discern
each bird's peculiarity and in that intimate sharing, learn

Of courtship and love, of a female's sharp wrath
if wooed out of time. Of the beauty of birth,
of regurgitation, growth and unexpected death –

Which came as a shock, when the fairest archangel
came reeling back in the first stage
of my apprenticeship – and I confronted old age.

Priesthood came with Barnabus's return, bringing greater rewards
as he presided over the registration of the ring, and I looked forward
to a fledgling's vow to dare. At first it turned back towards

Barnabus and my youthful captivity
to this sport – a mutual susceptibility –
indistinguishable in each shared activity.

So Barnabus taught me the final test of weaning,
when a bird could pick up corn from the floor, learning
like its mother, to peck and choose. And my old man discerning

My obsession, made me the dream gift
on my tenth birthday, – a real pigeon loft,
converting our old caravan by his imaginative craft

To house my first tired tippler, whom I acquired
from my Guru for 3 bob, which I had paid
with pride. The next was a tumbler, dearer but worth the quid.

... Soon I had them all, dove grey and dark slate,
speckled and blue tinged, their fragile fate
bound close to mine. I could remember each date –

When I bought them or found them, fullgrown
or new born, injured or lost, discarded or torn
from the flock by fatigue; and they thrived on my corn.

My greatest joy was when one evening
Barnabus hid my slight, nervous frame under his wing
of an overcoat and took me into the sanctum ring

Of his Racing Club cronies, whose pretence
of not noticing my underage presence
became for me their mark of acceptance

Of my pigeon racing days, which then, didn't seem in vain.
So we ventured, taking our pigeons in Barnabus' Volkswagen
to challenge our flying emissaries with ardour,
willing them to return again.

Dussehra *on Calton Hill*

While Edinburgh ruminates on a clear Autumn afternoon
a concourse converges on the generous expanse
of the summit of Calton Hill. The vision is unclouded
with the city reaching out to the Forth, gazing wistfully
at Fife. And caught at the edge of the cliff
is the startling trio, splashed lovingly
with the colours a hundred children strove to
clothe them with. While the crowd
waits mesmerised by Ravana, Kumbhakarna
and Meghnad – the awesome figures of the ancient epics
stand transformed into these harmless moulds –
gigantic, Mughal-coated, turbaned or crowned,
driven to the edge of a Scottish experience
unwilling to be hurtled down to the estuary,
they stand with amazed expressions, confronting
this western audience, who wait for the
towering Ravana to be kindled, then his
brother and his son, reversing the order of
the great Lankan battle, subverting the
history of Empire, as the East travels
to the West and explodes in stars
and streams of fire: the demons of darkness
destroyed not in battle but amidst
the festivity of people who
unite to celebrate the Festival
of Lights, presided over by
the old Observatory, setting aglow
Nelson's Monument and the forgotten Folly
as a chain in history is brought full circle
to greet the millennium and a new year.

Sally Evans

The Garden Sleeper

He slept for years out of doors
in a garden in London, his daytime
job, some sort of writer.

I didn't know him, but my path
as a young typist must have crossed his;
not only a bright colleger

but an abandoned lover, a philosopher,
a gardener without a garden
and a loafer in cafés rode to work with me.

From my north London window also
came the peck of a typewriter,
above the tired lemon shrub trees

hemmed in by dozing cats.
Trapped among statuary
lay summer-houses all year through.

He slept behind
the throng, the push of humankind,
the escalator pit,

the tall deaf buildings
connecting squares,
mind burrowing

in sentence-stretches, bits of maps
out of the libraries, museums,
much-loved bookshops.

Leaves opened out
in a city of millions.
We read each other, now.

A scrap in a plant-pot in my room
turned into a fuchsia.
Daisy-light shone by the railings.

At last, we all saw our
fought-for survivals
unfold. Each road led to another.

We do not live in London
and I have a garden
I am too old to sleep in.

Ivy and Margaret

Ivy Compton-Burnett and Margaret Jourdain

Margaret loves furniture: she goes
up and down the auction rows
feather bonnet, smart affair,
working at the V & A,
a woman among men at play.

The lonely Ivy, novelist
shattered by war. These two would share
a flat for more than thirty years,
a bureau with a book on top,
paper and highly polished wood.

Catty comments of London life:
"So late for dinner, but my dears,
it couldn't spoil, it was corned beef!"
and Edith Sitwell's poems are "bosh"
and "homos" so intriguing. Cheers!

Dear old Gollancz, he tries so hard.
Virginia and Stevie call.
Dear Cecil here will photograph
my hollow cheekbones. Let us sit
together by the silver teapot.

Her books are published one by one.
Margaret retrieves the paper from
discarded heaps, reuses them
as notepads at the V & A,
where, decades later, they'll be found.

"In no accepted sense were they
a lesbian couple," says my source.
"Each sought her own life and fame."
Ivy lost sisters and a brother.
Weren't there any other men?

Prewar years and postwar years
merge into one lasting household.
Margaret travels; Ivy doesn't.
More manuscripts, more scriptoires,
and more tea in the silver teapot.

Like many stories, this one ends
with death, of one then both these friends.
Their wars are over, and their shelves
of books are singing to themselves.
They mourn each other in the hall.

Reading a Sundial by Moonlight

timeless forest
under the midnight wall –

owls haunt dusk
and a deer's track leads to dawn –

sundial in moonlight, stronger
than wet shine from the road –

silent, before the roar
of a midnight timberload –

bats and swallows halted
under bridges –

disc lit dial
with a creeping shadow –

wandering mockery
of day's discernible hours –

the sky sleepwalker
showering white –

reading a sundial
by moonlight

At a Lectern

My father had his private room,
'the study', 'the library.'
My mother never owned a desk.
The thoughts she had were not for writing down;
her words were lost on children and the house,
they echoed in the garden, and the stream
that ran beside the garden rang with them.

I saw no mockery in how she'd say,
"you ought to write a book dear":
nothing odd in how he'd hide away
behind closed shutters while we sought the sun.
It was my dawn – I could not know
they faced their own dusks, one by one
before a court of children.

Our wigs and gowns were trees we climbed,
our benches boughs
and our reports were our own lives
whose streams ran into dangerous oceans.
I stand and write, at a lectern,
by a window, looking out,
alert for anything to call a sail
among these rafts of words.

London Scene *(1989) by John Bellany*

PC Version of 'Upon Westminster Bridge'

Earth hath not anything to show more fair.
Dull would she or he be of soul who could pass by
a sight so touching in its popular consensus leadership.
The commerce zone now doth like recycled clothing wear
the beauty of the morning: un-noise polluted, traffic-free,
ships, twin towers, Millennium Domes, theatres and places of worship lie
open unto the fields, and to the ozone layer,
all bright and glittering in the regularly monitored air.
Never did sun more beautifully steep
in its first splendour valley, outdoor climbing facility or hill;
Ne'er saw I, never felt a relaxation technique so deep,
the river glideth at its own fattening will,
Hi religious deity, the very residential units seem asleep,
and all that mighty heart is spin-doctoring still.

Brian Johnstone

Surfin' Safari for a Small Town Boy

The deuce coupe threads the dunes, back of the sands:
her daddy's car, but he will understand
that parties must be seized, she says, like days,
thrown as hand-made pots, agreed the way
they've signed their surfboards, waxed them down
like documents. In this grey town
the sounds of doo-wop only surface from the drains
that overflow, the malice of late summer rains
determined in their pock-marked progress
over sands and shallows, all that acned skin, to mess
up every wrung out joy that they display,
gleaming in convertibles: the Wilsons, Jardine, Love, gay
in some forgotten sense. The discs stack up,
the portable Dansette slaps platter on to platter, enough
to wind the provost up, his bike a solitary patrol
against the shameless pleasure of it all.
Awful in his cycle clips, flat cap, he gets around, his face
a sucked in breath of disapproval. Go on, chase
the blues away before he gets on to your back.
The surf is up. The wind is from the north. But fuck,
all summer long this is as good as it will get. The needle
hits the groove. Love's voice. You paddle
out beyond the waves, youth tied on with a cord.
She watches you, God only knows, holds your reward
in supple limbs. You feel the surge. You sing it. Sea
rips at your board. She says: sing it one more time for me.

Trace

When a man dies, his secrets bond like crystals, like frost on a window. His last breath obscures the glass. – Anne Michaels *(Fugitive Pieces)*

It was a recognition of shape. The long body bag
of our duvet rolled loosely on the floor and lying to me,
as your chrysalis of sheet had done in a different room,
late in the day you ceased being my father.

Deceitful, it caught my breath and threw it back
two deaths ago, to eyes that would not cry, as fingers
shaking, folded back the neat hemmed edge of cotton
to your chin, unshaven, your face, sunk cheeked and empty
as I felt looking at the husk of you, the mirror misted over
and obscure. But now I want to find you there again, unroll

this quilt, spool back to what we should have shared
with time and patience, pick the stitching out.

My father, you were rolled into that sheet before
my hand had eased its grip. I cannot feel
your fingers in my palm but only absence, the impress
of a word in pencil someone absent-mindedly erased.

The Old Poet Speaks

I am the old poet. I examine the tiny bones
of birds, their flight feathers, wing tips, down,

toy with the entrails of mice and voles,
divining my past in viscera.

I have a good friend in no-one.
He visits me at all hours, uninvited.

I watch for him from my window,
blinking in the low winter sun.

There is no sign but I know he will come.
I feel his footfall pressing on my skin.

I am the old poet. Women knit socks for me,
tie my feet with the persistence of yarn.

They will send me some through the post,
a brown paper parcel, its postmark illegible.

It is my life they consign to the mail,
shapeless and tied up with string.

Assent

The Whaligoe Steps, Caithness

Men tied these knots round bundles
of themselves, round gear and harvest,
bare possession, stuff. Hitched rawness
to the skin, bound tracks of rope and line
into the flesh, knots holding purpose,
sacrifices of their sex. Their being
burnt like tar about its ends.

With every climb, each gathering
to the hearth, a deeper cut, one firmer
in the hand, within the muscle of the arm.
Each pace the line held, each the cord
brought goods and chance discovery,
the step still firm. Hemp and sisal,
twisted straw: a guarantee, a bet.

Best of Three

Anne Donovan

1: Chappin

He took her tae an auld guys pub, somewhere down Partick. Doms and all. He liked tae sit at a table no stand posing at the bar; this was the kind of place he went wi his ma and da in Pollok. Her ma and da never went tae pubs, maybe have a wee drink in a hotel on their holidays right enough. She didnae know he was gonny say it the night, why was he so nice tae her if that was how he felt?

Gettin married. In a month. He still loved her. But he was gonny marry sumbdy else.

Yeez want tae buy a raffle ticket? Fur the sick kids.

Hand ower a pound. Two yella wans, 141 and 142.

Ah don't understaund. How?

Her da'll gie us the deposit furra flat if we get married.

Her da had a wee business out by Kirkie. Joiner tae trade.

But if you love me.

Ah love her tae.

Mair?

Just different. And she definitely doesnae want kids. There's no many women can say that.

She couldnae understaund him, this plannin, tradin aff wan part of yer life against another. She just wanted him; his smell, the feel of his skin, the way he done it like naebdy else. The way he got tae her. Inside.

She put her drink on the table. White wine, slitterin a bit. He hated that. Gied her a look. Always spoke his mind, never bothered if it'd hurt her, even tellt her when he didnae like what she was wearin. She'd never met anybdy like him afore, he was that definite. Everythin drawn out in thin black lines. You knew where you stood.

2: Still Chappin

He took her tae Edinburgh. In his motor. On their day aff. Naebdy'd see them there. And if they did, well they might of just met, bumped intae each other by coincidence, had a wee drink.

His shoes were beautiful. He always wore beautiful shoes, polished tae a high gloss. He polished all their shoes on a Sunday night; Helena's, the children's. She never saw him on a Sunday night. Her daddy'd polished all their shoes on a Sunday night too. Maybe everybdy's daddy did, she'd never thought of it afore. Maybe that was what daddies were for.

They had a bottle of red wine. He didnae say much; he never did, no much of a talker. It was fine. He paid for lunch. She didnae want him tae, tried tae gie him hauf the money but he wouldnae take it.

You give enough.

They wandered aboot the art gallery, looked at Leonardo drawins. She didnae know what tae say. He made her feel like a wee girl taken oot for a special treat. Tae make up for the fact that this was it, all there would ever be. Shadows in corners, chalky smudgemarks.

Later he dropped her aff, didnae come in like he usually did. She felt raw. Inside.

3: Doublers
She took him hame wi her. The place was a tip but high on two gins and nae dinner she couldnae care less; he was wi her and this was it, this was her chance and she couldnae afford tae blow it.

Kate. He always said her name. It was a stupit name, plain and dull and she'd always hated it but he said it as if it meant somethin.

They stood in the hall. She wanted tae touch him, but they just stood there in the hall, lookin at each other. They were that close she could smell him, sweet aftershave mixed wi pub smoke and night air. He was smilin. It was OK.

Want a cuppa tea? He's still smilin. Take a step forward. Touch his airm. Nice jaicket, soft fabric. She wants tae put her heid on his shoulder.

Kate. Katie.

Her arms round him, face buried in his chest.

You're that cuddly. I knew you'd be cuddly.

He's laughin. His body shakes. He holds her at airms length.

So you're no efter me fur my body?

What makes you think that?

They kiss. She leads him tae her bedroom where the bed is unmade and the curtains have been left hauf-drawn since she went oot this mornin but she doesnae feel embarrassed like she usually would. She pushes him doon on the bed and he pulls her on tap ae him and they fumble wi each other's claes. She starts tae laugh and he looks worried for a moment, then he's laughin too. She looks intae his eyes. They find each other's skin. Efter, they lie lookin at the light comin in through the gap in the curtains. They hear her neighbours clumpin into the close efter a night oot. She strokes the back of his neck and he rests his haund on the soft place just inside her hip bone.

Microfictions

He: Your hands always embarrassed me. I would watch women at parties with long red fingernails and smooth white skin, imagine the scrape of nail against the small of my back, a scratch fresh on my thigh. I wanted to watch you after a bath, smoothing cream on your hands. I wanted you to sit on the bed of a hotel room with a white towel round your head, filing your nails then painting them, slowly, meticulously in shiny scarlet, fingers outstretched, as if they would dry more quickly.

I never told you, of course. You just weren't like that, we weren't like that. Sometimes I thought I would drown in your scrubbed fresh skin, the clean line of sweat on your forehead. The things I longed for in those dark moments when three o'clock surfaces from a dream – they seemed such clichés compared to your unrelenting honesty. Even the way you left was honest, the words sharp and straight; a clean break, no torn-off edges, stained coffee cups, smudged mascara on a pillowcase. I could have done with messier surfaces.

She: There was always something missing, even at the beginning. Not missing, but held in check, like a fire that smoulders without ever bursting into flames. It was almost good, the sex. All the bits and pieces seemed to work; you made the right noises, the right parts connected, afterwards we laughed and talked and fell asleep, fitting neatly together. I thought we'd get to the next bit.

But where was the centre? When we kissed your tongue brushed round my mouth as though you were painting by numbers. There was that tightness, those little flickers of feeling darting randomly between us. Why no oh-my-god-warm-round-let-go-give-in-give-up? No darkness or fear or waking hours later, clinging together.

He: There were too many spaces between us. I wanted to colour them in, yellow and red and green, cross-hatch the shadows and spatter white from the tip of a fine brush.

Painting by numbers is easy; thin black lines define each section and colours are labelled for your convenience. The tiny brush fills each space precisely: the form fits. But what use is it to either of us, this messy love that stains and splashes? The love that belongs nowhere, the embarrassing kind which will not stay in its right box but keeps spilling out into the world and crossing boundaries, muddily mixing with inappropriate colours.

Prick your finger and observe the blood. It is red like fairy tale apples. The cloth which stems its flow is patterned with perfect red spots. Respectable. Taste it, suck it in public.

Oh, but the other one, the secret type; it comes clotted and blackened, mingled with mucus, rancid as regret.

She: Missing you. The true test of feeling – I read that somewhere. But what do I miss? I touched you once through a thin shirt, feeling the heat, not sticky or burning but human. Or is it the smell? Standing behind you wondering if you knew I was holding the moment, not listening to your words, just holding it: the smell, of fabric conditioner, aftershave.

Why couldn't we be honest? What difference would it have made in the grand scheme of things if I'd just said? Took you aside one day, a few moments of the day to say this is what I feel, this is what I want and for you to say, yes or no, just to say. But then I could no longer feed my sweet fantasy, dream freely. There is freedom in my wanderings: I can go anywhere, even where I do not want to go.

Was I afraid that if you heard the words, out in the middle of the room, suddenly the longings you harboured, beneath warm sheets at three in the morning, would evaporate like sweat and be gone?

How to know? When to seize the universe and when to lie along its edge?

He: You wake, when you wake, with that black hole at the pit of your stomach and emptiness behind your eyelids, prickling with sleep, dreaming of a friend's father's funeral in Benbecula with rows of men in black jackets, having a conversation about *Trainspotting* and philosophy, and a cold that won't go away and a sick line written on the inside leaf of a novel you've never read.

And it is finished, it is ended and the dream has gone. It's easy to live in dreams, their nourishment is light and digestible as thin soup made by white hands. Why did you think this time it would be different? You know that for you it cannot be different, you're not intended for the bright light: you are safer in the shadows, feel easier out of the light, your walk is unsteady and a fault line rips you from throat to thigh.

Coda

always

I would
imagine
never told
longed for

something missing

you
wake

it is
ended

INTERVIEWS
Diana Athill, Philip Pullman, Will Self

LITERARY FEATURES
David Daiches, Christopher Rush, Louise Welsh

COLLECTING
Lewis Carroll, Football Books, Book Trade Profiles

SHORT STORIES
Ali Smith, Ron Butlin, Ruth Thomas

Scottish Book Collector is not only for collectors or Scots
Find out for youself – ask for a free sample

SBC, 8 Lauriston Street, Edinburgh EH3 9DJ / Tel: 0131 228 4837
www.scotbooksmag.demon.co.uk email: jennie@scotbooksmag.demon.co.uk

Colin Kerr

Three Distractions to Clear Thinking

Philosopher's Stone

Into such depths I now plummet my mind
like a barnacle-clad anchor heaved overboard
into this storm-ridden harbour I call mine
Well it's still sinking   that anchor
for the chain I feel   is unravelling me
where I would stand   if my feet hadn't already gone

Sun Dial

I seek man's great thoughts
of the past to quench my memory
then forget to quicken
to their presence all around me
in new bodies my next door neighbour
for instance has a large sunflower
just like Van Gogh thought

Television

I sit at home most nights
in front of the television looking
for the picture of myself
coming when I switch off
There again this afternoon
when the room was flooded
with sunshine I saw myself
held between the hands of a newscaster
but they weren't my thoughts that he read

Monkey

Something so very appropriate
about a monkey made out of rubber
All that elasticity
the bounce of childhood
I shudder now to think
of the picking that went on
as if ticks existed even in those
far off times, when everything
was so clearly metaphor
The bunk-bed a canoe, the carpet
a deadly river-full of school chums

snapping at that Achilles heel in sight.
Monkey sat then at the back
of the boat and mouthed an ear to ear grin
His eyes dark and made from bubbles
while nonchalantly touching each finger
with his thumb, in a brazen show
of that old fellow what's-his-name's
new evolutionary course.

This Yawning Horizon

blue skies
over transparent wind
over water

A boat might float across it

The sun go down
Rise again   low
at first

It's too big an image
for us to manage
in just one night

So we dream
to make absolutely sure

Talking
over the breakfast table

my tongue has run dry
and I wait
for the boat to come home

captain nearly asleep at the wheel
His harbour   growing love

Blue

On the edge
of so many others

one swan

goes deep into
cold water for food

At the centre
of so many sensations

I understand

that deep blue
in the early morning sky

A half note   a bird call
glides slowly   across this vast surface

Yehuda Amichai by Hugh Bryden (commissioned for these poems)

Yehuda Amichai: Amichai was born in Wurzburg, Germany, in 1924 into a family of Orthodox Jews. In 1935 they moved to Palestine where he first served with the British Army during the War of Independence. He began writing in 1948 and published his first book, Now and in Other Days, *in 1955. During his lifetime he published 14 collections of poems and has been translated into 30 languages. Twice married, a father of two, he died on 22nd September 2000.*

Hayden Murphy

Yehuda Amichai (1924–2000) Five Poems

God has Pity on Kindergarten Children

God has pity on kindergarten children.
Less for those at school.
None for the adults.
He leaves them alone.
So at times he makes them crawl, splayed
On the desert floor
To reach the first-aid station
Covered with blood.

But maybe He will protect lovers.
Protect and shelter them.
He as a leafed tree shadowing an old man
Left to dry on a public park bench.

Perhaps we too will pass to press

The coin of compassion on their palms.
Those rare coins Mother bequeathed
So that the pleasure of content would pleasure

Us now and in our other days.

Huleikat: the Third Poem about Dicky

In these hills, even oil mountains
Are faint memories. Here Dicky died.
Four years my elder. Almost a father;
At the moments of fear. Now I'm the elder
By forty years. He is a son in memory.
A young son. I'm one old, grieving parent.

You who only remember the faces
Let you never forget the extended hand.
The feet approaching.
The words.

Remember: even the leaving of battlegrounds
Means you pass by the way of windows and gardens
Where the dog barks as the children play.

Remind the fruit at your feet of trees,
Leaves, branches, even the sharp thorns.
Recall the Springtime of green and softness.

Do not forget
Even a fist

Was once an open palm and fingers.

A Dog after Love

I entertained a dog
At your departure. Allowed it
Enjoy my body, get my scent.
Recognise yours.

It will, I so desire, tear
The balls off, chew the penis
Of your lover.

Later, I so hope,
It will return with suspendered stockings.

The Body is the Reason for Love

Body is love's base.
It guards it,
Imprisons it,
Yet even in death love is free,
Liberated
Like the gambling machine
Suddenly disembowelling coins.
Love's lucre
Is everybody's fortune.

I, May I Rest in Peace

I, may I rest in peace.
I alive say may I have a lifetime's peace.
I want peace now. Now while I'm alive.
I don't want to wait as a saint. Him
Who coveted the leg on the throne of Paradise.
I want a four-legged chair. A wooden seat.
I want my covenant of peace now.
I have survived wars, intimate battles.
Close-combat, face to mirror fighting.
Always my own face. My lover face. My enemy face.
Wars with the old wounding weapons
Sticks, stones, blunt axe and words.
The shredding knives of love and hate.
Even wars with modern weapons. Machine
Gun, missile, words, exploding landmines
Love and hate.
I do not want to be my parent's prophecy
That life is war. I want the body and soul of peace.
Rest me in peace.

Remembering Ian Abbott

Alexander Hutchison

I first met Ian Abbott when Joy Hendry paired us to read upstairs at Ryrie's Bar in the Haymarket during the 1985 Edinburgh Festival. We were scheduled to read from 7:30 to closing time – which was then roughly 11:00 o'clock. Even with Jo Miller also there to provide songs and give us music on the fiddle it looked like being a long haul. As it turned out, just about everybody had a good time, bobbing along on various enthusiasms; but, for me, meeting Jo and Ian was a pleasure that lasted.

We agreed to read in fifteen or twenty minute spells, with Jo in between, or taking over when it seemed right. Ian's reading manner was clear and deliberate, the voice setting out the measure of each poem so you sensed the shape as the theme was advanced. It appeared both formal and organic somehow, and he rarely mis-stepped or fluffed a line. "This guy is *good*," I said to myself, and looked more carefully at the sheaf of poems in my lap.

Later on (not out of material, but running a little thin) I cranked up and sang: getting through Patrick Kavanagh's 'Raglan Road' after a couple of false starts. When I sat down Ian leaned over and said in my ear: "If I'd known you were going to sing, I'd have brought my moothie". The impression I got of someone easy and convivial but with a meticulous and proper sense of his art was confirmed as we got to know each other better.

Ian had courage, and no false airs or graces. He also had a great fund of stories. One of my favourites has him driving down from Inverness with two hefty companions to pick up sheep at the Perth sales. When the sheep were stowed, and the pubs were dry, they set off North, with the sober Abbot driving. The two side-kicks fell asleep, and soon were jolting heavily together in the narrow cab as the lorry took the twisty road home. After a while Ian got fed up of being banged around by these two big snoring lummoxes, and stopped to sort it out. In a trice, the comatose *compadres* were roped together and lashed up snug to the off-side door. Sanguine, satisfied, free of encumbrances, Ian climbed back in behind the wheel.

A few miles later, who should it be but the boys in black come flashing up to pull the lorry over. They were looking for sheep-rustlers, or so they said, and they quizzed Ian close, checked over the papers from the sale, and made a quick tally of the woolly cargo bleating in the back. Before they left, one of the bobbies shone his torch around the cab, revealing for the first time Pinky and Perky, still trussed up and still oblivious. "I'm not even going to comment about this," says the disconcerted cop, just shaking his head and waving Ian on.

When *Avoiding the Gods* was published by *Chapman* I remember being disappointed by the reception it got in some quarters, since the poems were clearly as good as anything else appearing at the time, and I would have thought that earlier publication of many of the pieces – especially in *Lines Review* – would have prepared the way for an informed critical response. I believed we needed to sharpen our skills for receiving a book like that, and said at one point: "Norman MacCaig must heave a loud groan every time his name is pulled in and held up as an unflattering glass to his contemporaries. It's not fair to him – false comparisons benefit no-one – and it's certainly not fair to Ian Abbott, who has his own strengths and his own hard-won accomplishment."

Since that point, however, it's fair to say Ian's work has not lacked notice: Colin Nicholson and Tessa Ransford were two in particular who provided insightful commentary and support. On one occasion, reading with Sorley MacLean, Ian performed very well to a full house in the National Museum of Scotland. His name has not been missing either from standard anthologies – including the recent *Scottish Literature in the Twentieth Century* edited by David McCordick. Still, we could do with a new edition of his work, and a broader appreciation of his worth.

In McCordick's good representative selection seven poems confirm the distinctive elements of Ian Abbott's style. The work is not narrowly Scottish, although it can engage local or national issues with power and immediacy. The language is rich and beautifully phrased; the tone is both personal and measured. Dismissing the agents of a predatory supernatural world, refusing echoes of old liturgy, he says:

> Let us remain here, calmly
> Taking bread, and wine, and speech.
> And in the morning
> Take our limbs to work, and walk behind
> The swaying, fuming breath of cattle.
>
> And let us look for our salvation
> In the language we have come to teach ourselves.

Ian was too hard-headed to over-simplify; and he didn't aspire to mere rusticity. His poem 'Ewe against the Fence' is a corrective against any drift to plausible romanticism, as is the conclusion of 'A Crofter Buried':

> You thought to print the earth indelibly.
> But now let down, and burdened
> With the bare field's sullen weight,
> You must lie still and be content.
> The cairn begins to crumble
> Even as the final stone is being placed.
>
> Your footprints are already blowing shut.
> In time the earth accepts from you
> The price of everything you borrowed from it.

What the poet has to say at each stage is contained by the elegance and clarity of his forms – even in poems as dark as 'Ga-Cridhe', or when, before the guns, the "lean, red dogs" picking up the scent are

> floated forward, almost motionless;
> the dazzling harbingers of a day of blood.

Once at a literary gathering in Edinburgh I was trying, without success, to check on the origin of the word 'auspices'. I knew it had to do with divination, but couldn't remember how, and all the suggestions I got were haphazard or facetious. Finally I pounced on Ian and put the question again. "It's about birds," he said, "– interpreting the pattern of their flight." I recognized straightaway that he was right. And I dug up the bit from Spencer: "Time... taught me the sooth of birds by beating of their wings." Well, we must have thought for a little while we were the only buggers there who knew what was what.

Since he died I've kept looking to the patterns, and often he comes to mind: the crows on Salisbury Crags, spinning and dipping in the thermals; or down on the tarmac a chirm of starlings headed for crumbs. A while ago, on a drive up Cairnpapple Hill I saw a single magpie flap from a branch, and it took some time looking round to make the pair. Sorrow and joy are not so pat in Ian's poems, nor in the thoughts of his friends; but I don't expect one without the balance of the other.

I've made two poems for Ian since his death: 'The Holt' (from *English for a Butcher*, 1997), and 'The Hat' (*Sparks in the Dark*, 2002, both Akros Publications). In the first I tried to convey his mystery, his brilliance, his dark recesses and clear lines; in the second, his affection and vitality.

The Holt

(for Ian)

sinuous
from shadow

unsheathed
and silver

no pounce-work
no grudge-music

words are in
the breathing ground

this uncircum-
scribable air

The Hat

I thought I saw you.
I thought I could see you
come in and wander round –
I thought I recognized the hat.

Wherever it is you've clambered
off to, is there anyone there
to twist a story, lift a dram?

I could have sworn it was you –
my hand is out – even now I'm
smiling, waiting to say hullo.

Ian Abbot

An Educated Rabbit's View of the Snare

The universe is no more
than a bubble of soap
caught in the bright wire confines
of a simple frame.
The shape it makes is certain, and occasioned
by what they tell me are the lines of purest form.
That is to say
the universal geometries of least resistance.

How can I comment? All I would like to mention
is that I have come across that one barbaric wire,
that simple loop of universe
inside which the world was coruscating like a rainbow.
Naïvely, I thought that I might force an entry
and maybe write new chapters in the laws of things.

But what am I left with finally? Only a vision
of the radiant cosmos growing darker, a multitude
of clamorous small sounds ebbing
at the end into an awful, tinny mirth

which is that delicate
soap-bubble tightening its grin.

Cameraman

You say the poet's task is simply to record,
like the blind lens of a camera,
small scenes out of the world's
careering carnival
and to freeze them without commentary
in the page; like insects shut
in a kind of cellulose amber.

It's possible I could agree with this.
But if I do, who could explain
the sort of camera that I've been fitted with?
What geometry of lens is it
that on one side
can telescope the universe into its eye
one single, floodlit moment;
while on the other, simultaneously,
sends its calm, converging rays
to play minutely through the shuttered places of my heart?

Passing Through September

Sky cools. The earth
begins imperfectly to whiten
and the first uncertain skeins go wavering south.

Under the distant horns
a man in his solitary shell
is walking among the multiplied hills.
The slopes
have sloughed off summer imperceptibly: so from himself
the veils of another year
are peeling slowly like abandoned skin. Dry grass,
the empty bones of heather,
lie down finally beneath his feet.

His shadow in the low sun
leans backwards from his heels
under a sky of scribbled chevrons, flying
into the bright, receding season,
while step by step he moves
toward his patient, white horizon.

He is walking
into the thin line of the future;
into the numberless rising voices
and the terrible vistas of the ice.

On Certain Nights

On certain nights,
inexplicable tides
seem to set the earth rocking like a shell.

Raise it to your ear then
and you will hear that distant roar
which is like the beating of an immense sea;
but fainter still,
so faint that you may not be sure
whether you have heard them at all,
you will catch
a perfect succession of limpid notes,
a few strains of a rare and everlasting dance.

Then the dance will go on in your head forever,
leaving you dissatisfied
and ill at ease with the world.

Climbing Through Ammonites

Little spirals, scattered on the hills.
A litter of signatures, fastened
on the very soul of stones.

Let you and I move among them
casually, as if we did not hear
their curved, eternal voices
singing in the small bones of our ears.

As if, when we arrange them on the shelves
they will not speak to us
of what we think we have,
of what we think we hold forever.

Of how the sea bed of one age
rears into the mountains of another.

Stalactites

You wander through the caverns of his heart.
On the walls you trace
the patterns of rainbows, full
of delight you roam among the stalactites and stalagmites;
your skin holds colours of mother of pearl and gold.

But listen; drop by drop
those needles come together.
Imperceptibly they thicken, clot
to pillars of radiant stone.
Slowly the entrances are growing smaller;
soon there will be
no way in left any more.

Musteline

This is the one who, clothed
in her bright body hair will wield
her supple backbone like a carter's whip.

This is the one
who tirelessly will run you down, and show you
what it means always to have her blonde curve at your hip.

This is the one that you have all your life been frightened of.
The one who will transfix you,
steal you with her scent,
and print her perfect, bloody muzzle on your lip.

A Real Death

Behind a pane of curving glass,
under a rudely-painted desert sun
the python stacks his Shiraz coils on rock.

His head is sunk
in the tight, volcanic well of his body.
And as the crowd, transfixed,
stares at the essence of that painted stillness,
the sun
deploys imagined rays
about the limitless vistas of the cage: the snake
becomes one with the desert stones and nothing moves
that the crowd does not move there in imagination.
The pattering of insects, swirls
of overheated air, a slow pulse
beating in the body of the snake.

Until a flap slides open and a rat, alive,
is let loose in the cage.
Its pink feet whisper in the sand, its nose
is raised to sniff the air; while out of the sombre
well of coils the blunt head floats: eyes
lidless and fixed, the tongue
that tastes the air, the jaw
a long, unshakeable grin.

Held in a cage
within a cage the rat, transfixed, lies down.
And out of the placid, painted scene,
leisurely and real,
the slow uncoilings come.

The Poetry of Television

In the brittle light of midday
the corpses are arranged along the street.
Already, side by side, their devastated grins
are soaring upwards, flying
at a sky still trembling with the final shards of noise.

While here,
replete and lounging by the fire,
we juggle earnest, empty theories around the room

and notice how only the naked feet recall
a ruined field of silent, landed butterflies.

Landscapes

Evening.
The grey road mapped with ice,
scarred with hollows and pools.

The sky
is green-blue, transparent.
Along the horizon
a red flush lights the snowfields:
rows of black trees
stitch the sky against the earth.

I feel that I am passing
from a point to a point within a picture.
Icarus falling.
The centre of one world,
unnoticed in a corner of the other.

A Resurrected Long-Dead Soldier

Here he is at last,
discovered after centuries,
flung down headlong into the sodden peat.
He is bundle of geometries;
a huddle of lines and angles, hollows
where both his eyes were once and where
his ribs confined the spasms of his heart.

Time has imploded him
into a leather map
of everything we are that lasts: the skin,
the nails, the architecture
of his skull, the tiny perfect jigsaws of his hands and feet.
His brain is now
an aggregate of clays;
his heart a faceted, crystalline jewel.

They say
that when we sleep, we imitate the dead:
but certainly the dead
do not evoke the sleeping. His silence
as he hugs the earth in absolute. Only along
the sunken roads which cross
his forehead and his face
can we detect
the distant tramping of the future and the past.

Ian Abbot

Alexander Hutchison

Didn't Do

(for Norman)

Well, I'll tell you
what he didn't do:

he didn't have a neat
wee cunt and push it around;

he didn't lean on – or into –
not for a sense of *obligation*;

he didn't smear all over
like old tar on foreshore rocks;

he measured by what he admired
not by what he might get;

he thought there was more
to life than passable dentition;

he sometimes snarled and sometimes sneered
– but never at next door neighbours.

If he cosied up anywhere
he did it because he liked it;

he didn't say "ah hah hah" out
loud in buses just to draw attention;

he opted for chins and buttercups
rather than 'a forest of symbols';

his bucket always reached down
to the water in the well;

what it took he knew –
what it took to know he loved.

Mao and the Death of Birds

Because they took, he thought
more than their fair share of grain,
Mao decided the birds must die.

It could be this embraced concern
for the common weal, but economics
has its own imperative.

How did they do this?

Well, all one day, as long as it took,
the people banged on pots and pans
– whatever withering cacophony

they could raise – to keep the birds aloft.
Denied a roost, they flew until
their wings could not support them.
The people gathered every one
and put the pots to other use.

Was this not fine? The people, thus
instructed, dined on all that died.
Mao might have smiled; and no doubt
gathered in his own fair share.

Next year, without the birds,
the insects all enjoyed a carnival
in turn. The harvest failed
and failed again – until in millions
people died. Was this not then
resoundingly complete?

What Mao had to say when
all transpired, I must regret again
I have no note; but do recall
another claim he brought – with pride –
of intellectual numbers down: "more
than any Emperor that came before".

How that was done was less
spectacular than what removed our
feathered friends – merely
another bland imperative.

At least they didn't cook
them where they fell – he probably
would draw the line at that.

When arbitrary despots rule, we
all are thralled to blind obedience.
Innocent and ignorant the Chinese people
died; and songs and words of those they
killed will come again – though in
what form is hard to say.

But may some demon boil the bones
of Mao in Yangtse's seething flood
for evermore – with everlasting
death to his vainglory.

It Happens

I tell you, it wasn't
like looking out

through green trees
across the city.

It was more like
hooking into something
you wouldn't want to lift
into the boat.

I hooked into something
like that the other day:

belly hooked it
gaff hauled it.

Citronella

Lemon
sponge she
used to make

with lemon
butter icing.

I could think
of worse things

than sinking
in again to that
light sponge
astringent icing

the length
of those cool
dark citrus
afternoons.

Translations from Catullus's Carmina

Noli Admirari, Quare Tibi Femina Nulla

It's no mystery why no woman
seeks to place her soft thigh
under yours, Rufus – not even
if you stagger her with gifts of
next-to-nothing finery, or flawless
scintillating stone. The bad word
that wounds is this: you have
grim goat squatting in your oxters –
that is what they all dread;
not surprising, it's a rank thing entirely
and not something to lay down
next to a beautiful girl. Put that
poisonous smell out of existence,
or never wonder more why they flee.

Carmina LXIX

Egnatius, Quod Candidos Habet Dentes

Iggy, because he happens to have
white teeth, slaps on a permanent grin.
Suppose he approaches the plaintiff's bench –
the advocate plucking at the heart strings –
there's that smile. When tears are tripping
a mother bereft at the grave of her own sweet
biddable boy – he's smiling still. Whatever it is,
wherever he is, whatever else he may be up to,
you can guarantee his pan stays cracked.
It's an ailment he's got: in my view
neither flattering nor a fit state to be.
I'll tell you, Ignatius, old cheese, if you
were a Cockney, a Brummie, or a Geordie
or a lard-ass Liverpudlian, a blob from
Belfast, or a black and tusky Cardiff-ite –
or a Keelie (for nearest and dearest) –
or anyone else that cleans their teeth with
clean tap water, I still wouldn't want you to
plaster on that everlasting gob-stretching grin.
Nothing dies a death like a manufactured laugh.
As it is, you're a Mealie, and in Mealie-land
everyday the Mealies work their teeth and rosy
gums with what was pissed that morning –
so the more refulgent the choppers the more piss
you're seen to have downed or floated over. *(XXXIX)*

Disertissime Romuli Nepotum

To you, most honey-tongued of all the kin
of Romulus – those that are, those that have
been – Marcus Tullius – those to be in years
to come, Alexander renders warmest thanks –
of makars the nadir: as much the nadir of makars
as you of persuaders the zenith or apogee. *(XLIX)*

Caeli, Lesbia Nostra, Lesbia Illa

Kyle, oor Lizzie, yon Lizzie –
ane and the same Lizzie that
Cutty loved mair nor himsel, mair
nor aa his ain – these days at cross-roads
doon back wynds, pilks aa the
nevvies o Bonnie Prince Charlie. *(LVIII)*

wynds: alleys; *pilks*: peels, strips; *nevvies*: descendants, grandsons.

The Ancients

Donal McLaughlin

Enter THE ANCIENTS, en route to the POOLSIDE

This morning, again, the ancients take up position, just as he's eating his last bites of breakfast. He still prefers to stay indoors, not to eat on the terrace, though the louts of last week have flown home now. The ancients – who replaced them – strain to talk round the stairwell as they begin to sit down on the sunbeds.

"We've not got a toaster either," the auld guy complains. "Have you got a toaster?" From his reaction, her-next-door clearly doesn't.

"Ye'd think ye'd have a toaster, wouldn't ye?" his wife begins to reason – "We can't get no toast or nuthin!" he buts in, but.

Her-through-the-wall mustn't answer. Worse still: maybe can't see the problem.

"Ay, – and have you got a *kettle?"* he continues.

Your woman has been able to make do.

"Ay, heat it in pans, ay!" he repeats, sounding angry. "But have ye got a kettle? That's what I asked."

"Naw!" he repeats, as if to say, *"See?!"*

He pauses; looks at her; just timing the announcement: "They *have* them, though, ye know!"

He's got her this time. "Oh ay. They have them, alright. Over there –"

He nods to Reception in the corner.

"Ye have to pay for them but –"

"Pay for them!" his wife echoes. "Have ye ever heard the like? Imagine having to pay for the likes of a kettle and a toaster –"

"It's no right," says he. All he does, but, is scratch at his knee.

The silence continues. Time was he'd've read them the riot act. His wife, whoever saw her, would've joined him. Not now but. He's too frail got.

He takes off his T-shirt. Picks at his chest, sitting up on the sunbed.

His wife, on her feet still, unbuttons the blouse she wears over her T-shirts.

He turns to the neighbour again. "Last place we were in, they gave ye everything!"

"Everything!" his wife confirms.

"We'd a kettle. A toaster. Ye didn't have to pay for nuthin. There was even a grill, wasn't there?"

"Ay, a lovely grill. Ye know: to do the bacon under –"

"We can't do our bacon here!" the husband protests.

His glasses shake on his nose as he looks round and up to the neighbour.

His eyes are skelly. Even from a distance, they look skelly.

Your woman must've mentioned the pans again.

"Oh no! I'm no allowed no pans!" the wife says. "Everything I eat has to be grilled –" Another silence. This time, it could even be final.

"Lovely day yesterday!" the wife says, eventually, putting back on the blouse she's just taken off. She doesn't look at your woman. Speaks over her shoulder. Embarrassed, as she re-does her buttons.

"Yesterday was nice!" she tries, again, when she doesn't get a response.

Your woman must've agreed.

The auld guy takes over again: "Where are ye from, love?"

It's like he's trying to placate her.

"Edinburgh!" he repeats when she tells him.

Means something to him, looks like.

"Lot of Irish in Edinburgh!" his wife says. She's strangely proud of the fact. Again, doesn't get a response but.

"And when did ye come over?" he asks, to smooth the path.

"Thursday? Same as us! And when do ye go back?' The 6th? Ay! He picks at his chest again; his skin as ashen as the T-shirt beside him. Question is, what the sun'll do. There's no sign of him using protection.

"When we got here, there wasn't a bus or nuthin, ye know! Not a bus, not a rep, in sight. Nuthin!"

They're back on track. This time, he gets the response he wants.

"Ay! A disgrace! Isn't it? We had to get a taxi up here, ye know!"

"Ay, had to take a taxi!" his wife echoes.

"Arrecife to here's no cheap either!"

It's more and more noticeable how their comments overlap. Her voice is strong, whereas he talks through slipping teeth, it sounds like.

Sometimes, the two voices marry.

He fixes the glasses on his nose again; turns to the neighbour.

"Course, I'm made of money, me!!" he says, laughing suddenly and winking at her. His glasses go haywire.

"Ay, we're *loaded!"* his wife jokes, too. "I'd just like to know where it all is! Where it all goes to. That's what I'd like to know!"

Your woman must laugh at this, and all. The old guy's obviously encouraged.

"Give ye a laugh," he says. "We went to that Christmas Dinner yesterday. We'd put our names down, ye know. Anyway, I goes up to the boy at the end, to pay, like, and he says, There's nothing to pay! You've already paid, Sir! And I looks at him like that and says, I'm sorry, but I haven't paid nuthin. He looks down and checks his papers and says, According to this, Sir, you have. Then he says, Mr Donaghue, Sir? And I says, Yes – And he looks at me as if to say, There ye go! the boy does. But I looks at him and say, Ay, but which Mr Donaghue? Might there be another one? And he looks, and sure enough, there was!"

He laughs. His wife chuckles, too; her face lighting up for the second time. "Would ye credit it? Wasn't there two Mr Donaghues!"

At that, they both lie down to sunbathe; him fidgeting more to get himself comfortable. Your woman's maybe grabbed the chance to make herself scarce. They're side-by-side, now. Him in his trunks, less and less to fill them. Her in her blouse, top and shorts. She looks that solid; good for a few nights at the Bingo yet.

Lying down, he looks frailer still. His hair thin; like it's wilting.

He's probably just lying there, thinking, remembering; enjoying the sun, maybe even. He looks like he will when he's laid out but.

"Sean and Patricia went to Edinburgh, didn't they?" he says, after a bit. A brave bit. He doesn't open his eyes to talk.

He *sounds* frailer, now he's lying down, and all.

"Ay, right enough, they did," says she – just as ye might've thought she wasn't goney answer.

"They died young, too, didn't they?!" says he.

"Mm," she murmurs, in the sun.

"Fifties. In his fifties, he only was. Sean. She was, too."

"Mm."

"And here's us still going –"

"Mm." She sounds relaxed; peaceful. Like she's enjoying herself.

"Maybe that's what they're up to! What they're at! Maybe they're hoping we'll fade away to nuthin!" She turns to face him, laughing. Gutting herself, she is, behind her big round glasses. When she's done, she lies back down again.

"It'll take more than that, but, ay??!!" He can hardly speak, himself, for choking. They lie there, obviously settling for the complex again. Ye wouldn't believe there is an island out there. A volcano. The Papagayo beaches. Supermercado's about as far as the auld guy's got. And who knows if she's been that far.

"How many o a family did Sean and Patsy have again?" Like he's been lying there, trying to remember.

She struggles and all, so he starts to answer his own question.

"There was Sean, the eldest –"

"Ay."

"And then Paddy –"

"Mm."

"And then Roisin –"

"God, ay, Roisin!"

A cleaner passes with her bucket; a local. They're not even aware of her.

"And then –" He's starting to struggle, himself; to slow down. "Marie!" he remembers, just as he might've been bate.

"And – young Tony!"

He's pleased wi remembering that one. You can see it.

Another pause, then: "And the last wee one, her mother's double, God love her: Siobhan!"

His wife doesn't say nothing. He smiles, clears his throat, wriggles on the sunbed; stretches, flexes, then, finally, lies at peace.

"*Edinburgh*, eh?" Like it's his final word on the matter.

Switch to KITCHEN

He clears away his breakfast things; strangely choked, as he rinses the dishes. He'll chew on this for long enough –

No denying it: he knows, deep down, he'll chew on it. And for long enough.

Jen Hadfield

Planting for Peace

The Lord Provost's mudfilled pockets sway like udders
and his sovereign clanks the pitchfork
as he heaves it from an awning loaded with dirt

well, it's my privilege to be

she's running up and down
singing hi-o-hi-o and clapping
like a Morris dancer;
and all the kids wonder what's wrong

he says *it's my privilege to be here today*

She spins her padded moon.
They try to hold her
the sapling tilts like a mast in her eager sea

we'll take a seat

we'll take a seat now

want to end up falling again?

Downhill she orbits waists
– stripping the willow
of hips and thighs and torso
and reaching for fingers
like skinny leaves

falling

Vespers

At shutter-time
the apron slides from the lap of the sky.

The streetlamps are roosting
blackbirds tick as they set into silhouette.
And there are no leaves yet, no softening of the blue –
trees in winter voodoo net a jogger
from the pavement and hoist her into place

here

between Aries

and the police helicopter's
ascending
star.

Skerryman's Blessing

May you find your nuggets of claw
and coiled damp tail and splintered bone
and brochs of snails and seeds of fruits
all fortune-cookied;

may the light land every hour
differently on your bird-table:

tiger-black

mackerel-silver

Highland Postcards

Rannoch #1

charred wet wood
climbing tackle
the sob-stitched cheeks
of poor Sukie

Rannoch #2

The hoodoo trees jooking
some-old lateral truth
about scarcity

the leap of the fuel-gauge
a marvellous erection.

Great Glen

putain! ce sont
des vaches typiques!

Ullinish

Racing over the water   a sky
patched and manic as the next croft's
untethered Lucy.

The cat bolts from its throne of rocks.

Highland Giants

Glencoe's granite knees
steel toecaps of Cluanie dam.

Fratres *(Taking You With Me)*

I paint the low hill until I admit
how the light is on it.
Morning's coldest – working in thermals
and fleeces and socks in triplicate –
a lugworm, bundled bait
for the sky with the thunder-grey roe.

How is the light on the low hill now?
Blood through skin.
Once or twice a day sun opens the vein and
white is white of seagulls – sour Messiahs!
– then another two hundred
of Tommy's rainstained fleeces.

*

I said to Tommy (shifting stone)
whatcha doing and he said
playing at Nelson Mandela
what does it look like?

The layby's up for it, grips
your car with the windows mossed with thin damp.
Headlamps chuck out sticky webs to slide
from the windscreen and your black/bright forehead.
Headlamps – grasses giant
and shrinking – and us knotted in the hill's hair.

*

Now you turn the key and the gate's sudden
red iron – the last moment we've netted.
You've picked a sandtrack, you want
to say to keep it light, don't get attached
('no angel') and I want to shock you agreeing
yeh keep it light
and I can carry you a while. For a day or two
I'll have this cumulus bruise (your passing weather)
on my lower lip.

*

Up here it turns out it's less simple
a ewe's fleece
stained by the season of her last top.

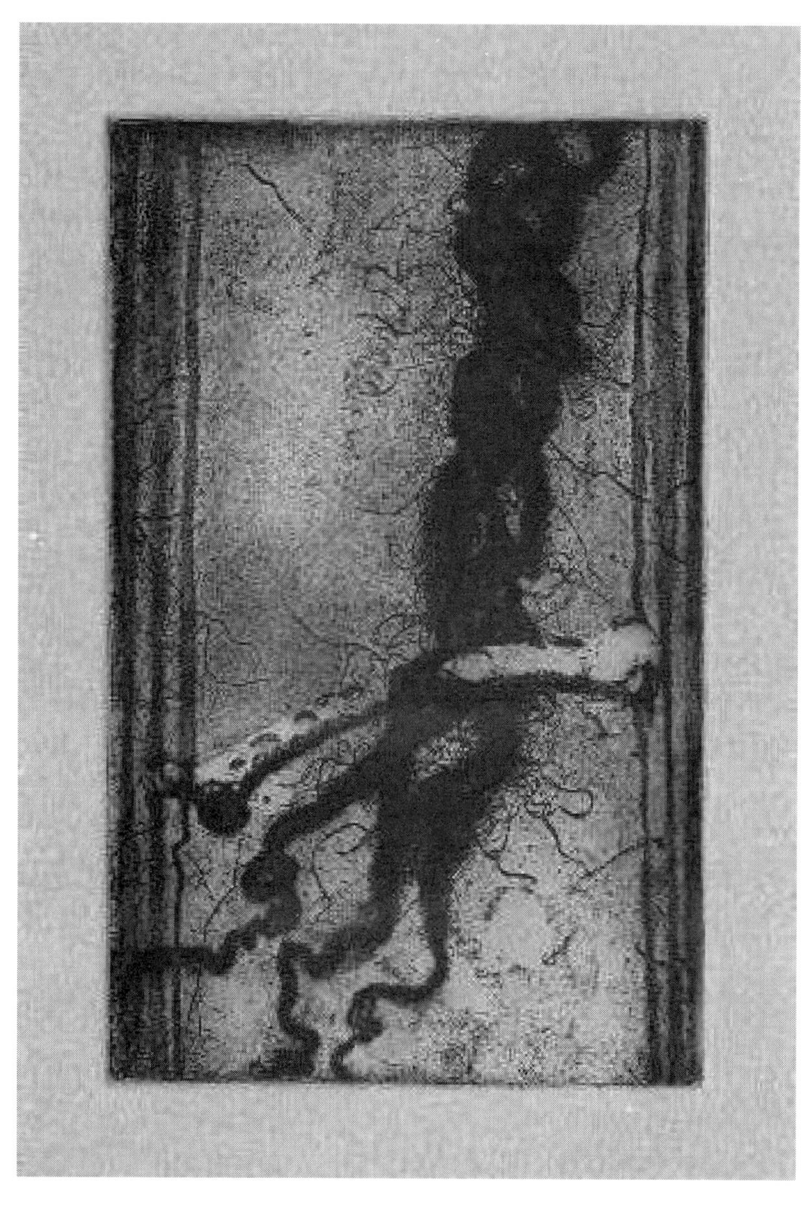

the softest fleece

Bill Duncan

Birdpeople

Thanks to the Being, the birds are come ...

Solan. The slopes of Stac Lee. March.
Puffin. The slopes of Dun. March.
Fulmar. The cliffs of Conachair. July.
Guga. The Rocks of Boreray. September.

The sky snows with birds, the sea is a drift of birds,
the street is paved with feathers, the house is carpeted with feathers,
the fields are speckled with feathers, like a meadow of white flowers,
the people work in a blizzard of feathers, our hair, our clothes
caught in a storm.

Thanks to the Being, the birds are come ...

Their oil stored for heat, light, healing.
In our feather store, a shipload of sacks, piled roof-high.
Their innards lure our fishing lines, their bones enrich our fields.
Fresh meat furnishes our table. Salted and stored, a Winter is survived.

Thanks to the Being, the birds are come ...

Winter Croft

The loom turns in every house.

Our time runs with the sea,
between tides, between suns.

The women spin from the softest fleece,
the men weave a broad cloth from their yarn.
In every house, a table cleared: a circle of women,
a rhythm of hands, voices, stories, songs, a garment shaped.

Between moons, between storms,
between darknesses, between seasons.

The loom sings in every house.

The Reverend John Mackay's Farewell to Hirta

Drawn from a black coat
on a loop of silver chain.
10.25am, October 5th, 1898.

"Field, sea and cliff await
their allocated hour. Moon and tide
retreat from the divide of day and minute,
the order of sermon and pulpit.

In my time they have learned better ways.
The Sabbath finds them thrice beneath my prayers.
Voices stilled and silent, save for psalms,
their poetry and dance a memory of shame.

Dead from lack of telling, their narratives fade.
My words have changed the way they see their world.
The Elders of their Church, my eyes and ears,
report an island altered through my years.

I think it is time I was leaving them now."

Lines from Morvern, Argyll, Autumn 1931

This is a beautiful country, but strange.
There were no trees on Hirta.

Finlay is content: a wage, a ceilidh, a dance.
Lachlan has drifted away to a city.
My father returned to Hirta for the Summer.
Christina misses the village street and says the house is lonely.
The women live apart, the men work a long day in the forest.
The nurse visits Donalda, who is much changed.

I had never heard my father curse on Hirta:
the Summer boats, the tourists, their money.
He slurs in a low bitter tongue of the pulpit.

I plant trees that I will never see harvested
on a hillside miles from my house.
There were no trees on Hirta.

The Village Street, House Number 14

Space of a missing door
framing a cold moon.
Behind a broken grate
the black of a dead fire.

A wind blows
through the bones of the house
between ruined stones
echoing an old song.

a memory of shame

Illustrations – etchings by Susan Wilson, in collaboration with Bill Duncan, printed at Dundee Contemporary Arts Print Studio

Ian McDonough

The Hills at Night

Here is a path to try your eyes,
steer your shadow,
sail a sullen navy
through the hills at night.

Inch over umber rises,
past deepened violet light,
into the gloomy cupboard
of the hills at night.

Run towards the quiet reaches,
pale and faintly glowing,
where the witch's black cap
sinks in a bog of its own jet terror.

Let us travel, hand in hand,
into the unfamiliar hills of night,
for you and I both know it –
we must brave that landscape anyhow.

Photosynthesis

Clouds banked up, darkening my steps,
and the Assynt hills
became a backdrop
for a far-fetched, ill-considered play.

The air thinned to almost nothing,
until the whole of Stoer
began to wheeze and hyperventilate
gasping for an atmospheric change.

Then you snared a little sunlight
in your gaze, cracked the very atoms
of the day, spreading oxygen
like lifebelts in your wake.

The Weather's Engines

Devices have devices,
and we, like all machines
breed intimate dependencies
with those who calibrate our gears,
apply the viscous fluids,
transport outputs
to a final destination.

Who drives the weather's engines?

Cows and clockwork mice and Hamlets,
herded by extraneous forces,
churning up
with feet and hooves and wheels
the regulated fields of engineers.

Diamond Sutra

New Year in Thurso,
shining with the flu,
shedding all my layers
I uncover you.

Love, the Sutras asks us
to walk a path
knowing there is no path,
nor even the illusion of a path.
But in this sweating bed
I feel the coolness of your feet,
the adamantine succour of your touch,
and if this is illusion
it is of the finest water.

Bells ring to count the passage
of one more phantom year:
we hold each other,
stare backwards through a lens
to marvel at what wisdom tells us
we can never share,
because it is not there.

And like the child of carbon that I am,
I realise I couldn't care a damn
for all their phantom wisdom.
I am tired of diamond geezers
with their vanishings,
their mind abiding nowhere

their inconceivable rewards,
their Sutras sanctifying illusion.

Love, the asteroids are crashing
into earth, distributing a diamond dust
which permeates our world.
Here, at the Northern edge of land,
where the sea whips glittering sand,
let us trade our common atoms,
feel them buzz, combine and shimmer –
absorb the real light together.

Fish Fingers or –

The Predicament of the Scottish Playwright

George Byatt (from Chapman *35-6)*

The proposition that a new and vital Scottish Theatre based on new writers and new writing had emerged in the last ten years seemed self evident not so long ago. *The Great Northern Welly Boot Show* of 1972 can be taken as the starting point of this development. But, it is now equally self evident that all is not as it should be.

The Predicament: – Glasgow Citizens' Theatre continues to add to its European a reputation without saying anything of any consequence about, or for, Scotland. At the Royal Lyceum Theatre in Edinburgh, the Leslie Lawton Gang Show continues to gives the same old tired programme of faded Broadway and West End 'hits'. Like the Citizens', but in different ways, it has a programme equally at home in Watford or Weston-Super-Mare. The Traverse Theatre, the root of the whole Fringe theatre movement in the so-called British Isles, has moved far from its *avant-garde* beginnings. After a period of partial commitment to new Scottish writing, it has moved into a new phase that has not yet crystallised. Elsewhere in Scotland, Perth, Dundee and Pitlochry – with minor variations – continue to bend the same suppliant knee to Broadway and the West End as does the Lyceum.

A limited amount of tokenism towards new Scottish writing exists, but not enough in any of the above theatres to alter the overall impression that none of them are in Scotland. They seem rather to exist in some cultural cul-de-sac of the middle-class, middle-brow mind. And an English mind at that. The Citizens' is no exception to the rule. It is simply a quirky, up-market version of the status quo.

Thus the predicament of the Scottish playwright lies in the nature of what might be called, without too much irony, the 'commanding heights' of the Scottish Theatre. For at those rarified oxygen-starved heights there is, as far as can be judged, no vision. There is no vision of the theatre as a place where the vital issues of our culture can be explored; no awareness that the theatre should be the people talking to themselves; not a hint that Scottish culture is still a vital oral culture and that the theatre is the natural high point of social communication in such a culture. To be fair none of these ideas may have occurred to those responsible for running these theatres. That is, if it is fair to accuse them of crass, mind-bending, bewildering ignorance of their own cultural context and the way in which they relate to it. Or, as in the case in question, the way they fail to relate to it. For most of them, the anal count, or 'bums on seats' as they indelicately put it, is the index of theatrical success. There's vision for you.

The Monopoly Game: apart from the lack of vision of theatres is the problem of their limited number. They constitute an artistic monopoly and act as a built-in barrier to future development. None of them has the kind of studio theatre in which new writing can have a place to try and triumph.

Or, equally important, fail. True, there existed for short periods of time such places as the Close Theatre in Glasgow and the Young Lyceum in Edinburgh. Fire destroyed the first, and what looked like a sword destroyed the second. Both parent companies seem relieved rather than distressed at the premature deaths of their not-quite-legitimate children.

Outside of the theatres mentioned, there are what we might call the theatres without a theatre, the touring companies. The two largest of these at the moment are the 7:84 company and its music orientated offspring – Wildcat Theatre. To 7:84 belongs the honour of pioneering a new kind of touring company in Scotland – politically orientated and populist. Wildcat is in a related mould. But despite 7:84's recent re-kindling of Scottish popular plays of the Forties, neither company is able to offer much opportunity to writers other than those who are already members of their respective organisations. This is not a criticism, but simply notes a fact that is the result of the origins and histories of both companies. Nevertheless the Scottish playwright's predicament proliferates.

A Death Worse Than Fate: but suppose for a dreadful moment that one of the 'commanding heights' theatres did produce a play by a new Scottish writer. What fate would await the writer's work? Not, surely, a fate worse than death? No – worse. Just the death of the play as the writer has conceived it, and this because all these establishments operate on the same hierarchical model as the Broadway and West End which they ape. They employ a director, usually male, to 'direct' the play: an authority figure re-interprets the writer's work to fit the theatrical pre-conceptions of the status quo. The idea that the writer could produce the play in conjunction with the actors is met with amused and patronising contempt. Such an attitude is of course completely ahistorical. The director as we know him, (I use 'him' deliberately), is a product of 19th century naturalism (the pretence that actors are 'real' people talking to each other, unaware of the presence of the audience). This is the prevailing mode in the 'commanding heights', a mode that comes trailing clouds of unexamined social and political implications. The director is the blind servant of this mode.

Perhaps the best way to illustrate the such handling of a play is to tell a story: – And it came to pass that a playwright went forth to fish with rod and line. For days, weeks, months, years, a lifetime even, the writer patiently waited for a tug on the line that dipped into the limpid pool of the collective unconscious. Finally, there was a ripple on the surface, and after an exhausting but exciting tussle, a great, gleaming, living, silver fish was landed. Then, still living, still struggling, it was presented to a theatre.

Ah, we too are excited, the theatre said. This is the most beautiful fish we have ever seen. See how silver it is. See how it turns and twists. Above all, it delights. This one will twist and turn and turn forever. Lo. Behold. Here is your director. He will, with your approval of course, choose your actors. And he will show your fish to all the people. And so the director did take the fish, and, with his chosen actors, at his behest, and accepting his wisdom and with great effort, they did kill that great, living, silver fish.

And they did turn it into fish fingers. And then they held them up for all the people to see. Woe. Woe.

Some writers and most directors might dispute the truth of this story. Many playwrights will recognise its bitter relevance to their own experience and it may go some way to explain the failed promise of new Scottish writing in the seventies. It's fair of course to say that writers in other cultures have the same kind of problem.

The Fringe That Grew: in England in the late 60s and into the 70s there was a related upsurge of new theatre writing. This upsurge did fulfil its promise in a spectacular way. Taking their cue from the Edinburgh Festival fringe and from the pioneering work of the original Traverse Theatre in the Lawnmarket, low budget theatres appeared in pub rooms and basements in many parts of London. The Soho Poly theatre, founded in 1969 by the late Verity Bargate and Fred Proud is perhaps the best-known and most successful example. Through this tiny basement theatre went, and still goes, some of the best and freshest writing and acting talent in the whole of England. Other small theatres like The Bush and The King's Head also continue to flourish. Around them, a stream of such theatres live and die and are sometimes re-born. New writers in London have some hope of performance, while here in Scotland there is almost none.

This London Fringe or Alternative Theatre altered the direction of the mainstream. Today many of its writers now have plays performed in their 'commanding heights' – the West End, The National, The Royal Shakespeare and The Royal Court. Whether this has been a good thing or a bad thing is a matter for debate. They have directors in abundance in England and they also make fish fingers. In Scotland there never has been an Alternative Theatre in the London manner, and because of this lack, the 70s upsurge of writing here was absorbed directly into the fish finger industry.

No Way Out or Round or Through? To summarise: there are too few theatre outlets in Scotland. Their monopoly constitutes a barrier to developing writing talent and the values they live by are more likely to destroy new talent rather encourage it. So where can the playwright, new and established, turn? Is there, as H G Wells said, no way out or round or through?

Fortunately, a way out is emerging for Scottish Playwrights in the eighties. Soon there may be ways round and through. The way out is the Workshop movement now beginning to expand here. The best example of this kind of theatre in Scotland is the Edinburgh Playwrights' Workshop. Founded by writers, actors and others, the EPW has been running regular programmes of new writing by writers both new and old. Each play in the series has a deliberately restricted rehearsal period (to keep as close to the original text as possible). Each is presented, script in hand, by professional actors to a public audience. There are no sets or costumes and no light changes. Props are minimal or non-existent. Where possible, the plays use a limited amount of movement. Plays presented in this way have to be good to survive and the survival rate among these plays is an index of the strength and quality of a body of new works that cry out for production.

More than fifty plays have been presented by the EPW in this way in the last three years. No other professional theatre group in Scotland, and possibly in England, can lay claim to such an output. The plays have ranged from the reworking of a neglected early 17th century verse play to contemporary plays about oilrig workers. Radio, television as well as theatre plays are included in this programme. Several plays have gone on to production but not as many as could do so. In every case the writer concerned has been primarily responsible for their presentation. Ideally this is done in full and free collaboration with the actors involved.

After each presentation, the plays are discussed by audience, actors and writers. The discussions are structured so that all present are given an opportunity to comment if they wish. The weekly 'anal' count at the time of writing is between forty and fifty and is on the increase.

The initial workshops were financed from their own box office returns. Later the Scottish Society of Playwrights gave its support. And now the Scottish Arts Council provide a minimal budget for what could become the Scottish Alternative Theatre of the near future. The critic Joyce MacMillan has described the workshops in Scottish Theatre News as "a completely new form of theatrical event ... cheap, informal, immediate and heavily dependent on audience participation ... their contribution to theatrical life in Edinburgh has already been substantial". The EPW's declared aim is to encourage other Scottish cities and centres to set up their own similar enterprises. Surely, here are the seeds of the future?

Alternatives: but after the way out, where is the way round and through? It is not provident to be too specific about coming developments. They will take their own course based on the initial impetus derived from the workshops. Already several new production companies have emerged and more than one has put workshop plays into full professional production. All these companies are based on the work of particular writers. Theatre Vortex has Christina Johns as its writer. Rona Munro is the writer for Stage Traffic and older established companies such as Mental Guerrillas and Theatre PKF are in close contact with the new companies. And new works by the writers George Gunn, Katy Gardiner and Rob Laing are planned for production. Other companies in Edinburgh and Glasgow are also consciously or unconsciously part of what begins to look like a new phase in the life of the theatre in Scotland. In months rather than years, we should begin to see results that will show the way round and through.

It is an exciting prospect for writers, actors and audiences. The river is full of living silver fish. The banks are crowded with fisherpersons. There is a growing awareness that co-operation and not competition is the real law of life. Scotland is small enough and big enough to create a new theatre that could take its place in Europe and the World. If we go about it in the right way the predicament of the Scottish playwright could disappear. An Alternative theatre could take us round the 'commanding heights' and who knows, the fish finger industry might itself be led to find new values to live by. But that's a story for the future, one that we look forward to writing.

George Gunn

Winter Barley

Ode to the Coming Summer

(For P B)

The coming Summer swims across the North
& breathes a cool May into an eager June
to coax the growth from beneath the earth

so the little heat can come & soon
the barley will green the ochre of the park
& the thrushes trill their grateful tune

in dawning's that shed the need for dark
& swallows can execute their figure eight
gathering up their strength to put the spark

of joy back into the fibre of their fate
which is to be the seasons crowning glory
nothing is too early, nothing is too late

It is the Summer coming, neither sad nor sorry
giver & builder; this is her story

The sky may be grey but there is no need for tears
like the promise of an open hand
the season is a warning & welcome of fears

which can be nourished across the land
cultivated in kind & hopeful furrows
& turned to warmth as nature planned

for we have no need of the weed of sorrows
the living bloom across the field is spread
& defies the desperate & the doomed to their burrows

to play endless dice with the dead
a game that needs neither sloth nor slurry
for the colour of life is constant red

& Summer has a mind it's time to marry
the blue space for birth; this is your story

A perfect pibroch from the Pentland Firth
Summer circles the ever-moving shoal of meaning
the days stretch & meld the myrtle of their mirth

from Hoy's high sandstone shelf, leaning
their elbows on Morven's accommodating prow
to the velvet slipper of Kildonan's dreaming

in her hill locked cradle where now
the acres are aggregated in a computer's bleep
the days caress the wrinkles on the brow

of history which is the subject of Kildonan's sleep
this northern landscape of calm and fury
where action & reaction are twenty feet deep

on the soft nether-bedrock of nitrogen & slurry
sweet Summer music; this is your story

If I were a deer made from rays of light
I would run with you across the hill
& splash through burns from day to night

& never stop my itchy running until
I had come to the high mountains of Kashmir
& break out your bright crayons of creation & fill

the blank pages where blood is white & death is near
& you would melt the metal of that moments quarrel
& summon the colours of possibility to appear

to take the roaring from the sky & oil from the barrel
& shed the light of plenty that only Summer can
that pibroch which feeds the inaccessible

peaks of aspiration & the straths of our shame
oh, early Summer, put the woman back into the man

Make me your messenger & your skaldic tongue
season of laughter & light & love
when youth is broadened & the old grow young

take these sunlit thoughts & throw them above
the cacophony of the pitiless market
& let them sing so that their blood can move

that necessary mountain of passion & thought
& like the breather corn growing in a Caithness field
it roots in the stars to earth what it is to what it is not

food for only a few so the dead can wield
a steel blanket around the earth
& shut out the light & imprison the yield

of the labours of the Sun. Ah, my firth
is the world a seabed to the salt-rose of our worth?

Rough Weather

(For John McGrath)

It snowed in the north the day you died
the white powder lay across Rogart
like a negative
I kept expecting Bill Paterson
or Johnny Bett to come prancing
over the top of Strath Fleet
to make us laugh
Then I realized your power

These flat green swathes accumulate in the sea
how hard is time & its apprentice
& will we hear the rolling clack
of these dice of chance & destiny
"I am innocent of life's communion,"
whispers the deer, the eagle

here is highness enough
for all those low gods of denial

the fields approach the ocean
slippery as ideas
& it was ideas you had
a-plenty
in this theatre
of the world

ah, McGrath, you were a dawn
& now there is darkness in the heart of a Gunn

John McGrath (courtesy of Elizabeth MacLennan)

Young Rowan

The summer's failure rose above the sodden county
until its very art became invisible
Below the grey listless clouds
the black-haired woman sleeps
By a stocky wall a young rowan shivers
in the dying promise of the wind

The decommissioning buildings come together
in the conversation of a camp
& like that enforced eloquence
will leave no lasting imprint
on the carefully scarred map of this voyage
charted by CCTV cameras & industrial gloves

From their urban bothy they looked across
the unbuilt ground to the maternity hospital
in which no longer anyone is born
Accident & Emergency too has gone
Soon fog will roll in from the firth
covering Olrig Hill in a hazy skin

That ungiving summer was when the Free Kirk split apart
one too many times & this time for money
Another squall argues in from the west
& the young rowan now is bending
bowing seawards in forced supplication
Here on the cliff's edge the town is hermetically sealed

Around the place the lucky & the afflicted
build dubious mansions in which to dress
the excellence of their absurdity in the necessary material
it takes to need a double garage
looking ever inwards through soundproof windows
The Atlantic drums out an architecture of sea anchors

to the very ones who will never hear that rhythm
for as the rain abates it is the dog walkers
who will inherit the tarmac & the neon light
A blue van is parked by a brown wooden shed
inside the deal is done
afterwards the mobile phones are switched on again

Brutal

We feed the birds
but the black crows come
21st century
in the white snow
of February

Struggle

The sky is cathedral black
across the north
& we paint our dreams upon it
& harbour them there

so the Xmas night
is a series of candles
hidden behind peats
& nothing is forgotten

& everything is remembered
in the orange flickering
of the future, of our memory
of our imaginings

of a time when the world was green
& cream white cows
with long red ears
roamed over the link-lands

& the bronze beach was awash
with silver shells
& the sea's moon-woven
tapestry of tangle & phosphorus

& we danced to the music so magical
that the peat lamps
of the morning lit up
a welcome across the sun's brow

to the angel of the sea
& the star of the morning
beyond seasons & anchorages
from firth-end to firth-end

the psalm of the sea
a headland of hymns
in the sermon of sandstone
we will hear them

at the day's opening & at its close
remembering the story of the flame
& the still candle of silence
the flickering light of life

Changeling

William Hershaw

In a quiet neuk o Stratheden Psychiatric Hospital on a caller, muinlit Sabbath een, a senior doctor is takkin a young student on his round o the wards. They gae alang a green corridor till they reach a chaumer that staunds on its ain. Afore they gae in ben the doctor keeks ower his glesses tae tak a bit neb at his haundfou o files.

"A most interesting case, this one, Mr Kerr. A queer bugger. A local man. Highly delusional. Speaks very little, which makes a precise diagnosis and subsequent treatment extremely difficult. The fascinating aspect is this – on the few occasions when he does speak he insists in doing so in a form of rhyme. Unfortunately, he usually starts to become agitated and his mood fluctuates wildly. I have been forced to prescribe heavy sedation when this occurs. Watch him carefully and tell me if you notice anything, because, frankly, I'm at a loss. He has been with us for a number of years and I have got precisely nowhere with him so far – with any form of treatment. Maybe you can give me a clue … maybe they teach you students something at college these days …"

They gae ben. A chiel sits bi the winnock, gaipin up at the bricht fou muin. When the twa doctors snaik in he disnae muive or tak ony tent o them ataa. It is like he disnae ken they are there. The young student luiks at him. He is a maist eldrich sicht tae see. The student speirs at him in the siller licht o the muin. He is happit in an auld fisherman's jersey and a plaid shirt ower big for him. He micht be an auld man, he micht be a young ane, but ye cannae tell. He has a fell o thick corbie-black hair on his pow. His face micht be auldren if it were no for his twa bricht emeralt een. They sparkle and lowe and glaim like fireworks. His lang thin face draws out tae a stickit-out pyntit chin. His lugs are ower muckle for the size o his heid and are sherp and saft as a tod's. His body is streetched out and as nairra as twa ply reek. The student taks tent o his pale white haunds that splay out intil lang fingers like twigs. He micht be a Guy or a tattiebogle. Doctor Kerr ettles tae strike up a blether wi him.

"How's tricks then, Ian? A lovely night … I see you're studying the moon. And how are we getting on today? Are the new tablets helping you?"

"What do you see, Ian?" asks the student.

"C'mon now, Ian," says Doctor Kerr. "You mustn't be rude … we're only trying to help you."

But Ian juist ignores him as if he was a flee that was bizzen on the wa. He luiks up at the muckle black bow o the nicht-time carry and his green een twinkle like the sea on a gleg day. The blae starns wink back tae him. He lauchs.

"He seems to be looking for something," remarks the student.

"God knows what!" repones the Doctor. "I think we're wasting our time here. We'll discuss him in the office. I think there's a case to be made for extreme measures ... last chance saloon. C'mon, I'll get you a coffee."

They gae out and shut the door. When they are awa, Ian lauchs tae hisel aince mair and in a sing-sang voice chants saftly:

> Fiddles tae bow and pipes tae blaw,
> There's music tae hear ablo Largo Law,
> Tirl at the yett, birl round the key,
> It's ablo the lintel but nevermair free.

Ian the Fiddler was comin back fae a weddin in Kettlebridge Toun Ha. It had been a richt guid nicht. The haa had been fou, the swippert feet o the dancers fleean tae his jigs and reels. His lang soupple fingers raxin tae the magic notes, his elbuck jinkin up and doun like the clappers. He had gaun doun richt weel and tho his fingers ached, he had grinned a daft sloppy smile as he stuck tae his darg and filled the haa wi pleesure. His bow scrapit and screiched and danced up and doun on his fiddle. At the hinner end o it aa, the best man, hauf seas ower, had bocht him a dram and stuffed some faulded notes intae his tap pocket.

"Weel duin, Ian! Yer a lang dreep o a laddie but there's naebidy can touch ye when it cams tae the fiddlin. Ye should dae it fou time – turn professional raither than be droukit and drouned on the high rollin seas. That fishin boat o yours is gey wanchancy. The weddin wadnae hae been worth a tinker's breeks without ye. Mind you, whase gaunnae play at yer ain weddin next week? Ye'll be ower thrang wi Mhairi!" He winked, coorse like. "Here man, dae ye think I've ony chance o a dance fae that mither-in-law yer gaun tae bide wi, Auld Peg; ocht, I'm juist kiddin – tak anither dram then gie us 'Maggie Lauder'."

The hours had been fleean past quicker than poppies bloom and fa. Bi the time the last guests had stechered hame out the haa, it was weel past midnicht. Luckily, the minister was drivin tae Coaltoun o Wemyss and Ian was gien a lift as faur as Largo in his black Ford. He had a lang walk afore him till he reached his hame in Saint Monans but he didnae mind because it was a braw caller nicht. The muin was out and he wad hear the souch and sang o the sea as he daundered alang the road hameward tae the East Neuk.

As he waved cheerio Ian was weel contentit. He flung his fiddle case ower his shouder. His heid was fou o pleasant thochts o his ain dearest hinney, dark and douce ee'd Mhairi. He lippent tae her gentle Heilan weys. He looed her accent, like music, blythe and no like the roch-tongued lallans fisher-lassies. They chappit the heids aff herrin at the key-side wi sherp knives and their voices could peel pent. He had been a fish-erladdie fae when he had taen his first shougly steps. Mhairi was the finest catch that ere he had taen and the luckiest ane as weel. She didnae even luik at the ither men. He pictured her lang, sleek black hair that fell doun around her comely waist. As he walked alang the road he could imagine her smile and the wey she birled her heid and swished her hair. He wished she was wi him nou and he thocht o hou if she was he wad gie her cuddle. She wad whisper tae him in her saft Heilan lilt and he wad say "wheesh" and tell her tae haud her peace. "Aa thing will be awricht," he wad tell her.

Whit did she want wi a fuilish, ugsome thing like him? It worrit him. He wisnae braw or swack or strang and some fowk lauched at him ahint his back because o his strange luiks. And yet he kent she loved him wi aa her hert. They wad be merried the neist Setterday and Ian howped the weddin wad be as guid as the ane he had juist played at. Yet there were times that Mhairi said and duin things that Ian thocht were unco. She wad luik at him wi troubled een and tell him no tae gae out tae sea. She had tellt him 'the sicht' ran in her faimily and fae time tae time she wad hae dreams that left her thrummlin and white wi fear when they met up at some secret tryst. She never tellt Ian whit they were but he kent they were about him. Never heed dreams! Cam Setterday they wad be couryin doun in their ain wee bield. And so he walked the lang road hame.

Ian never kent whit made him dae it but he mindit later it was if a voice in his heid caad, "Turn around, Ian, and luik at Largo Law". Gin he had kept on walkin, nane o it wad hae happened. As it was, wi him aye bein a nebby chiel, he birled around and saw the lichts.

They were flashin on and aff and dancin out and in on tap o the auld hill. Betimes there were ane, syne twa, syne three and fower circlin round in a gird. Syne there was juist ane and syne there were nane. They were like siller starns. They were like bairn starns that had fawn loose out their velvet happin in the carry and had skailed doun tae the Earth tae play tig and chase and dance wi each ither. Their mithers and faithers wad caa them back up suin. Ian gaiped at them, entranced and delichted bi these ferlie fairins. He had passed ben Largo Law mony times. He had heard tell o the fairies wha were supposed tae bide ablo Norrie's Law, the wee plooky hillock that sat on the shouder o the big ane. He had heard o a treasure that was buried there. He had never believed ony o thon havers. He thocht o the hill as juist an auld, cauld, lang extinct volcano. Nou he speired the antrin muvin lichts. He saw the fower lichts jined as ane and the hale croun o the hill was lichtened up in a siller radiance for a minute. Was that shadows shiftin aroond up thonder?

Wha micht be up there at thon time o nicht? He jaloosed Mhairi's face if he walked throu the door wi a muckle kist o gowden treasures – coins and rings, tassies and bracelets!

Without a thocht o the danger there micht be, Ian lowped ower the waa and sprauchled throu the fields as fast as he could gae. He fairly stottit aff stane and tussock and his lang spindly legs cam intae their ain as he scuttled up the brae o the Law, like an ungracefou attercap. In nae mair than ten minutes he won tae the tap, pechtin and pantin and sabbin for breith. Wi his neives on his knees he spied out the lie o the land. Not a sowel! Aa was dark and still. He scartit the gress wi his big tae. This was fell disappointin. "Onybody there?" he caad out. His voice singsanged back at him. He sat doun for a minute tae hae a blaw afore settin aff doun the hill for hame. He tuik aff his fiddle case and opened it. It had gotten a sair rattlin as he ran up the hill. It was an auld fiddle his grandfaither had gien him and the pegs were gie loose. It wad be out o tune richt enough. He taen it out, liftit his bow and ran it ower the rosined strings. E A D G – The fower notes sang out intae the cleir nicht air and the muin keeked out fae ahint a cloud.

Ian luiked up and speired the first o them richt awa. The instant the first note had sounded a sma cratur o hodden grey had appeared tae his left. He was nae mair than three fuit high wi a big heid and muckle black een. He didnae seem tae hae ony claes on tae hap hisel wi, even though it wasnae that warm. It wad be wrang tae say that Ian wisnae feard. His neive shuik and it dirled the strings on his fiddle. At this anither ane kythed up on his richt. Ian thocht o makkin a run for it. The twa o them juist stuid there, watchin him. Ian luiked round. They were aa ahint him, aa around him. He was surrounded. Tae his horror, Ian watched mair and mair o the sma grey figures rax out fae the shaddays. There were at least a hunner o them. They didnae mak a sound and juist watched him. Hou was he tae escape? He couldnae run without gaen throu them. Wha were these queer – like wee men that didnae mak a sound? Yet they never liftit a finger tae herm him either. Efter a minute Ian had the presence o mind tae speik.

"Hou dae ye dae, Gentlemen?" he blustered. "Ma name is Ian the fiddler. I'm pleased tae mak yer acquantaince. But nou I maist be gettin hame ... Excuse me."

Ane o the grey chiels solemnly pyntit a lang runkled finger at Ian's fiddle. That was it! They were wantin tae hear music! They wad lat him be if he played them a tune.

Ian struck up a chord. Aa the grey men lowpit back, as if in fear, then muived in, close in a ring. Ian stertit tae play his fiddle.

He began wi a slow air, a tune aboot an immigrant leavin his hame and gaen tae a strange place. As he played, the sma grey hauflin men began tae swey in time tae the tune. Then he began tae warm tae his task. He gied them a medley: 'Ye Jacobites', 'My Love's She's But A lassie Yet', 'The Piper Cam Tae Our Toun', twa o them in E minor, the ither in D major. Nou the grey men slowly jyned their hands and began tae circle round, wi muckle gracefouness and solemnity. Neist it was seasangs and hornpipes: there was 'The Keel Row' and 'The Boatie Row', 'The Sailor's Hornpipe' and 'Harvest Home'. Nou the fleet-fuitit grey men were daen a whirlmagig around him and Ian had tint aa fear o them as he sawed awa on his auld fiddle. He couldnae mak sense o their fremmit language but he kent fine they were haen a fine time. They were aw singin nou. The faster he played the faster they danced their jig around him ...

But it had been a lang nicht for Ian and efter a while he felt fair wabbit. "I'm deid duin wi aa this playin!" he caad and sat hisel doun. They clamoured round. It was gey strange, he thocht. He couldnae mak heid nor tale o their words but he seemed tae ken whit they were sayin.

"Cam ben our boatie and we'll gie ye a dram that'll tak the weariness awa," they said. "And while yer at it we'll ask ye about thon wuidden kist wi wires on it that ye hit wi a stick. Neither wonder it screams when ye belt it! Shaw us hou tae mak ain. Come wi us. Ye'll like it in our boat. We'd like tae pick yer brains, heh, heh ..."

They tuik Ian by the haund and led him throu the prow o their siller steel boat. He hadnae seen thon berthed up here afore but he could nou. Whit was a boat daein up on the tap o a hill? He was haunded a gless tube wi green liquid in it. Cheers! Fiddlin is thirsty work. He had a slug o it then, neist thing he kent, he was waukin up on the green gress on tap o Largo Law. The sun was shinin in his een. It maun be Sunday mornin. "That was an unco dream!" he thocht. "I maun mind it and tell Mhairi when I get back."

Yet it was a dream that he couldnae seem tae shake aff. As he walked hame alang the road he was shair that somethin was no richt – like he was still dreamin and had juist thocht he had waukened up but hadnae really. He couldnae pit his finger on whit was wrang. The hill was aye there. The sea was aye there. Awthin was in its place yet naethin seemed richt tae him. It was gey early still wi no mony folk on the road. Aince or twice cars went fleean past him at an awfou lick. They were makes he hadnae seen afore. "They're no juist makkin them in black nou, I see!" he thocht.

At last he trauchled his sair feet intae St Monans. He came in fae the Ainster road and past the Kirk. He heidit up the brae tae the harbour. On his wey he had tae pass the hoose whaur Mhairi steyed wi her auld mither, Peg. "I'll chap on the door and scrounge a cup o tea aff them," he thocht tae hisel, "and I'll tell Mhairi aboot thon weird dream and the funny wee men."

He noticed the snab's had shut doun. Funny – when did that happen? There wasnae onie boats in the harbour either … The auld wumman was up and about that Sunday morn. Staundin on the doorstep he heard her slowly hirplan ben the lobby tae answer the front door. Mhairi maist be haen a lang lie. Throu the gless panel he could see a blurred black shape, back-bent and aa crippled wi arthritis, the puir auld sowel. Her shilpit fingers fumbled wi the sneck. At last she opened the door tae him and liftit her wrinkled face tae him, her heid crouned wi siller hair, poued back in a ticht bun. She had her peeny on. "It's juist me!" he said.

For a second Ian thocht she was haen a stroke. She turned a grey colour, her jaw drappt, her mooth gawpit. Her een were neir streetchin out her heid as if she was a lobster being biled .

"Ian!" she gasped and stechered back intae the lobby.

"Whit's wrang, Peg?" he caad, his hert hammerin like a clapper in his chist.

"Peg? I'm no Peg, Ian… ma mither deed in the War…" chokit Mhairi and faintit clean awa …

Up by in Stratheden, the muin had gaen doun. But the unco-luikin patient in the fisherman's jersey was at the winnock yet. Saftly, he sang tae hisel.

> "If time were a thing tae be bocht
> And I had great ritches tae spare,
> I wad buy aw the years that hae gaen
> So that Mhairi and me could be young aince mair."

Tom Hubbard

The Temptation of Michael Scot

1.The Wandering Scot

We remember him as one of our own:
We could not tolerate that he went beyond us.
He was a boy like many of us:
His parents' cottage set upon a slope,
By the townhead pathway straggling to the fields.
Maybe in the smoke of an autumn evening,
As he left us after school, he saw his destiny:
His mother stoked the coal, it formed in the sky
Lands that were strange, events yet stranger;
Stranger as the smoke dissolves
In our poor forgettings and forbiddings.

He seeks the stone, this boy;
There are many stones in our land.
He finds one of the right shape and weight,
On the track from the lonely shieling;
Aims it at a puddle, flings another one.
Ripple against ripple, circle against circle
Hold him. He watches. His attention outlasts
Every attempt at knowledge. Stone after stone
Serves him for a while, then he must go on seeking.

Michael Scot, proud provincial.
He was resolved to mould his land anew
When he came back, and brought his devil with him,
To cleave the Eildon Hills, to dam the Tweed.
His moulding we scorned as meddling;
To cleave, like Satan's foot; to dam, damnation;
"Confine your schemes," we cried, "to foreign courts!
Your fancy ways are not for the likes of us!"
His fancy ways now profit us forever:
For coin, we'll blast the hills, and stink the river.

Michael, uneasily universal;
Stammering and drawling
Among the Sorbonne sophisticates;
This sober young laddie
Seeks in the constellations
The mysteries and movements of the nations;
He is schooled the less
In the turn of a face or the fold of a dress,
The night's laughter that swirls around him.

Your homeliness, Michael, is a charm:
Folk hear from you how the axis
Of heaven is the axle-bar
Of a mill-wheel near your Scottish home;
You make them see, in your serious way,
An orchard bearing the universe
In an apple, rounded and complete,
Hiding its future in its seeds;
And God, for you, in giving soul
Anew to body, is the father
Who gives a notebook to his child
To write within "whatever he will
Be it for good or ill."

As the years fell from you, Michael, you felt lighter.
You left Paris a poised young man,
A head of knowledge upon you,
Widely to be dispensed, and through a smile.
The mountains seemed to welcome one of their own;
Your steed passed over rocks as with a jig.
Sunrise and sunset on an Alpine pass,
As Michael Scot surveys his continent.
You were not a man for the weeping, till you marvelled
That here, at last, was Italy. At Bologna
You studied law, but others studied you
– For here, at last, to them, was Michael Scot.

You were called to Sicily,
As tutor to the king,
Frederick, sober young laddie:
The future Emperor of the Holy Roman Empire.
It is owing to you
That art and science will enjoy
His patronage, and he himself compose
Poetry in the new Italian tongue.
At the boy's wedding
To Constance, princess of Aragon,
Your present is a manuscript:
Your version of an Arab text –
Medical lore from Tripoli –
Secret of Secrets: so do you share
All that you seek with all who care.

Satisfaction, though, began to elude you.
Who seeks the stone, in time will seek for miracles.
Only a miracle could have saved Palermo
From the plague: ah! Not a single learned book
Could keep the court together. The survivors
Escaped from Sicily: you sailed to Spain.

Toledo!
A spectre-city, blanching the ridge to strange horizons,
Drawing in the moonlight to its bare stone
Yielding and resisting with equal pride,
Quivering over the scorched sand, the cascading glen;
The glower of the night dissolves into flecks of pink
Over the wall-towers to the citadel:
Toledo takes on flesh
As by a miracle.

From the hills around, for the first time,
Michael Scot approached Toledo.
From the hills around, for the first time,
Michael marked out the library.
He knew exactly where to find it,
Although a stranger to Toledo.

From the shelves of the library, sheaf after sheaf,
Learning of Greeks, preserved by Arabs;
From the transformation of the word,
Michael with his Jewish scholars,
Raising the science from the silence;
Speaking it far beyond Toledo.

"Al-khem! Al-khem!"
The alchemy of the Arab sages:
"Al-khem! Al-khem!"
Michael would almost have it cried
From every spire of his Toledo.
Secrets buried deep in earth,
Substance forming in its womb:
Lead to iron and to copper,
Silver and to GOLD.
He who transforms the elements
Transforms himself:
Michael Scot brings from the deep
Michael Scot reborn a god.

It was then he came back to us.
His new life jolted old feelings:
He yearned for Scotland and its years behind him.

> "*Whan I gaed oot,*" he told us then,
> "*You aa thocht I wis fu o blethers.*
> *I wis a young lad, stung at the hert,*
> *And whaur it stung, it haurdened;*
> *I wad gang oot, and lairn ti greet again.*
> *My wark is dune, and I hae lairned ti greet.*"

Down every close and wynd of Edinburgh,
The prodigal was welcomed, for a time.

We had our banquet, humble as it was,
To hear strange tales from this our traveller.
He picked the fatted calf clean to the bone,
And we had wine for him in readiness.
From bone to wine, much wine, then back to bone:
Many were the sunken eyes and broken grins
In the corners of the howffs, where Michael shared
Secret of secrets with all who cared.

The sudden spread of wizardry
Was checked, as sudden, by a stronger power:
The hooded crows of the Scottish Faith.
We remember (almost) their proclamation
Posted at every mercat in the land:

IT IS DECREED THAT THE SAID MICHAEL SCOT
DENUNCIT AT THE TABLES O OOR LORD
BI CERTAIN JUST AND SOBER CITIZENS,
HAEIN HARKED AT THIS UNHALY HERETIC
O HEATHEN NOTIONS LAIRNED IN GODLESS AIRTS:
IT IS DECREED THAT THE SAID MICHAEL SCOT
SUFFER THE DUE PROCESS O DESAIRVED CONFINEMENT
BAITH SOLITARY AND PERPETUALL:

AND THE LORD DAURNA HAE MERCIE ON HIS SOWEL

2. Ballad of Michael and Old Nick

He seeks the stone, some fourteen years
Into captivity:
He seeks the stone – at last, it moves –
Our alchemist is free.

His stone of destiny! That cell
Dried up his hope, his youth.
What's learning now, he asks himself;
What's effort, virtue, truth?

"No more abstractions! They were masks
I wore upon my rump.
From now, my study's but for power:
I'll make the bastards jump."

For the first time, he studied *folk:*
There's none had gone so deep.
What moved him most, he found within
Himself, in his own sleep.

He lolled in perfumed palaces;
He fairly bathed in wine;
A ripe young empress in the haze:
Cried Michael: *"She'll be mine!"*

All vanished. – Yet the subtleties
    Of his own soul were gleaned,
And mixed in just such quantities
    To call up the Arch-Fiend.

"Michael, mon frère: your soul's a catch:
    One's bored among the mob."
"Nick, you old faggot, cut the crap
    And get on with the job."

"Michael, your boyish company
    Will make it less a chore.
I've never known the formula
    Work quite so fast before."

Michael demands that Nick supply
    The best of girls and booze.
The women treat him like a prat,
    The wine just makes him snooze.

"Michael, what next? Rewrite our text,
    Experiments in Bliss?"
Poor Michael knows that Hell awaits;
    The devil takes the piss.

"Fetch me that floozie in my dream:
    No longer I'll be chaste!"
"– Old FLAME?" The devil smirked. "– So sorry!
    – Joke in terrible taste."

The ripe young empress in the haze
    Lived at the edge of town –
Called Agatha. A servant lass.
    So what? Her eyes are brown,

He likes her laughter: yes, she'll do.
    She's lonely. Enough said.
"Michael, what next?" – "I'm wanting you
    To help her to my bed."

She kisses him: no more; she pleads
    That he'll respect her trust.
Michael begins to look at her
    With something more than lust.

Old Nick is nervous. "Michael, what next?
    There's more to be enjoyed,
But little time, –" "– Back to your pit.
    Our contract now is void."

Nick kicked the ground: it opened up,
    Took him without his prey.
Of Michael and his Agatha
    There's little more to say.

She died in giving him a girl,
  Who sang him into age:
"Who seeks the stone, will find it soon,
  And study his last page."

Michael removed his scholar's cap;
  A stone fell on his head.
They placed him in his daughter's arms,
  And Michael Scot was dead.

Galley of Dreams *by Marianna Lines*

Valerie Gillies

Below the Surface

The Well Meadow won't lie fallow, the ploughland
speckled with pits like a field freckled with new shoots:
over a hundred hidden wells sealed with clay stopping,
all air excluded. Pillars of earth send down taproots,

underworld-dark, they lead away, out of sight.
Suspended shapes are shining in the soil. There!
Look! A blaze of light coming up from the pit wall.
Golden yellow, brass. Red glaze, Samian ware.

The earth's gate opens. This is the lined well
down which the oak-staved Roman bucket drops.
Their place on the Via Trimontina is the showcase
for their camp kettles, big jars, cooking pots,

adjustable padded helmets, earpiece and face mask,
and for everyone who makes it to the end,
medal backing-discs and saddle-horn stiffeners,
someone's hat of hair moss. It's the stuff of legend.

For anyone who ever scratched his name,
a *graffito* on a white bronze cup says "Maximus".
An iron handle marks "the property of Niger".
Dometius Atticus and Lucanus too have left us.

Our own names lead the march by a phalanx
of men wearing headsets, Gucci sunglasses, overalls
from Beyond Retro, mesh vests by Rokit, Galliano
hats, Moschino sandals. Shine on, robot metallers.

How can we value the instant flash of this faceplate
visor with the world's steeliest eye-to-eye stare?
Or these bones and skulls of nine horses and the slender
girl groom lying across the pit below them? A charioteer

now driving nine red horses across the heavens.
For the well is the way to the other world, where a rattle
sounds in the hiss of the sistrum, the beak of a raven
barks above the wave's thrash and the wind's whistle.

Long-jawed hounds guard a Pompeii of the north.
A child's shoe in one piece of leather: the outpost of the dead
is not far away. The leg-bone and spur of a cockerel:
for a moment we hear it crowing in the land of the shades.

Hazelnuts, the matter in a nutshell. A hazel twig
freshly cut with a sharp tool, bright and silvery,

at the bottom of the well. What's sealed up is a mystery.
See the twig and long to see the whole tree.

Place of peaks and pits. Night soil and ritual rubbish,
wells drawn into vanishing point. This remote outer
edge of the earth Newstead, it's the pits that make it.
How deep it goes, our thirst for their first water.

After the rites are over, these are left for the hallowed well:
the water-filled cup, a splash of scarlet, the ceremonial flask.
A row of lights moving in the evening. The land herself
holds a lamp and a battered helmet mask.

Roman Gemstones

life as you'd like it to be –
huntsman carrying his spears
his hound in at heel

glass intaglio
Cupid holding up a torch
and a butterfly

dolphin in agate
wavebands, nose on top, tail up
soul across the sea

winged Victory
carries palm branch, laurel leaf
on tiptoe, flying

naked eye carving
wheel rotates, sand grinds
cutting in lines

a personal seal
gemstone for pressing in wax
a half-sucked sweetie

Tipu's Amulet

He wore it on his upper arm, next his skin,
so there must be something in it.
He fastened the talisman of destiny to him
which should never be taken away.
Finding Tipu's body, still warm,
Captain Young untied it from his arm.

Sewn up in flowered silk, a bubble
of brittle metal is hidden from sight.
With its Arabic manuscript, the flat capsule
slides around as if alive, inside.

The blowers on knots chant powerful words,
musk in the ink and a sharp Persian sword!

Given to wear with love, no amulet
is a piece of dead matter, cold or inert.
How many times can it protect? Two
musket-balls passed through his chainmail shirt.
A stolen amulet, losing its active powers,
can withhold them from its new owner.

Overgrown with jungle, the old Gajalhatti Pass
still shows what's called *Tipu's Road* in places.
His amulet harms no-one. The angel's writing
is shut up among crowded gems in glass cases.
This is one relic which can restore
a hero, a future, to the state of Mysore.

Chairm

whurl stane
whurl bane

canny ane
ne'er forgane

mare stane
lig alane

whaur nane
maks a mane

ringled ane
wide wauken

Tinto Kist

a wish – a mist – a kist
a sound – a round – a ground
a cairn – a bairn – a Lanimer

a word – a bird – a chord
a track – a torque – a ringfort
a turf – a tuff – along the Garf

a knowe – a howe – a brow
a cone – a bone – a drone
a haw – a jaw – to Wildshaw

a fell – a bell – a well
a briar – a desire – a beaconfire
a glade – a glide – into the Clyde
a billow – a hollow – by Sornfallow

An Angel, Grounded

Alice Galley

Of all the buildings in the City, it was the cathedral that Evelyn returned to, stepping through the wooden door into the vastness beyond. She wanted to see again the disparity between the human figures restricted to walking over the flagged floor and the space above them. That part of the architecture that no one else saw; an area considered empty. For her it was full, teaming with energy and spirit, held in place by the ceiling and, like a hot air balloon, secured by the guy rope walls. Extra stone was required in the form of buttresses, to keep the cathedral from floating away.

She had seen, from her attic room, the air above the slates shimmering with this escaping force. She wondered, if she climbed up onto the roof and lay there, would it fill and lighten her? Evelyn had always liked tall buildings, particularly old places, with spiral staircases, where each stone tread was worn away in the centre to form a series of crescent moons. She was not afraid of heights and even as a child could stand on parapets and laugh at the fear in the faces of her friends.

Most of all she enjoyed the privilege, the solitude of these elevated places. Of an evening, after work, she would sit on the windowsill of the tenement, her legs dangling over; the hot air rising from the street beneath and flowing between her toes. From her lofty position she would watch the scurrying people below her; people who studied the place where the next footstep would fall, or stared into the middle distance, their minds on something else or some place they wanted to be, now. Not one person ever looked up. The only creatures that ever met her eyes were the pigeons lined up on the stone sills opposite, cooing encouragingly to her.

She had videotapes of programmes made from the perspectives of birds, which she would watch for hours, first carefully angling the television so she could lie on the table, peer over the edge and look down on the screen. On holiday she only booked into hotels that had the swimming pool on the roof. That way she had the knowledge that she was high in the air and something of the sensation of flying, naturally, unaided by machines. Despite it being only second best, she did enjoy plane journeys, propelled out of the cloying city atmosphere to trace a path across the heavens.

There was one part of the cathedral she did not like. The crypt. She would never willingly go down a mine, or take up pot-holing. It was torture enough every morning: to get to her job she had to force herself down into the earth, pack herself into the underground and hurtle along the tunnels. The carriage was a tube of aftershave, perfume, deodorant and sweat. The people pressed so close around her she could smell them on her clothes all day. Each time the train left the station and entered one of the semi-circles of blackness, she was convinced she was entering the gates of hell.

After fraught tube journeys she would turn away from her flat and seek the cathedral, knowing exactly where on her walk she would first see the spires and towers. She passed couples lounging on the tiny triangle of grass in front of the building, a green beach in a sea of cobbles; they were sprawled out as if on sun beds. She preferred the coolness inside, pausing only to look up and envy the man checking the lead work on the roof.

The height of the spires reminded her that as long as she could remember she had wanted to live and work in a lighthouse. To stand on the gantry at the top of the tower, and stare out over the sea, with nothing beneath her. To see the gulls float past, their wings barely moving, just the occasional beat to direct their flight. To hear in their calls the true sound of freedom. To listen to the waves trapped on the shore at the base of the cliffs and to know that she was above such mundane forces as gravity.

When she mentioned lighthouses, other people mentioned solitude, long dark winter nights with only the wind for company. Loneliness is not to be found between land and sea. It lurks in city flats where neighbours bang car doors, bang the close doors and then, just to spite her, bang the bedroom door. There were some nights when even the stars deserted her, and she would look out of her window to see only a line of street lamps, their heads turned determinedly downwards, away from her.

So, in the absence of lighthouses, she went back to the cathedral. Walking amongst the pillars, listening to the sounds swirling around the giant dome above her head, leaving behind an echo, an energy ghost.

She remembered the shimmering power. It was calling to her. She walked around the building looking for a way upward. There were a few doors, thick planks of dark wood, securely bound by iron bars, to prevent them being warped by the energy inside the building. They were all locked.

The door was protected. She knew as she tried the handle that gargoyles watched her from the frieze above, and down the panelling snakes hung like vines, waiting to strike, camouflaged from the unwary by the wood's grain. She risked their venom, and the admonishment of staccato footsteps, to trace out the wooden carvings with her fingers.

On the doorframe, beside the keyhole, angels waited in silent contemplation. She felt the smooth lines of their wings, in her mind's eye swan white. She recognised these angel carvings, her fingers found their form familiar, their watchfulness reassuring. They were like family to her.

She tried the door handle again. She needed to escape. This was the doorway out – if she could only travel through it, her future would change. The angels watched her with their two dimensional eyes, felt her fingers caress their faces, heard the lonely thoughts inside the dome of her cranium. They understood the frailty of humans and kept the door closed. The angels knew that she would never fly, not until she had hope and soaring spirits inside her body. They watched her and then watched over her.

Evelyn turned away, disappointed. The feeling sapped the strength from her muscles; she walked around the wall of the cathedral, so that she could rest against it, her hand connected to the solid stone. Before leaving, Evelyn paused, leaned against the green baize of the notice board, felt the small cold dots of drawing pins against her bare arm. She looked down to find the word 'Vacancy', projecting from her elbow. She moved her shoulder and read the uncovered words, 'Cathedral Guide Required'.

They never spoke, the angels and Evelyn, but Evelyn knew they watched out for her. They were always pointed out to the tourists on her tours, just before she unlocked the door to the spires and took those who dared to the very top.

Illustration by Shona Dougall

Robert Alan Jamieson

Ootadæks

(In Shetland, the land outwith the community dykes, as opposed to 'innadæks'. Metaphorically, 'alienation' or 'exile'. There are cases of unwed mothers-to-be cast 'ootadæks' in the early history of the islands.)

Kæl-jærd

Dy æteent voar is kaald as stø-blaan kloot
apo da briests o dem it wilfilie
dø gjing agenst da wintir gæl;
du's adrift athoot a sæl,
as dem dat koort da storm's upstierin
most ken dir koors will mæstlæk be.

Lass, du'll turn de fit an truk de owir
da riggs fir filska; du'll mak dy varg
a klæm dat laas ir nivir lang
afoar dir døin wrang t'sumien;
innadæks, da merks dy mynd
wid nætril draa hjing skæv;
dy boosin's fit t'siekin aa.

Næ kæl-jærd stied sall sær de;
du winna tak de sok; da waas
du'd bigg ir boond t'derilikshin
on ert sæ røtit wi tradieshin;
apo sumiddirboadie's laand
quharivir du wid sit, dir sumeen sittin.

Quharivir du wid dell, dir sumien dellin;
ay njaagln on quhar du most set de spad;
fæ Jøltyd's eld is twirmt in Janwar's mirk,
till Östir roars at aa mann wirk
dan sall du fin dy æn wy furt, awa fæ hier;
fir nane'll bær de mukkil mær.
Innadæks, dy teddir's tyed.

Kailyard

(an enclosed area, generally to the rear of the croft house, used for storing crops and growing vegetables)

Your eighteenth spring is as cold as wind-blown cloth on the breasts of those who go against the winter gale; you're adrift, without a sail as those who court the storm's beginning must know their course will finally be.

Lass, you'll turn and trample over fields for mischief, your nonsense claims that laws are wrong because they're old. Inside the dyke, the shapes your mind would naturally draw go squint. Your blustering hurry sickens all.

No farmyard steading's big enough to hold it. You won't take up your knitting, the patterns you'd create are wasted here on those so governed by tradition, they're always cramping somebody. Wherever you would sit, there's someone sitting.

Wherever you would dig there's someone digging, nagging on where you must put your spade, from Christmas embers dwindling in January's darkness, till Easter orders everyone must work. You must find a path away, for none will bear your presence here much longer. Inside the dykes, your tether's tied ...

Trøba

Ootieköst, mak lood soonds; ootby heir,
næ niebir lissins t'dy reksin rel an flyt.
Gjing light an saft wi særwoarn fit.
Dir næn t'fors dy boo-bakkt flit.
Bit kiep du de dy waddir ee opin:
mebbie næ mær sistir fæmieljir waaks wi de
næ mair, she taks dy mæt, dy plæs, dy Sundie shön
mebbie næ mær dy briddir wrassils an laaghs
dy birss up – bit still an aa, du's stød owir aft
afoar dir blaa, ta gjing awa an no tink lang.

Afoar du quhets dy fæmlie lot du'll raag
tree tyms ootby, tree tyms du'll drittil hæm,
hoopin ta fin sumthin du's left ahint de
or else sumeen – still dær ida aald hoos,
waatchin fir da prodiegil hæmmir waandrin,
t'shak an sit, twa freens, two haafs tigiddir hæl.
Bit quhan du kums, dir næn gien oot t'siek fir de,

an du fins noght t'warm dy frozint haand,
noght firby a soor wird fir niebir
apo dy shilpit tung, becaas dej lat de gjing
an nivir baad de bide. Hent du!
Dy gæt's awa, owir da stank
quhar broun ert's sib tæ green.

T'Framhoga, du'll take da ky an lag a simmer,
du'll æs da spægie idy limms, lat da voarmø pass.
Quhan herdwark's skoars itidy løf ir hæld,
du'll turn dy haand ta luv, an quhan
da nort wind haalts its oostrin brøl,
du'll kok de lug an lærn da lævrik's chön.

Trøba

(Old Norse 'troð': a small piece of land not included in the division of allotments among families in a village.)

Outcast, though you make loud sounds, here no neighbour listens to your spluttering arguments. Go softly with sore-worn foot. There's no one to force your bent-backed bow – but keep a weather eye wide open. Maybe sister familiar walks with you no more, no more she takes your food, your place, your Sunday shoes.

Maybe no more your brother wrestles and laughs your temper up. Still and all, you've stood too often in their company, to go away and not to miss them. Before you leave your family, three times you'll go, three times you'll drift back home, hoping to find something you've left behind – or maybe someone, there in the old house watching for the prodigal wandering home, to shake hands and sit, two friends, two halves together whole.

But when you arrive, no one's gone to look for you, and you find nothing to warm your frozen hand, nothing but a sour word for neighbour on your bitter tongue, because they let you leave and never urged you stay. So move yourself. Your path's away, over the ditch, where brown earth's next to green.

To the far pasture you'll take the cattle, and while away a summer, you'll ease the stinging in your limbs, and let the spring exhaust you. When the spade-sores in the palm of your hand are healed, you'll turn that hand to love. And when the north wind halts its wild, loud roar, you'll lift your ears and learn the skylark's tune.

Settir

Dir's næ fær noo ida emptie laand,
we mann aa gjing dær quhiles.
Dir næthin heir t'mak de hadd fæ heddin oot
at nyght t'tak a bræth o air
an, glindrin up apo da møn,
t'fin dy wy t'meet dy laad
amung da örnin heddir.

Ju'll koort da kölin wiet in waatirie hols
an be da japplin ström, ju'll trist an kjiss,
du'll tak his haand an waandir flooirkled laand
Skjin trivlin skjin, mooth presst 'po mooth,
saft wirds'lll piestir quhar da wintir roart.

Here ju'll bide, ju'll kærie stæn t'mak a bø
jur jærd, jur plantikrub, jur krø
Ju'll set a brokkin bransh t'grow quhit röts ju nied,
fir ju hæ neid o littil, hæin ennaniddir.
An he his broght a livin jæst
itida skjinbag kæriet at his bellie.

Bit dir aj a faa t'rummil simmir's waas
A sneck, a slap at lat's da ootby inby.
Dy laad an de'll koorie hæmir, eens quhaarvin,
Koalin's kaad fir, an treshin, stookin haands ir niedit,
T'help t'tak da hærst sæf insyd da jærd.

Settir

(Old Norse 'sætir: mountain pasture, dairy land, summer pasture for cattle in the out-fields)

There's no fear now in the empty lands, we all must go there, whiles. There's nothing here to stop you going out at night to take a breath of air and peering at the moon to find your way to meet your lad among the heavy scented heather.

You'll court the cooling wet in watery pools and by the yapping burn, you'll tryst and kiss. You'll take his hand and wander flower-clad land. Skin feeling skin, mouth pressed on mouth, soft words'll whisper where the winter roared.

Here you'll stay, you'll carry stone to make good your house, your yard, your fold. You'll plant a broken branch to grow what roots you need, for you have need of little, having one another, and he has brought a living yeast in the skin bag at his belly.

But there's always a break in the dyke to let the flock back in. Your lad and you'll cower homeward, when hands are needed, to help to gather harvest, safe inside the yard ...

Skattald

Fir aa ju'r anst an gien bakk innadæks,
ju'll haankir t'be bakk ootby,
quhar simmir's opin hert allooed jur raag
till hærstwark's ærnist klaag began,
an med jur boadie's swaal an æk. Insyd agen,
ju lang t'truk jur sækrit gæt o trespis.

Am hit's no dattin lang till trespis is dy sang,
quhan simmir's siedin's shaain hit's first syns
An da fok at hem mak mukkil i dy swaallin wæm
An quhitna ill-kint laad wis døn dis t'de,
an quhitna shemlis rönnin hoor du wis.

An mebbie dan da hærst's no aa hit myght be,
Fantashin's gost is sookin wintir's bens –
a grietin nied'll krø da en at seeks a nju bø
up abøn da dæk at marks da ootset,
tym apo tym. An dær dy laad'll kum agen t'de.

Ootiköst, du wisna ment t'tak dy pæs
In an oot da brukkit grind fæ bærndom,

Du'll rowl an staag, a sowl misplæst
Bit raag du, fir bettir stæns sood rowl an rummil
dan lie derilik, læk aa da faan hellakröss.

Fram, ayont da briggstæns, stook an dess,
da laand's aniddir læklie aatigiddir,
aaned no be laas, bit be da fit dat, ida akt o passin,
klæms hit. Quheddir hill or lonlie daal,
hit's emptie t'da ee it's seekin fir its aaner.

Skattald

(Old Norse 'skattr': a tax or tribute, especially to the Crown; hill-pasture to which the 'skat-briddirs (brothers)' had rights)

For all you've done as you were told and gone back home, you'll hanker to be back outside, where summer's open heart allowed you roam till harvest's work began, and made your bodies sweat with ache. Inside once more, you learn to tramp your sacred path of trespass.

It isn't long till trespass is your song, when summer's seeding's showing its first signs and folk at home make much of swelling – what lad of poor family, what shameless whore?

Then the harvest isn't all it might be, and famine's-ghost is sucking winter's bones. A crying need will drive the one that seeks a new life up above the dyke that marks the cultivated limit, time after time.

Far beyond the door paving, the corn-stacks, and the land's completely different – lined not by laws but by the foot that in the act of passing, claims it. Whether hill or lonely dale, it's empty to the eye that seeks the owner's house.

Outcast, you weren't intended for a life of peace. In and out the broken gate from childhood you will roll and stagger, a soul misplaced. But you should roam; it's better far to roll, than drop and then lie derelict, like all the fallen gravestones ...

Ootset

Aald waas mann be remeid.
Past dæs ir aft a tæl o fæljir
o da willin haand t'set da perfik sied
o toghtin wirthie died. Sens rins awa
akross da ægis, waarpt an oot o chön.

Sær vext, ju turn jur pashin inta hæt,
rub oot a syns o luv, mak knevs,
rædie t'læ oot onie en at skjimps ju.
Dan jur rædie t'ontak jur nætiril task
Middir an fædir in aniddir laand, da bærn
Itidy wæm will kaa dis unkan ert hit's hæm.

An ju'll grow aald on stænie grund,
ilka jeir upgaddirin mær an mær
t'bigg nju waas. Quhan tree tyms hæmir
du's gien an seen du's næ mær hæm dær,
du'll kum agen t'dis baald hill, sæ strewn
Wi histrie's unmæd gær, an tink it is dy peksins
T'opin grinds an lat dem faa.

Bit shö enjogh da kolli's flukkrin makkadø'll die,
da rim o lyght will lift da moarn,
dull waakin t'da bryght syd o desel,
Brakkin trow dy døl, an fillin de wi glæmin lyght.

Oot heir apo da shaald ert, du'll undirstaand
Dy lentin's just a swallin o da mærch, an dat
dy turnin fit his broght nju laand, nju lyf, nju toght.
An unkin fæs med kyin, a laand ootset
a pattrin sprett an med aniddir wy.
Lass, læv dy sok. Du's mær t'spin as oo –
Devys desel.

Ootset

(Danish dialect 'udsæt'; the addition to a house or a room; Jutland. Old Danish 'udsætning', an outbuilding; the extension of a cultivated allotment, new land brought under cultivation.)

From time to time old walls must be remade. Often the past's a tale of failure, of willing hand to set the perfect seed of thought in worthy deed. Meaning runs across the ages, warped and out of tune.

Sore-vexed, you turn your passion into hate, rub out all signs of love, make fists, ready to knock out anyone that dares make fun of you. Then you're ready to begin your natural task, Mother and Father in another land, the child inside you'll call this strange place its home.

Together you'll grow old on stony ground, each year gathering more and more, to build new walls. When three times you've gone homeward and seen you've no more home there, you'll come again to this bald hill, so strewn with history's unmade gear, and think it is your penance to open gates and let them fall.

Soon the flickering pretence of day will die, the night will follow. You'll hold your fatherless child against your breasts to keep it warm. The first daylight will herald morning, and you'll awake to the bright side of yourself, breaking through your sadness, and filling you with gleaming light.

Out here upon the shallow earth of exile, you'll understand your striding's just a tramping of the marches, that your turning foot has brought new life, new thought; new land to cultivate.

A stranger's face made kin, a bond extended, a pattern pulled and made again. Lass, put down your knitting. You've more to spin than wool.

Devise yourself.

Ach Caledonia:

Notes to accompany a performance tape

Tom Leonard

[In the mid-seventies I made a number of works for tape recorder, some to be performed with added songs and words, and the holding up of placards. The first of these, My Name is Tom, was published as a soundscore by Good Elf Press in London in 1978. Ach Caledonia *was composed in 1975. What follows is not a description of the tape itself but a description of what took place alongside the tape when* Ach Caledonia *was being performed. The tape featured a number of different 'voices' and registers, saying "Ach" in different ways, "how day ye spell it", "ma mammy's doon it the laundry", "discipline! discipline!", "not before time", Scottish country dance music mixed in with a piano version of* The Rite of Spring, *and a woman describing a restaurant where you could get a pot of tea with four cups of tea in it, breast of chicken the size of your hand, etc. The tape lasts just under 6 minutes. – T L]*

The placards used during this work are as follows: –

a) T I C K L Y M I N C E

b) A B L U E S K Y

c) A D E A F E G G

d) O V E R

e) A D I E T I N G K E T T L E D R U M

f) T H E N E W S O F T H E M U F F I N

g) T U M U L T U O U S C E N T I P E D E S !

h) CELTIC

1. THE WHORE OF BABYLON
(OUR HOLY MOTHER THE CHURCH)
2. SENSUOUS RITES
3. INSISTENT DEPENDENCE

i) RANGERS

1. THE OLD TESTAMENT GOD
2. AUSTERITY
3. INSISTENT INDEPENDENCE

j)

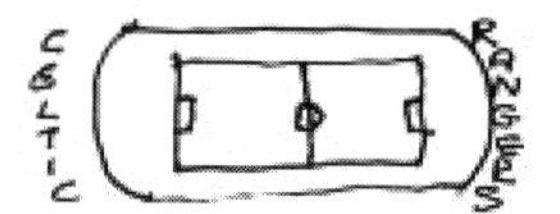

OEDIPUS SCREWING HIS MOTHER
AT BOTH ENDS

k) T H E C O N C E P T O F B A T M A N

l) T H E R E N A I S S A N C E O F T H E P O K E Y - H A T

m) T H E E X I L E O F T H E V O M I T I N G D A N D E L I O N

n) M O H N J I L T O N

o) M R S D A L E ' S B R E W E R Y

p) D E L I R I U M T R E M E N S O F T H E O S T R O C C O P U S

Soon after tape starts, narrator reads:

O Caledonia! stern and wild,
Meet nurse for a poetic child!
Land of brown heath and shaggy wood,
Land of the mountain and the flood,
Land of my sires! what mortal hand
Can e'er untie the filial band,
That knits me to thy rugged strand!

Placard sequence a, b, c, d, Then begins telling quickly:

well as I said to Tom

Let's be honest. Let's talk about a language,
I mean a sound-system, a Glasgow sound-system,
though Belfast has similar features. Let's talk
about kinetics, e.g.-

Man: – Ma mammaizdoonit thi lawndry
Woman: – Ma maaaaaamaiz doonit thi lawwwwwwndry

Placards e, f, g held up.

Right? That's where the tactiles are at, often. The
man uppercuts, the woman clings. Let's talk about
the body, let's talk about the church, let's talk
about the bevvy. AND the industrial revolution.

well as I said to Tom

Let's be honest. Sin = sex = shame of the body,
and: –

1. Posh people use their bodies, eyebrows and things, while talking.
2. Bodies are sexual.
3. Posh people communicate sexually while talking.
4. Posh people are poofs and cissies.

or why do you think we've so many doctors and
engineers? OK? A computer could have predicted
R.D.Laing, fifty years ago. Glasgow's
instant existentialism! Boom boom.

well as I said to Tom

Take the molecular family, and that. The father
as moral arbiter. But. Father O'Leary and the
Old Testament God. Both upped and snipped
the molecular father's balls. PLUS. The industrial
set-up: "You wait till your father comes home!"
and, "My daddy's a plastic button-pusher!"

The next paragraph usually wasn't reached. Once or twice it was added somewhere:

[So-shu churned. Sorry. Socio-economic factors,
as per – shat on, and their language. Right.
Let's talk about the bevvy, looking for mummy
at the bottom of the glass, the "dependent" personality,
the wish to be a muscular version of Frank Sinatra …

well as I said to Tom

I'll have a pint of lager, he said.]

Football placards h, i, j held up. Then narrator reads, angrily:

Ah, Sun-flower! weary of time,
Who countest the steps of the Sun,
Seeking after that sweet golden clime
Where the traveller's journey is done:

Where the Youth pined away with desire,
And the pale Virgin shrouded in snow
Arise from their graves, and aspire
Where my Sun-flower wishes to go.

Placards k, l, m, n, o, p held up.

Then narrator in high, thin, sort of heckling Wee Free minister's voice:

In order that the spectator may be stimulated into self-analysis when confronted with the actor, there must be some common ground already existing in both of them, something they can either dismiss in one gesture or worship. Artaud intuitively saw myth as the dynamic centre of the theatre performance. Only Nietzsche was ahead of him in this domain. He also knew that transgression of the myth renewed its essential values and "became an element of menace which re-established the divided norms." He did not however – (wags finger) He did NOT however – take account of the fact that in our age, when all languages intermingle, the community of the theatre cannot possibly identify itself with myth, because there is no single faith. Only an act of confrontation is possible.

Placards a, b, c, d.

John Bellany

> The art of exploration looks at places
> Nobody has yet explored for fear
> Of finding out too much and so we stare
> Alarmed, alone, before the frontal faces.

So spak Alan Bold, a man much missed and a huge force in Scotland, about John Bellany in his poem 'The Voyage of John Bellany: A Triptych'. The cross-overs between important Scottish writers and painters is something someone, somewhere, no doubt in the University of Texas or Aukland or Southern Maine or Germersheim should write a thesis about.

John Bellany has been doing this for years. He has had important relationships with George Bruce, Hugh MacDiarmid, and of course Alan Bold (and through him many others). Last year he was 60. Time and time again, in my brief forays into the world of Scottish painting, and knowing the relative ignorance of most writers of my acquaintance, I am deeply ashamed about just how curious they are about what we have to say, and how indifferent we literary lot are to anything outside our immediate world. Not so the painters; they go around with books of poetry in their pockets. They are shockingly well informed of everything we do. What's happened to us!

When asked to write a page of intro (for which this is a poor substitute) we had a long telephone conversation which both he and I wished we'd had the wit to record. John said quite simply that he wouldn't write anything for this purpose, because people relied on and were in fact tyrannised by the written word, which, being infinitively manipulative, boxed all of us into some kind of concrete cul-de-sac. He spoke about how he spent days not looking at anything printed, just looking about him, at things, and trying to understand what they meant or represented. But the loud world of print, other people's tawdry, ill thought-out if well-paid for options, shut that reality out. You need to spend days looking at wallpaper, taking as your starting place a kind of disorientation, a 'not-knowing-where-you-are' sort of feeling. You need to accept the discombooberation of that, and build from there ... by looking, and looking – not be thinking, and thinking, and reading words by other people.

As John has been very open about, he's gone through the slings and arrows himself, his artistic drive turning to self-destructive impulses:

> You die the day you see our death.
> You succumb to the ultimate and avoidable defeat.
> You see the contours of your face
> As fraudulent and you know you're done.

Many of the illustrations we give here are self-portraits, and each one illustrates a different self. But they are not just self-portraits; they each reflect a different vision of the world as seen through the perspective of the artist. Bear in mind that this is an artist who just wants us to look and feel. Not think and say. When you're almost dead, you know the value of light.

Light is here, in abundance, and insight into the world of the lobster, the crab, the fisherman, his wife/ lovers (who cares which) here is a man with his nerve ends cut, who sharpens us up with the clarity of what he sees, and his omnivorous urge to collaborate with us, to create a better world in our wee place. We use his works here further to celebrate the energies and positive force of other artists such as George Bruce and W Gordon Smith. Most of all we remind ourselves that in a world dominated by words, there are, if you can find the time to let it happen, many other worlds, which it might be better to inhabit than the controlled, word-governed world that we all sadly live in, time to let pictures, vision, speak.

Look at it: no-one can control what you see: "The curves that hold the earth together speak/ A language of their own, a tone defines/ An area of understanding: lines/ Control emotions as the colours break/ The barriers between the talk and look/ of Life."

> ... You recognise the folk,
> You know the feeling, what the artist means,
> Or think you do until the stunning scenes
> Knock back your senses to a state of shock.

That's real humility; not that we go into a state of shock because of whatever fix we might be in, but that we are knocked back into a sense of our own smallness, by the hugeness of the world around us. Enjoy and savour John Bellany and the sheer delight and colour of his looking, seeing, mind.

You're 50 Today, John *(1992) by John Bellany*

John Bellany

Self-Portrait with Accordion (1974);
from *John Bellany* by John McEwen,
Mainstream (1994), p. 100

The Star of Bethlehem (1965-6) – JB, p. 14

Three Fishers (1966) – *JB*, p. 16

The Kiss of Life (1984) – *JB*, p. 130

Bethel (1964) – *JB*, p. 12

Lobster Fetish (1971) – *JB*, p. 95

Woman with Albatross (1998)

Bonaventure (1986) – *JB*, p. 138

Scottish Family (1968) – *JB*, p. 67

Pourquoi? (1967) – *JB*, p. 52

The Persecuted (1969) – *JB*, p. 70

Woman of the North Sea (1994) – *JB*, p. 196

Self-Portrait with Jonathan (1967) – *JB*, p. 73

George Bruce

To Colin Dunbar for his Drawing of Me

Yes: I am that guilty party,
savaged by the years, damaged goods.
Time to say goodbye, but that the
too kindly flesh bids me stay
a little while, shuffling my winter
way among the autumn leaves. How
they glow, even as now from the
poverty of absences – the beloved
Elizabeth – I catch in my ashes
their dying fires. No escape
for this word-man. I look upon
the self you made of me. You
looked within, saw the years
of blizzard, of thought, thought, thought.
Have done now for you have me there
on the page – wordless. I look upon
the white silence you have generated
about me. You caught me in that moment
each glittering and dark moment of my
being, caught now in the red-yellow
of this Fall, bringing out of memory
the watcher in me of the other. This
you set down of me in the eyes,
with tenderness in your art. So
I look on you: so we know we need
the forgiving and critical eye. Thus I
would have my being take all
in their differences into it. The
despairs, black night's depths, rage
against the unpropitiate absolutes,
ecstasies, you take care of all
in the sweep of your line, and in
fading shades. I should do likewise
in the word. A single leaf falls,
passes my window, rocking
a little in still air, veined as is
the back of my hand. Still it burns
with life as it joins with others
to make a mould. One Fall I
walked along University Avenue,
with her, my wife, when two
are one – above, the leafy riches

of red oaks, as if intact, yet
upon the floor a wealth of hues.
Heaven above, heaven about
our feet, hand in hand we moved
until we stood in the broad, blaze
of sun. I am not deceived. This was
the illusive touch of memory.
Your line says: "This is what you are
and may become." I submit to
that presence that looks at me.
Then let the talk be from the
black marks on a sheet of paper.
But let it not assign to me that feature
of the tribe – the killing hate of human
kind for its own kind. Not that,
that stigmata. It is of the past,
should be, but that if one
is stained all are. Out of the
silence on the page it is the now
I would have speak to me. The tree
is undressed of its leaves. Stark, black
it stands, as if its life's on hold: yet
concealed in earth's chest, stored
through hard frosts to make anew
the waited-for new day. As if for me
you gave new eyes with clearer
mental sight that brought the past
and present as one time, one thing,
yet put at risk this single being.
For with such sight how could
one hold the self together as little
children, worn to the bone, walk
their *via dolorosa*. The nations are
as nothing until no child cries 'lost'
upon the road. Have you given me
a face that may look (unshielded)
on the face of the Nazarine?

The Crescent, Spring 2001

The Crescent turns its face to the sun,
its shadow falls from it. Now
for the first time this year the girl-
mothers pause with their prams for talk.
They wear trousers, of course, work at
part-time jobs, supported by husbands
partners, boyfriends – not the traditional

garb or mind of the Crescent. When
it was born there were social prop-
rieties not to be broken. There were
man-servants to answer the door-bell.
Chopin came with his man to number 10,
Cadell, even in near poverty, came with
his to number 4. There was an upstairs
and downstairs in the heads as well as house.
There would be no end to this time,
The British Empire and the Crescent were
forever – earthquakes, social upheavals,
political violence happened in another place.
The Crescent has moved into the sun,
the shadow gone. A thousand terrors
lurk on the edges of the mind, but
the Georgian face of the houses and the
faces of the girls with the prams,
as the light bounces as she puts back
the hoods and covers, and lives
in this now which stretches to
the Springtime before the engulfing
computer was dreamed up, and this
Crescent the outpost of this proper
classical street. One constant –
the Crescent turns its face to the sun.

Epistle Three

To Elizabeth Grace Cumming; The Botanic Gardens, Edinburgh

Thinking of you now in the completeness
of home and friends – as far as circumstance
has allowed – now that the great endeavour
of the book, the testimony of the skill, imagination
and virtue of the artist, James Cumming,
is completed, which has in it part of my being,
the conception yours, the determination yours,
and family, to make a book – with friends – I,
sitting in the setting sun, witnessing
two pigeons, one iridescent green in the neck,
the other purple, scuttering about my feet
in fussy conversation stirring the dust,
I ask myself – why should I interrupt?
The moment of need is past,
I shall not achieve such completeness –
my desk strewn with papers, imperfect poems,
unfinished business, will be so at my sundown.
I sense your letter in my pocket:

would have me believe otherwise: so be it.
A bee at the yellow azalea draws nectar.

A New Year

Finally the word that mattered more
than victory or defeat – 'forgive'.
The trees that still grow about
the President's home on the campus,
as he assumed his peaceable office.
On leaving the house I walked
remembering the sky-blue curtains
of the bed room, the whiteness
of the pillows. It was a fresh morning,
the wind blew the curtain to and fro. All was as
he had left it – his home. In the University shop
cards were for sale. We might care to buy one of
the house itself. Some find it of special interest.
As she left she said
"No one lives now."
I did not contradict her.

The Dancer

the maquette by Degas at the National Gallery of Scotland

Stepping aside a little from his ballerinas
in paint, his hands found themselves shaping
the clay and she was there before him
at the fine point of balance. She is beyond
what nature gives, yet grows from nature.
There is the virtue of the man, the attentive
skill of his hands, the warmth of his being.
Her lodging is the National Gallery of Scotland.
Breathe more gently as you approach.
For all the permanence of clay and bronze
she has an air of evanescence – that grace
which has shed all human impurities. She
creates her own atmosphere. At any moment
she will make her silent take-off into
white nimbus clouds and the blue.

A Photograph

taken by Norman McBeath

I met a face blossoming
into light from dark,
as if the dark of time's abyss

photograph of George Bruce by Norman McBeath

had yielded up the gift of life
which yet engaged to both,
to dark and light, it must
return as to its first home,
nor should I protest, 'No'
to this condition since
it may temporarily show
the transparent beauty of humanity.

Dear Norman,
When I look upon my self
as in the creative interpretation
through the eye of the camera
with the co-operation of light,
I see not my self but *the* self
that recognition of the condition
of living for every human being.
In the marriage of light to dark
is life – in time and beyond time.
Praise be for the dark.
Praise be for the light. – George

Sheena Blackhall

A Brocher's Farweel: George Bruce 1909- 2002

Farweel tae Pitullie, adieu Mormond Hill
Fur the virr o a Brocher is sattled an still
He is takkin a voyage, grey oceans tae cross
An the skreich o the scurries rings lood wi oor loss.

He will niver lie weel in a lang timmer sark
He wis niver a Makar fa coddlit the Dark
Kandinsky, Nijinski, Beethoven an Blake
Ye've a fier comin ower will kittle yer claik

Oh there's mony he'll ken o the fowk fa bide there
Fur it's thrang wi the ferlies o speerit an air
Wi Pound, Yeats an Eliot, weel he'll belang
Tir nan Og's far the gowden an gracious are thrang

The price that the ferryman takks is his braith
Fin a life's at its lees syne richt kindly comes Daith
An aff tae the lan o Tam Linn he is gaen
Like a wave skelpin dolphin that's breistin the faem

Farweel tae Pitullie, adieu Mormond Hill
Fur the virr o a Brocher is sattled an still
He is takkin a voyage , grey oceans tae cross
An the skreich o the scurries rings lood wi oor loss.

Valerie Thornton

L'Eglise de St Julien Le Pauvre, Paris

Let's have some light.

Here's a candle.

Thank-you.

What's the matter now?

Maybe we could put the candle on something?

An old saucer?

Maybe a little brass lamp base, with decorative chasing around the edges.

On the floor.

No. Hang it from a chain – three chains – with ornamental links and a bulb of orange glass around the flame, for warmth. And maybe a pierced brass disc to draw the three long chains together, before a final chain, rising ...

I'll get a nail, shall I?

Well, maybe a kind of hook in the form of a bird's-beak, attached, perhaps, to the rest of a bird, made of bronze with its wings spread wide for balance.

On the wall?

Maybe a rail, a little wooden rail up there, sort of carved and inlaid and long enough for, say, eight birds to perch on, all with their wings stretched out, and we could have little painted panels below inset with gilded images of haloed angels and holy people. And the arching stone roof ...

Who said anything about the roof? What's wrong with a ceiling?

... and the arching stone roof, above carved pillars and stained glass windows and gargoyles looking down on the little wooden chairs with rush seats and carved backs and the stone floor with peach and orange rugs and a wrought iron stand with a big vase of white lilies for peace ...

Why bother? I've got a torch here. See?

La Alhambra, Partick

You don't have to go
all the way to Granada
to see a bit of La Alhambra.
It's right here, across the road

from number sixty-two.
Stand in the sun and avert
your eyes from the windows
but gaze at that old rose tree

coiling up red sandstone
with those Moorish curls
drooping with heavy flowers
in an ancient shade of pink.

Climb between a Glasgow accent
and a glass of *vino tinto*,
up the arrowslit stairway
to the roof of this redstone tower.

See! Spread far below, Granada,
La Catedral, a scree of white houses
and cypress trees and beyond,
the plains of Andalucía.

Don't look north behind you
where the Sierra Nevada bare
their snow-capped teeth.
In such cold light, only Partick lies.

Hace Muchos Años

Hace muchos años
many years ago
aprendi el español
I learned Spanish
pero ahora he olvidado
but now I have forgotten
most of *las palabras*.

Many years later
estamos aquí
here we are *en Cataluña*
hunting sights and words
with equal assiduity.

'Yesterday' is lost
in the small shadows
below the ash grey leaves
of the olive trees.

'Tomorrow' is in the red dust
we have yet to raise
from the baked dirt road
rising through fields of sunflowers
to our *casa* on the cliff-top.

'However' may be
at the bottom
of a bottle of *ratafía*

sipped under drifting satellites
in a night which belongs
to the gecko
in the wall lantern.

'Still' is certainly somewhere
in this early morning
which belongs to the golden light
spilling into the far-below valley.
Our window opens
above the almond tree
where two woodpeckers drum
and young goldfinches flurry
in the dry bushes.

We do not belong here.
We do not speak
the same language.
I look far away, far down
from this window to a new day
while you, in this gold wood cabin,
whimper in your sleep.

Hace muchos años
once upon a time.

PC

Yesterday
we clicked
at first sight.

We merged,
inserted symbols
created a new template

but we could not
find and replace
our pasts

escape the cursers
undo and redo
the shattered windows.

Today we are cut,
cancelled beyond restoring
the arrow broken.

I have been saving
for such a rainy day:
tomorrow, a Mac.

In the Wardrobe

Valerie Thornton

It's when I shut the cat in the wardrobe, like she did, that I'll know for sure. Know not that I've shut the cat in the wardrobe, but that I am the one in this generation. There's been one all the way down, for centuries.

She, my aunt, was the one ahead of me and it started simply, with typing errors. She, who had been a perfect typist, started sending letters on her Basildon Bond, the white pad with the red rectangle and glittery gold lettering on the front, with silly typing errors like: "Thank you for your better. I hope you are all wall."

Then a 'joke' about going out into the world and being halfway down the street before realising her trousers were on back to front, or inside out, or upside down or something, and not fastened properly.

It's earrings, not trousers, which are worrying me, although I did go out with my T-shirt on inside-out a couple of months ago. My favourite pair of two-shades-of-green Parisian stars have gone out, just because they were my favourites and I was greedy and wanted pink ones too. I've looked everywhere, again and again; they might as well never have existed.

And my glittery diamanté ones from Tyndrum have vanished even before I could bring them home. I bought them very quickly, greedy again, three pairs at once, during a very dark thunderstorm which also had flashes of brilliance. There were clear ones like diamonds, blue ones like sapphires and pink ones like nothing on earth.

And because I was going alone to an island with huge skies where no-one would look at me, and where diamanté earrings were inappropriate for the seals and the sea otters, I stashed them, in their little leopard-print paper bag, still pinned to their display ovals of plastic, in a safe place. I didn't even treat myself to a quick look at them, saving their brightness so they could surprise and delight me once more, later, at home.

I'm home again now in the dark city with small dull bits of sky, and rain clouds hiding the stars. Where diamanté earrings are needed to be seen, but I cannot find them anywhere. I seem inadvertently to have put them out, or rather, failed to bring them in. No point looking in the fridge, in the butter compartment, where my aunt eventually found she'd put her missing wallet, which wasn't even a yellow one.

My only consolation is that the cat's not in the wardrobe yet. Maybe that's the dark place where I'll find my bright earrings. If I had a wardrobe, that is. Or a cat. Or any pretty earrings to lose in the first place.

Sam Gilliland

Tae Willie Neill

Sic wale o cauf-kintra's leid I hae,
Whanged oot o Coila's mou,
It gars me greet that gaitlins dinnae
Jig ahin the gudeman's pleugh.
Och, Willie, the warld haes left ahent
The likes o us lang syne,
Wi suddron yis chields maun be content,
Whilst Scotia's fare maun dwyne.

Lang had I warslt wi the thocht o't,
Heezed in my hert its soun,
Mergh i my breist at sough o't,
Lallans sae faur dinged doon,
Yet hae I thigged anither sang,
Tae daff attour the braes,
An skeich my fit the hale day lang,
Foremose the muse sweet Alba gaes.

My plaid upo ae shouther wecht,
A glint in these twa een,
Wi Soutar I maun brawlie fecht,
Wi Dunbar lauch an preen,
I'll sowth a sang for Scotia braw,
Haud forrit auld MacDiarmid's prees,
Ilk birn fae lirkit brou maun fa,
Gif Fergusson my trauchles mese.

Leeze me on the Heids o Ayr,
The auld Strath's rins an glens
And in my pooch a makar's quair,
Aiblins the wark o Spens.
As I gae brankin ower the braes,
Wi kith an kin sae leal,
I'll kittle up the pipes an play
A lilt tae Willie Neill.

William Neill – a Poet

Brent Hodgson

One thing is certain about William Neill these days is that he is unlikely to found either in the cab of a turbo-charged tractor or behind a team of Clydesdales. Not that he is unacquainted with the tilling of the soil. When he was a lad he often followed the ploughing, and at other times he was reading with delight the adventure stories of R L Stevenson. The books by this Scottish writer he came upon by chance inside a cupboard, and, without any telling from his elders or from school dames, took to reading them. The opening lines of Neill's poem 'Ayrshire Farm' speak of his childhood: –

> I remember the black chains that hung
> on the swee above the fire, and I remember
> the men who sat in the farm kitchen;
> they wore stout boots, and their hands were no less rough …

Farming today is not the same as in the days of yore. Now a wheat farmer can sit in the cab of his combine harvester, press the right buttons, look at the screen installed inside the cab and be advised if he should proceed with the reaping of the crop. On board the combine are instruments to measure the moisture content of the wheat.

For centuries the action of the plough was similiar to the dragging of a hoe through the ground, which only fractured the soil as a result. The word 'plough' is related to the plot and the patch, and according to the *Encyclopaedia Britannica* was a unit for the assessment of land. The Old English word for plough was 'sulh' or 'suit', and its root is seen in the Latin 'sulcus' – a furrow. In Scotland the ploughgang was the area a team of 8 oxen could plough in a year. Furrows undergoes a contraction (the same thing that happened to the place-name Gretenho) in Willie's poem 'The Choice': –

> Eftir yon wearie daurg frae burn tae heidrigg
> cowpin the furrs owre in the droukin rain,

The *Encyclopaedia Britannica* of 1911 consisted of 29 volumes with a word count of 4 million. A tiny reference is made to James Small, a blacksmith of Berwickshire who invented a cast-iron, one piece swing plough. James Small was a clever man because he changed the shape of the plough so that the mouldboard turned the slice of furrow over. The inversion of the earth was an agricultural advance of great significance, something fully recognised in Alastair Moffat's recent book on the history of the Borders.

Is there a connection between the ploughing of the land and the art of poetry ? Clues are seen in the Latin versus – a turning, by analogy a furrow, and in Old French verse – a stanza. People new to poetry or who intend writing poetry, should note that a stanza is a group of rhymed lines adjusted to each other in a definite scheme. A stanza is a *neat* thing, and so is a field that has been ploughed by an expert ploughman. A field ploughed to a regular pattern is attractive to the eye. When viewing such a sight it must be plain at least that the ploughman turned out a neat and tidy field. Neill is fond of verse that adheres to a regular pattern, and here is an example from his poem 'Nausicaa': –

> 'A ghruagaich òig an òr-fhuilt bhuidhe
> co an duine tha 'nad dheoghaidh?
> le coltas air mar mharaiche?'
> 'Fhuair mi esan air an tràigh!'

The staple metre of Greek and Latin Epic poetry was the hexameter, a line of 6 feet. Poets of the calibre of Longfellow, Coleridge, Southey and Kingsley wrote poetry in hexameters, and none of them were alive at the same time as the Greek and Roman poets of antiquity.

If William Neill was asked to write poetry in lines of stressed iambics consisting of 15 syllables with a pause after the 8th syllable, could he do it? Would he understand the requirements that are necessary to write in this measure of Greek poetry, a style that was usual in the 4th century? As he has consistently demonstrated competence in the writing of verse, there is no reason to think he would be incapable of doing that.

Could he write rhymed couplets in a combination of tetrameters and trimeters, the stanzas often of 15 syllables, a form that bears a close relationship to the Greek form of stressed iambics of the same number of syllables? The answer is yes, he could. What does any poet need to know to write poetry? A basic knowledge of the foot, the dactyl, the spondee, the trochee, the division of rhyme into masculine, feminine and triple rhyme as well as the 4 types of metre would be a start. Writing poetry in regular hexameters wouldn't be easy for any poet. If something is difficult to do, most of us tend to avoid that method or scheme. An unbrave poet could get it into his or her head that if they were to write in hexameters, why, they might wind-up being ridiculed for their efforts.

Nowadays we might all be thinking poetry in the form of stressed iambic lines of 15 syllables is old-fashioned or simply out-of-date. Why would any modern poet bother with it? One response is that it is a traditional form. Heroic or 'high-flown' poetry written by a knowledgeable and competent poet would mystify those said to represent the powerhouse of Scottish poetry, because present in such would be two things that are largely absent in their own poetry: lines that are memorable and pleasant to read. Is the last stanza of the old folk poem 'Bonny Barbara Allan' well-composed?

> O mother, mother, make my bed,
> O make it soft and narrow.
> Since my love died for me today,
> I'll die for him tomorrow.

Yes, an ancient Greek form of verse can be traced in many popular English and Scots ballads.

The question whether William Neill would write in five-foot iambics or hexameters is, of course, hypothetical. But what would without doubt appeal to him is the quality of the verse. He would have no trouble at all between distinguishing between patterned writing and the writing of prose. A favourite poem of Neill's is Burns's 'Holy Willie's Prayer': –

But, Lord, remember me and mine
Wi' mercies temporal and divine,
That I for grace an' gear may shine
Excell'd by nane;
And a' the glory shall be Thine –
Amen, Amen!

The poem is an historical object, a product of a particular mind and vision, and it has a rhyme scheme. Like the poetry in the 16 volumes of Neill's work, 'Holy Willie's Prayer' meets a definition of poetry in being an imaginative expression of emotion, thought or narrative in metrical form.

Neill's voice can be heard not in just one language but in three, for he is a skilled versifier in Scots, Gaelic and English. His use of the Scots did not come out of book-learning; he heard the language spoken as a boy and so it comes naturally. His belief is that Scotland is rich linguistically and one should understand the different tongues in order to understand Scotland. The world of Dumfriessian place-names supports his view: –

Ecclefechan : Church of St Fiachan. Gaelic *eaglis* – 'church'.
Drumlanrig : Ridge of the clearing. Brittonic *llanerch* – 'clearing'.
Gretna : Gretenho - the great hollow. Old English *holh* – 'hollow'.
Langholm : The long meadow. Norse *holm* – 'meadow'

Another contention of the poet is relevant here. Neill would say that Scotland as a concept has yet to be expressed politically because it has been a mess from its beginning. And speaking of messes of the present day involving sectarianism, elitism, nepotism and parochialism, we have recently been made aware that the ex-First Minister Henry McLeish may be facing expulsion from the political party that spawned him, and that the cost of the new Scottish Parliament continues to soar. Is it not shameful that no elected representative of the people insisted on the setting of a fixed budget for the building? Even more disgraceful is the fact the final cost of the building has been declared by our politicians to be uncappable.

A pub sign in England is a source of amusement to Willie. The name of the pub is 'The Honest Lawyer' and the pictorial representation of the name shows a lawyer – with his head tucked under his arm. In his book *Wild Places* is a poem written by Neill titled 'Bull'. A contemporary story concerning a bull may inspire another poet to put pen to paper. During the foot and mouth disease epidemic of 2001, the Isle of Arran had not a single case. Yet when John McKinnon of Hillhead wanted to shift a bull the distance of 10 miles from Shiskine to Bennan, the Department of Rural Affairs in Edinburgh very kindly sent him the rules and regulations and an application form to authorize him to carry out the move. All the data from the department was contained in a fax; a fax that measured 35 feet in length.

Once upon a time a poet was a figure who could be relied upon to give a fresh, independent outlook on current conditions in society. Those days may be gone, although there is evidence that the opinions of poets were sought in America after the events of September 11. A few comments made by William about the world at large are of interest: –

> In Celtic society to be regarded as a poet you had to remember poetry as an oral tradition and if you couldn't, you were not a poet. The tribes of Britain were quite sophisticated people and not barbarians when the invading Romans arrived. The worst thing that happened in Europe was the expulsion of Moorish/ Arabic scholars under the compulsion of a bunch of pseudo-Christian bigots. Philosophy, art and linguistic studies in India were centuries in advance of anything in Europe when the invading (and ignorant) British arrived.

Writing prose can be easier than composing verse, is a belief of William Neill's. The prose writer can get into a flow and write away at length. Not so with the poet who is writing concisely, who may be acutely occupied with including in a poem such things as rhyme and the rhythmical arrangement of words. The pattern of the poem may have to be adapted to match and reinforce the theme of the poem.

What advice does William Neill have for the poet? Write coherently is one message. Write in different forms and vary the subject matter. Write poems and send them to your friends. Post your poems on the Internet. Poetry that makes sense will probably be written in a patterned fashion. Poetry that rhymes and scans is more likely to be memorable than unpatterned verse.

Getting a book of poems published is hard. Do not worry about winning glittering poetry prizes. The settin ower intil Scots o the Romanesco sonnets bi Giuseppe Belli, brings to the fore Neill's love of satirical poetry. Why is Belli, a poet of the early 19th century, so highly regarded? Because Belli 'gets to the point' – as simple as that. Neill himself admits that the problem of getting 'bite' into short poems is never easy. Nevertheless, he accomplishes this in 'The Audience Wi The Twa Scots': –

> Twa Scottish chiels gae roun in whit thay think a proper
> sign o gret cleverality, daunner aboot
> contentit, and maist shamelesslie athoot
> breiks, in claes mair fittin for a horse-coper.
>
> Thare canna be ower monie hairtie blaws
> o wund aboot the heathen kintraside
> whauriver 't is thir ferlie skellums bide,
> wi sic wanchancie gear aboot thair baws.
>
> Ti think a Paip that kens o graund societie
> wad hae fowk ben for a fu audience
> o siccan bare-airsed raiscals, bauld an braisant.
>
> God's truth ! Ti risk sic ugsome improprietie
> as bou in sic a Presence wi the chance
> that aabodie see a sicht that's haurdlie daicent.

Some more advice to poets from William Neill – write poetry for fun. If you want to make money from writing, write prose.

A major achievement for any poet would be the learning to communicate through the medium of poetry. Neill's sonnet 'Poet's Walk 1796' is worth examining in this regard as it does communicate. With the "exciseman Burns staucherin roun an roun frae White Sands ti Midsteeple", we see at a glance the setting is rooted in reality. But there is also a hint of the afterworld. Only the three words 'daurk St Michael's' are employed to arouse the imagination of the reader to the impending fate of the poet, who after his death was elevated to the rank of national bard. In the sombre sestet we discern the emotion of sadness, restrained in a remarkable manner: –

> Exciseman Burns wannert the kittle toun,
> his wame aw wersh wi drink, his hert wi gaw ;
> wha tentit him in this thrawn bit ava?
> Nou nocht tae dae but staucher roun an roun
> frae White Sands tae Midsteeple, up an doun
> the banks o Nith, aye waitin for the caa
> o the Caledonian Muse. The bitch had fled awa
> an widna yield a sang tae a gauger's tune.
>
> Thro grey Dumfries the cauld broun watter gaed,
> droonin the speirit as it smoort the rime
> oot tae a stick's tap on the causey stanes.
>
> Whiles the faur city flittert in his heid.
> As daurk St Michael's bydit for his time
> the smirr o Solway stoundit in his banes.

In the poem 'Poet's Walk 1796' we are assured, that over the last 80 years William Neill has learnt the craft of poetry well. (*A list of William Neill's published works is available from* Chapman)

New from Chapman Publishing!

Wild Women of a Certain Age
by Magi Gibson

Rejoicing for an age when children have grown up but energy still springs, Gibson's title poem has become a classic for women everywhere. The rest of the collection doesn't disappoint either – variously combative, sensual, longing but always full of life. A must for women (and men) of all ages! *£8.70*

Clan MacHine *by Ian McDonough*

Going on a magical mystery tour through inner and outer space, past, present and future, McDonough's first collection is a feast for the senses. Worldly yet sardonic, *Clan MacHine* is a far-ranging voyage for the open mind.*£7.70*

Prices include p+p. From Chapman, 4 Broughton Place, Edinburgh EH1 3RX
Tel: 0131 557 2207 Fax: 0131 556 9565 chapman-pub@blueyonder.co.uk

The Ruit an the Flooer

William Neill

Whan I wes a bittock o a laud in the Auld Toun, I wes obleeged tae be bilingual: the leid o the skuil wes Scottish Stannart Inglish an in the case o twa teachers 'Received Pronunciation'; the leid o maist ither fowk in the toun wes Scots o varyin depth an lexis. Houiver, lang weeks an weekens pit by on a ferm shuin fullt ma heid wi a mair mensefu getherin o Scots wards. It is aye on ferms an crofts that the auld leids are maist lastie an strang. Forbye that, I am muckle behauden tae twa leal teachers wha shawed me that oor ain hame-leids were a necessar lugmairk o Scottishness, an no juist the yae leid ither. Sae I hae made a pint o stowin a bing o Gaelic intil ma heid tae. For aw the modern yammerin agin Rab Burns, he wes a chiel o gret mense, virr an manheid, an I hud an auld-faither wha wad say owre sic maisterpieces as 'Holy Willie's Prayer' in guid Ayrshire Scots, the baith o us gey near lauchin oor heids aff atween duans. Forbye that, I hud a guid learit teacher wha tellt me tae listen fur the twa Gaelic souns in Carrick o thay days, an no tae forget anither native o Carrick, Watt Kennedie, whae gied Dunbaur a richt mellin in the maitter o the Gaelic tung, that wes still vieve thair in thon days an for monie a year eftir.

The haill crux o the maitter, a pint made eidentlie an aften by Christopher Murray Grieve an George Campbell Hay, is that a *kennin* o oor twa native leids is a necessar lear tae onie scriever wha wad gie himsel or hirsel the epithet 'Scottish'. Scotland is the yae place whaur a man kin tell ye he kens Latin, Greek, Icelandic, Javanese, Arabic an Serbo-Croat an naebodie wull tak onie tent o't in the wey o thinkin this onie gret ferlie; bit juist lat yin say he kens baith leids o Scotlan an thay'll wag the heid in disbelief.

The wark o baith Grieve an Hay in pintin oot the integritie o Scotland is mair aften than no unduin bi the menseless poseurs wha divide Scotlan, like Gaul, intil three pairts; the Linguistic Fitba Teams as I caa thaim. Baith o the twa makars I hae quotit yaised the three leids o Scotland in thair wark, awbeit in variant meisure. It is nou heich time that the linguistic depairtments o the Scottish Universities made shair (or siccar gin ye'd hae it!) that thair modern resairch cam tae the skuils, sae that the bairns growe up kennin thair ain true grunn. Gaelic wes the vernacular o Scotland until 1380. Twa leidit Hielandmen (an thare hes aye been monie o thaim) yaised Scots as thair saicont tung as the Buik o the Dean plainlie shaws. An even gin the Teamsters dinna want tae see yon sempil truith, for the maist pairt the Scottish population is nou, tae yaise Garioch's rare line: 'jurmummelt thegither like unctioneer's lots' sae the Scottish Linguistic Fitba League dinna hae a leg tae staun on. I hae aften taen tent that monie o the loodest skirlers anent the brekkin o Scotland intil twa pairts, Gaelic an Scots, cudna cry oot for thair mait in yae leid or the tither. Scotland is stuffit tae the mairches wi awkin clubs an societies for the Scottish This,

That an the Tither, an gin ye want tae mak maist o the members lowp aff the flair or luk as if ye hud duntit thaim owre the heid wi a hemmer, juist address thaim in guid Scots or Gaelic. A glaikit gant cams intil thair een an thay steer til the lythe side o ye as suin's thay kin. An thair's fouth o thaim that think the ootward signs o Scottishnesss are eneuch; the bre-chan maks a bonie garb, an it's eith tae pit a sash owre yir shouther or a philabeg roun yir dowp, but it disna, on its lane, mak a bodie Scottish.

Gey aften ye'll hear the cuif's aff-pit that 'nobody in educated society speaks or writes Scots or Gaelic' frae sic as luik doun thair nebs at onie leid forbye thair ain fushionless cletter. It is haurdlie warth pintin oot tae sic tykes the excellence o the native scrievers the past threescore years has brocht oot, an tae sic as are learit in Scots an/or Gaelic thair's nae caa for me tae mak a leet o thaim here.

I hae, yince mair, hud ma birse pitten up by the Scottish Philistine Soci-etie, findan fouth o past-maisters o't in an airt I hadna suspeckit, a journal dedicatit tae the heizin up o patriotism. A vizzy taen on the journal's behalf hes brocht oot the paradoxical fack that maist o its readers wadna gie a docken for oor Scottish leids an cultuir. Wha wad credit it? Thair luve o Scotland seems tae be a maitter o siller, altho yon's aye buskit up wi the graund name o Economics. For ma ain pairt, altho I canna see why oor ile an ither walth sud gang tae mak the sooth o Ingland rich while they hae the nakit impidence tae caa us puir, I wad raither sowp sowens day in an day oot an caa masel Scot, than forleit ma ain cultural heirskip tae mak masel intil a saicont cless Inglisman, in the fain howp o better-ment. Scotland is siccarlie made Scotland by its leids an cultuir, the harns o its scrievers, penters, sculptors, musicians an no by its latitude an lon-gitude, usquebae, ile, coal or politickers. O I ken we wad hae dowie days athoot material walth; ye'll find wark an walth in an eemoch-knowe but as faur as I ken they haena made a piperor a poet yet. I expeck, tae, that aw thir neipheids gang yince a year tae the Januar haggis-dirkin in the name o The Immortal Bard, tho it's yin on the modern wunners o the warld hou the Bard's immortalitie hes lastit athoot being smoort tae daith ablo thair thowless annual cletter.

Monie a year syne, I attended a Mod in The Gret Plook (London). Et nicht maist o the singin wes in a howff near St. Pancras Toun Haa, gin ye cud hear it abune the reels an jigs frae assortit fiddles, pipes an melodeons. Intil this hellish dirdum cam a chiel wi a bouler hat, black jaikit, strippit breeks, brief case an umbrella ablo his oxter. He stuid at the baur aside me.

"What on earth is going on here?" says he, in the maist perfect suddron panloaf.

"It is," I reponit, "A Mod."

"Oh, yes. A kind of Gaelic Eistedfodd. Strange how these barbarous dead languages continue."

I ettled tae keep a grup on ma tung an ma temper, pitten it aw doun tae invincible ignorance, but he blethert on in the same daft wey, gien oot

William Neill, photograph by Gordon Wright

wi the kin o trasherie warrantit tae mak onie Scot lowpin mad. I wes a guid wheen years yunger than I am nou, an forbye I had taen a guid dram in the coorse o the celebrations. Juist as I thocht maitters hud gane faur eneuch an hud turnt roun tae pit him richt on a few maitters o cultuir an politicks he gied a grin an proggit me wi his elbuck.

"Nach thusa tha fas fiadhaich, a bhalaich," says he. (Aren't you getting mad!)

I sud hae jaloused that naebodie but a Scot cud hae thocht up sae monie pints for the heizin up o Scottish birses. Frae then on he jined intil the ceilidh wi gust an Gaelic. Nou this man cudna yaise Gaelic aboot his wark in the Ceetie. But Gaelic wes in the smer o his banes, an ablo his weel-steekit jaikit an breeks wes a chiel wha hadna tint his cultuir. He wes shair, in ither wards, o his identitie in the warld; but then, belike the leidless, learless ile-patriots dinna care aboot identitie. If yon is thair true thocht on the maitter, whit are thay daein in yon gallery o wrastlers for the Scottish ethos?

The pint I am makkin is that it is eith tae maist mensefu Scots tae keep a grup o Scots cultuir houever needfu a veneer o Inglishness is tae thair means o economic survival, as Grassic Gibbon's Chris shaws plain. The ruits ablo the grunn are stranger than the flooer abune it. But the great Scottish mistak hes aye been tae feed the flooer at the expense o the ruits, sae that the haill plant dees, a pracktick that is aye bein gien a heize bi oor saicret enemies, learless social sclimmers, an thowless dominies.

Nou it isna for me tae say whither Gaelic or Scots can yince mair become the tung o the feck; that is for the yunger generation, no auld boddachs o threescore plus. But Scots an Gaelic are still wi's; thair are bairns wha speak thaim still, an oor native leids will last intil the twintie-first centurie, sae thair is nae raison why they sud be kickit owre the doorstane afore thair time bi North Britons. Thare are still chiels scrievin in thaim, yunkers wha can gie thair scrievins a guid, burnist glent. The teuchest daurg is tae get sic wark accordit its proper status in the minds o the fowk, an tae spreid its effect in the skuils an colleges.

Tae feenish; I maun threip on again that I hae *never, onywhaur* said that a Scots writer maunna scrieve in Inglish. Whit wey wad I hae the gaw? I scrieve in Inglish masel as maist o the Scottish writers dae. Whit I hae said, an am no the least blate aboot repeatin, is that gin ye'd be a Scottish scriever ye maun hae a kin o wal o Scottish culture within. Itherwyce, whitiver kin o scriever ye are, ye maun seek anither epithet, for style an attitude baith pro an contra in onie question is ruitit in native lear raither than geographie, ootside the realms o mathematick an science.

But gin ye wad be a 'cultured Scot' in the ainlie true sense o the ward, ye maun hae a big hert, tae face oot the muckle clan o ill-educatit snirters wha, athoot kennin a ward o oor native leids, set thaimsels up as its critics.

This essay was first published in Chapman *41, Summer 1985.*

Pablo Neruda

Translations by John Manson

II: The Inventions

Do you see this little trisyllabic object?
It's a secondary cylinder of good fortune
and operated, now, by coherent organisms
from remote control, I am, be certain
of such a resplendent efficacy
that grapes ripen to their unknown pressure
and wheat is transformed into bread in the open field,
mares give birth to vermilion horses
that gallop the air without previous advice,
great industries move like centipedes
leaving wheels and watches on uninhabited sites:
Gentlemen, buy my tertiary product
without mixture of cotton nor lacteous substances:
I bestow you a button to change the world:
buy the three-phase before I regret it!

V: The Guests

And we the dead, echeloned in time,
seeded in planned and pompous cemeteries
or fallen in pits of poor Bolivians,
we, the dead of 1925, 26,
33, 1940, 1918, nineteen o five,
nineteen hundred thousand, in short, we,
the deceased before this stupid figure
in which we're not living now, what happens to us?

I, Pedro Moor, Pedro Seed, Pedro Nobody,
wasn't I entitled to four figures and the resurrection?
I want to see the resurrected in order to spit in their faces,
the precocious who are about to fall
in aeroplanes, on railroads, in the wars of hatred,
they who hardly had time to be born and present
arms to the new century and remained cut short
rotting in the middle of the fiestas and the wine!
I want to rise from my grave, I who am dead, why not?

Why are the premature going to be forgotten?
All are invited to the banquet!

It's another year, it's another century, with dead and living,
and we have to carry out the protocol, lay down not only life
but also dried flowers, rotten wreaths, silence,
because silence has a right to beauty
and we, delegates from death,
we want to exist for a single flowery minute
when the doors of the coming glory open!

VI: The Men

I'm Ramón González Barbagelata, from anywhere,
from Cucuy, from Paraná, from Río Turbio, from Oruro,
from Maracaibo, from Parral, from Ovalle, from Loncomilla,
no matter, I'm the poor devil from the poor Third World,
the passenger from the third class compartment, Jesus!
in the luxurious whiteness of the snow-capped cordilleras,
hiding among the orchids of slender idiosyncracy.

I've reached this aforementioned year 2000,
and what do I draw out,
what do I get drunk with, what do I have to do
with the three illustrious zeros that flaunt themselves
over my own zero, over my non-existence?
Cry of that heart that waited for its flag
or of the man laurelled by the most tender love,
to-day nothing remains but my indistinct skeleton,
my disturbed eyes facing the initial time.
Initial time: it's these lost huts,
these poor schools, these still in rags,
this earthy uncertainty of my poor kin,
this is the day, the initial century, the golden gate?

I, at least, without saying too much, well, reserved
as I was in the workshop, patched and absorbed,
I proclaim the superfluousness of the inauguration:
here I came with everything that went along with me,
the bad luck and the worst jobs,
poverty always waiting wide open,
the mobilisation of the overcrowded people
and the numerous geography of hunger.

VII: The Other Men

On the other hand I, sinner fisher,
former avant-gardist already out-of-date,
from these years dead and distant
to-day I'm at the threshold of the millennium,
frenzied anarcho-capitalist,
ready to stuff both cheeks
with the apple of the world.
A more flourishing age not even Florence knew,
more flowery than Florida,
more Paradise than Valparaíso.
I breathe at my ease
in the banking garden of this century
which is finally a great current account
in which I'm fortunately in credit.
Thanks to investment and subversion
we'll make this age more hygienic,
no colonial war will keep this name
so discredited and reiterated,
pulverizing democracy
will take charge of the new dictionary:
it's beautiful this 2000 equal to 1000:
three equal zeros shield us
from all unnecessary insurrection.

VIII: The Materials

The world filled with notwithstandings,
with unfounded fears and sorrow,
but we must admit that besides the salty bread
or next to this or that iniquity
the plants, when they weren't scorched,
went on flowering and dividing
and continued their green work.

There's no doubt that the earth
delivered other things with great difficulty
from its trunk that seemed everlasting:
the copper dies, the manganese sobs,
oil is a final death rattle,
iron takes leave of the coal,
coal already closed its hollows.

Now this century must murder
with other masks of war, we go
to inaugurate death in another way,
mobilise blood in other warehouses.

Coulter and Pleuch

Some Ideas for an Approach to the Poetry of William Neill

Colin Donati

Thow tynt cultur, I have cultur and pleuch – Walter Kennedy

Like most members of the tribe of poets, William Neill is a polymath with magpie instincts, bound by little more than his own disparate curiosities and observations. His direct plain-speaking voice and straightforward commitment to well-crafted prosody on one hand, his commitment to questions of national cultural integrity on the other, usefully limits his canvas. But to itemise the full range of subjects and concerns of his work would quickly reveal a vast depth of interests and he is able to employ a broad compass of registers from the comic to the serious, often binding the two characteristically in one poem. He is always intelligent, always honest. He never makes a secret of his opinion about things. A true makar.

Similarly his famous employment of the three leids, English, Scots and Gaelic, all vastly different in tone, register and effect, imparts yet further variety. Scots is his language of birth. He still holds it his first tongue even after all the smooring pressures of English-language education. The Celtic tongue he learned in adulthood. Ask what inspired him to do this at a time when it was nowhere near the fashionable drive it has become today and his answer is immediate: "I didna see hou I culd possibly be a Scotsman and no ken Gaelic". His first published poem was in that acquired leid, and in 1969 he was the first non-Gael to win the Bardic crown at the Mod.

These facts show us a natural poet with an unpretentious, casual mind open to everyday matters, accustomed to working as the fancy takes him, darting from interest to interest, observation to observation, even jouking from tongue to tongue. Add in his numerous translations and the results *seem* all hither and yon. Not so. Despite the disparate contents of his poetic kist, Neill's poems form a surprisingly consistent body of work.

So what gives his work its characteristic stamp, its unity? Voice is one reason, but not the whole story. There are two further reasons: the first is his approach to prosody, the second his Scots cultural commitment. To use an analogy both agricultural and literary, think of one standing to the other as the coulter does to the pleuch. Neill takes a thrawnly-held individualistic position on both in his cultural landscape.

He is a poet of the Hamish Henderson generation, that period from the late 50s which builds on the achievements of the earlier Renaissance of MacDiarmid *et al,* and extends its legacy right across Scotland's civic life; a movement which contributed towards and culminated in the establishing of a devolved parliament in Edinburgh in 1999. This was a real watershed moment, and minding ourselves back to the prevailing cultural and political atmosphere decades before the 1996 referendum already begins to feel quite difficult, so much has shifted. But it is important to do so. Neill's work forms part of that context.

A landmark of the Henderson generation was the great 'folk culture flyting' of the early 60s. MacDiarmid famously resisted the folk movement, calling it a manifestation of 'peasant' culture, dismissing it as a "fortunately irrecoverable" way of life that Scotland had "happily outgrown". Its prosody, he argued, was typically limited and backward-looking. He referred to this at its best as "crambo-clink" (see *The Armstrong Nose*, selected letters of Hamish Henderson.) Henderson championed the upsurge of folk culture and argued that it was a democratic cultural expression essential to "human wholeness". Others like David Craig went further and claimed to hear 'Homeric' heights in some of its products "equal in quality, in beauty and truth, if not in scale, to the great European epics". Doubtless there were extremes on both sides. Where does Neill fit in with this?

Neill's work combines both camps and synthesises them, achieving some highly characteristic effects. In fact his position as a bridge between the two is almost uncannily perfect, lying in the combination of his upbringing on an Ayrshire fermtoun, and the education he studiously pursued throughout his life culminating in Honours Celtic Studies and English as a mature student at Edinburgh University. So here is a man who has (as he puts it) "skailt sharn and stooked corn", but who also knows his Homer direct from the Greek.

The first gives him his physical and practical connection with that world which MacDiarmid, aye the Marxist, was so eager to consign to the midden, a world Neill so frequently describes with potency, accuracy and graphic force in poems such as 'Kailyard and After':

> When I wes wee I hud tae dae ma share
> mulkan the kye wi the weemin in the byre;
> I mind hou I wad scoosh lang streemin jaups
> that loupit in the luggie makkin froth
> rise oot frae yon rich deeps

And this in a day, as Neill records it, when members of that 'peasant' community could still be sweirt for instance to adopt tractors, those "mitherless dreggans breathin the reek o hell" ('The Auld Grunn'). On the other hand the mature student in the capital "seeking yearned truths" bielded in cells "a little warmer than Lindesfarne/ a little less remote than Icolmkill" ('Edinburgh Don 1971'), brings these natural philosophies into contact with the more comfortable urban world of bureaucracy and teaching which both anglicises and inculcates a myth of progress.

So the two 'sides' of that debate are married with an almost ironic neatness. His education has not dispelled the 'peasant' aspect, the 'rural pride' ('Cartwheels'). The two together have given him an unromanticised commitment to traditional values rooted in history and the soil. And if his poetry is anything to go by, these are values he has assiduously maintained and strengthened throughout his education. The bond is strengthened and confirmed in his love of prosody. His poems always take the long view and frequently imply that we lose these values to our peril.

It's doubtful that Neill might have had a 'program' in expressing this.

That would be too overblown, too 'MacDiarmidian'. Manifesto-like 'statements of intention' in many poems could just as easily be examples simply of his typically thrawn voice. But note the title of his recent long collection, *Caledonian Cramboclink* (2001) and its key choice of noun, an aizle from that past flyting still secretly hot. Surely not altogether an accident.

An ideal candidate to effect a synthesis. The two camps are married so neatly in his work, with its natural philosopies born of practical and unsentimental commitment to traditional values rooted in history and the soil, that it seems an ironic comment on the flyting. These values were maintained and strengthened in his education. The 'rural' and the 'urban' are given uncompromising equivalence in his work. His poems always take the long view and frequently imply we lose these values at our peril. The marriage is confirmed in the characteristic prosody. Neill likes to claim that critics consider his regard for traditional verse forms as unfashionable. In doing so he gives himself license to make a stand against many prevailing poetic orthodoxies of the last half century for which he has contempt.

Neill perceives these values as a wisdom under threat. He associates this with his sense of national identity under pressure. All through Neill's lifetime modernity appears to have been tearing both these up at a rate of knots. He thus equates erosion of Scottish culture with erosion of the wisdom of the long view. This might explain why he seems so personally driven to shore up his sense of Scottish identity in his poems, whether through extending his sense of its compass, or by dispassionately investigating the consequences of its loss, as in 'That's Gone and This Has Come'

> I speak just the fine English now,
> my own ways left behind …

He is not just adding his 'chuckie to the cairn' (to borrow Garioch's phrase); it goes further. The poems in Neill's extensive *oeuvre* are like stanes o aw different shape an size, some big some sma, biggit til a lang dyke, violating unity of place in the metaphor, no so much a Gallowa drystane dyke as mair a Dutch sea dyke tae shore back a threatened tide of cultural engulfment. Anglicisation is usually his overt target, but that could just as easily stand, today, for the larger ocean of globally corporatised homogenisation.

So Neill aspires to perceive the most far-reaching continuities, the most durable verities, the deepest tribal echoes in the bone. This of course makes him a profoundly conservative poet. To be conservative in Scotland means to embrace the radical tradition which comes through Burns and is more in line with Paine than Burke, one that still enables us to hear an incisive relevance for modernity even in the mediaeval (anti-capitalist) Henryson. Neill works very consciously in this line.

It is time to elaborate on Neill's approach to prosody as seen as the 'coulter to his pleuch'. The image is from Walter Kennedy, Gaelic poet in the court of James IV, and an emblematic bard for Neill. It appears in his defence against Dunbar's attack in 'The Flyting o Dunbar and Kennedy' and is one of the great lines in the Scottish canon. Its meaning is precise. The coulter is the sharp-edged wheel, or vertical blade that cuts the soil in advance of the plough and so helps keep it true to line, leal to the rig. A plough that lacks its steering influence could hardly cut soil effectively and would tend to wander. When Kennedy says that Dunbar has 'tynt cultur' he is saying that he may possess the 'plough' but lacks its most vital component. Dunbar (he is saying) is a wild, undirected upstart poet, one quite literally (for it is probably the *true* root of the word) 'uncultured'.

Neill is drawn to identify himself with neglected figures from Scotland's literary past. Kennedy, being a Galloway Gael who had the capacity to bridge Scotland's tongues, is a wholly appropriate precedent for Neill's purposes, and he frequently cites his example. Yet the 'Carrick bard' is a figure that lies largely forgotten. Neill is acutely aware of the effects of Scotland's cultural amnesia. It accounts for his 'embattled' mentality (a thing he shares with many contemporaries who pursued the Scots muse) his sense of the makar always being fated "tae lieve amang but aye abreid frae men" ('Poetry Reading, Edinburgh 1787'). But it also rewards him with the whiles dreamlike capacity to see what the feck of us no longer know how to:

Chunnaic mi Bhaltair Cinneide
a' coiseachd troimh clach mo shùl
fo sgàil a' Chaisteal Dhuibh
aig am laighe na greine
is grinneal fo chois
air tràigh liath Dhùn Iubhair.

Ach cha robh e an lèirsinn
duine air bith eile ...

('Cumha Bhaltair Cinneide, 1450-1508?')

And elsewhere he is moved to anger and indignation. 'Canto Macaronach' is as good an example as any. A long poem, wild and wandering in structure, that switches 'macaronically' from language to language, almost as if Neill allows his muse licence to run amok *without* the controlling influence of the coulter for once. The exception that proves the rule.

A good instance of his concern to connect linguistic issues and cultural identity comes in what I regard as the Canto's climactic stanza. After citing various European nations and arguing that their 'true totems' exist in the lasting works of those creative writers who have generated their words, not the passing ploys of soldiers or 'economists', he states:

Likewise, I tell you, Scotland lives in words:
if you care nothing for the speech of Scots,
Scotland is lost to you: elsewhere are hills as high
rivers as long and deep and fields as green.

But why is this question of cultural identity so important? Angus Calder has written (in *Scotlands of the Mind)* that Scottish identity is "a myth ... given substance only in the corporealities of persons who imagine that they have it" for there can be "nothing outside consciousness which is identity". (One presumes he has to apply this to all national identities, not just Scots). We therefore (he says) 'invest' our individual identities in 'externals' such as landscape, sport, literature, industry and so on.

Calder (deliberately?) avoids including language in that list. Neill makes it key. If language is one of the 'externals' we 'invest' ourselves in, then it is without doubt the most intimate, for it sits both within and without, flags both our sense of 'self' and of 'tribe'. When language is challenged or eroded, when that particular 'investment' is prevented from giving its return, then we are potentially creating an extremely deep faultline in the psyche which touches on the question of national identity in both the exterior and interior realm. Neill sits himself bang on top of a particularly critical and profound example of just such a faultline, and one that exists in his own life and experience.

Consideration of this helps us understand one salient feature of the 'nationalist' expression in his poetry. It is the way that concern for national awareness manifests in Neill's work as an intensely *personal* endeavour. This gives his work some of its quietly persuasive meditative qualities in tandem with the more characteristically blunt, plain-speaking and didactic elements. Further investigation would be fruitful.

Incidentally, the image of 'investment' appears at the end of 'Crofting Piper'. Here Neill adopts the persona of the piper 'MacCowal' in order to escape the "drip, drip, drip/ of the Saxon natter-torture" (BBC broadcasting) and visualises himself playing perfect *piobaireachd* to the "baffled" tourists who grin, the "righteous [that] look down their noses". Each variation, the "*suibhal, tuarluath, crunluath,/ crunluath breabach, crunluath a mach* ...

> a kind of gold that in this sunken time
> pays up the interest due on history's usury.

And on that note, finally, we turn to Neill's sense of (eternally unjust) history, and the use he makes of it.

The opening poem of his first long collection *Despatches Home* (1972) sets a standard. This is the imagined letter of a Roman governor discussing with contempt the colonialised social structures of the Britain his Rome has vanquished. The native masters he says with contempt are "well fooled, well tamed/ they use our baths and lard themselves with oil ..." Up in the hills are the bands "ungovernable ... growling in their own speech" that remain hostile to the Pax Romana. They "hate us as we hate them". The speaker's punchline comes in his closing words:

> We both despise
> the Latin-lisping traitors of the town.

There is nothing ambiguous about the set of relationships Neill succinctly establishes here. The invitation to draw parallels with his own pre-devolution Scotland is obvious. We suspect Neill thinks of his own 'countrymen' (a word he uses with irony in other poems) as people who have similarly sold out on their own traditions. Again the issue of language is locked in:

> The squireens speak school-Latin and affect
> misunderstanding of the kerns from their estates ...

We might also note his association of 'sell-out' with towns, another common motif in his work.

But the Roman's comments are presented without gloss and Neill draws no conclusion. As soon as we seek political parallels, the poem does not close onto one single interpretation. In fact it could open on a whole number of different conclusions. It presents an explicit image, but with no single simple moral. We are perfectly free to apply it as we please.

Despatches Home does not contain a single poem that fails to stand in some way as a metaphor or an image for some aspect of Neill's contemplation of Scotland's cultural predicament or the predicament of modernity. Once we sense this, even a poem that seems to have nothing to do with such questions, 'Island' for instance, resonates with suppressed implications. In fact the meditation in 'Island' is steeped with the dream of national reawakening, though one that expresses infinite loneliness "No desert is more unvisited than this dark peak".

He repeats a similar trick in *Straight Lines*(1992), though here it is questions of 'modernity' versus the 'longer view' that are more the issue. There is a sort of woven pattern in the sequencing of the relatively short poems as if each is regularly picked up on and turned by another one three or four down the line. The impression of intention here is strengthened by the way the 'title' poem so to speak ('Fairy Tales', by virtue of its containing the lines that the title refers to) embeds a metaphor for the inadequacy of the 'educated' mind that loses more in wisdom than it gains in intellect, a metaphor that can shape our approach to the whole collection.

So Neill's poems are not reduced by this 'reductive' seeming approach. Resonance and interest survives and grows. Indeed, the more we attempt to take the lid off what he is saying and lay it plain on the table, the more subtle, ambiguous and complex the message gets, even in his more comic squibs or 'neutral' poems such as landscape descriptions.

There is much I have not had space to mention, like Neill's fascination for the sonnet. (Something to do with the plough in his blood, each turn of the horses at the heidrig a physical correspondence for the turn at the eighth line?) 'Pride maun hae a Faa' is a devastating and characteristically Scottish example. His translations of Belli's are superlative, better than the Garioch in his knack for that artless meshing of street speech and sonnet form avoiding all pretension and maintaining the full slow-burning force of political indignation and irony. Then there are his equally remarkable selections from the Odyssey rendered intil a Scots gey different in tone and quality, sonorous and hypnotic, plain (even harsh) as well as hinting at some uncannily familiar non-aristocratic qualities in that (alien) Homeric world. And its stories clearly fascinate him beyond his translation. Compare Neill's 'Nausicaa' with MacCaig's, both similar in length and focus, and consider which might be the more spiritually 'Homeric'.

Neill's works are like a rockery strewn with tiny alpine plants half-hidden among boulders. The more we look, the more we discover. Now that we can start to put the Henderson age into some kind of perspective and attempt a proper appraisal of its poets, let Neill be among the first of those to be considered. A proper assessment of his work will be a cultural litmus test. I hope this article helps to provide some sort of streeking of the field.

David Purves

Nine Poems in Scots from the Chinese of LuYu (1135-1209)

Lu Yu was a major poet during the Sung Dynasty. He is understood to have written over ten thousand poems. He lived in the south of China in the period before the whole country was overwhelmed by the Mongols under Jenghiz Khan and his successors. His patriotic resentment against invaders was expressed in his poems and this ensured his popularity in twentieth century China following the Japanese invasion.

His poetry does not, perhaps, reach the heights attained in the eighth century by his predecessors, Li Po and Tu Fu, in the Golden Age of Chinese poetry. The fame of this illustrious pair of heavy drinkers seems to have cast a shadow on later poets, to judge by a piece by Chao-I (1727-1814) from 'On Poetic Geniuses'

> Li Po, Tu Fu – aye on awb'die's lips,
> duin ti daith wi foustit raens.
> In ilka age an immortal genius is born,
> ti swan it ower us aw for cuddie's years.

Nevertheless, Lu Yu has his own distinctive voice and his own valuable contribution to make to the wonderful tradition of poetry in China established over a period of over two and a half millennia. His poems are loose and casual and many pieces are useful social commentary, throwing light on life in China in the society in which he lived. Some of the poems in this selection (for example, 'The Courtesan', 'The Herd Loun' and 'The Wyld Flouer Man') are skilful pen-portraits of people he had encountered. Although Lu Yu was a member of what have been called 'the scholar gentry', he was not wealthy and well able to relate to the poor illiterate farmers among whom he lived.

The English neo-classical poetic tradition was long preoccupied with abstractions, rather than the perennial concerns of living people. When versions in English of wonderful ancient Chinese poems were published by Arthur Waley early last century, they were actually regarded with disapproval in England, because they did not fit into this entrenched, sophisticated tradition. However, since then, several published collections of renderings in English of ancient Chinese poems have become popular, while the neo-classical tradition involving rigorous rhyming and the regimentation of language into metered formats, has declined.

Furthermore, English has now developed into an international scientific and technological language employed by hundreds of millions of people with many different cultural backgrounds, living in different parts of the planet. It is sometimes argued that, because it is no longer the language of any specific community, and has lost contact with its original social roots, English is no longer a suitable language for poetry, which is properly concerned with the life (and plight) of Man as a social being. Although the

Scots language is certainly closely related to English, this argument cannot be applied to Scots. Scots is an intimate social language which is much less concerned with abstractions than English. It is specific to an identifiable community and it has a very different emotional flavour from English.

Versions of ancient Chinese poems in Scots have a vigour and emotional quality which was not always evident in the English versions from which they were derived. The Scots language can be powerful, tender, earthy or humorous, and the best poetry reflects the sentiment expressed by Burns: "the hert's aye, the pairt aye, that maks us richt or wrang". The compatibility of the Scots language with ancient Chinese poetry is no doubt because it is usually straight from the heart. Scots has its limitations, but it does not lend itself to pomposity or affectation, and may in fact be a more suitable medium for recreating these poems.

Whether these versions do justice to the original poems in Chinese is a question for the judgment of the select band of Chinese scholars who are also familiar with literary Scots.

The Wyld Flouer Man

Div ee ken thon auld caird that
sells the flouers bi the South Yett?
He fair leeves on flouers lik a bee.
In the forenuin he sells mallaes;
In the forenicht, he haes poppies.
His shantie ruif lets in the
blue lift. His rice girnal is
aye tuim. Whan he haes
ingethert aneuch siller frae his
flouers, he heids for a tea-houss.
Whan his siller is gaen, he
gethers mair flouers. Aw throu
the Spring wather, whyle the
flouers ir in bloom, he is lyke
in bloom, tae. Ilka day he
is fou the haill tyme. Whit daes
he care gin new laws ir posted
at the Emperor's pailace?
Whit daes it maitter ti him
gin the government is biggit
on sand? An ye mak ti speak
til him, he winna aunsir; but
onlie gie ye a drukken smirtil
frae ablo his tousilt heid.

A Dauner at Nicht

The muin is that hie, it is
amaist inti The Plou.
A walk oot the ceitie
alang the gait ti the Wast.
The damp wund bumfils ma coat.
The dewie gress drouks ma sandals.
Fishermen ir singin awa
blyth lyke, on the ferr wattir.
Tods lowp on the connacht lairs.
A snell wund gethers an fills
me wi dowiness. A try
ti think on the richt wurds
ti claucht this unco lanesumness.
A stodge hame late. The nicht
is hauf duin. A staun for
a lang whyle bi the houss door.
Ma wee son is aye up, readin.
Aw at aince, be bursts oot lauchin,
an aw the birn o dule o the
gloamin o ma lyfe is awa,
lyke winnelstrae afore the wund.

Blyth Days

Aince we haed a chapper
on the front yett.
Nou we haurlie open it.
A dinna want fowk
skliffin up the green fug.
The sun growes warm lyke.
Spring haes fair cum at lest.
Whyles ye can juist hear
on the lown saur,
the dirdum o the street.
Ma guidwyfe reads the classics.
She speirs at me the meanin
o the auld characters.

Ma son fleitches for a sowp o wyne.
He gollops doun the haill cappie
afore A can stap him.
Ir the oniething ava
better nor a wawed gairden,
wi yallae ploums an purpie ploums
plantit tyme aboot?

Forenicht in the Clachan

Here i the Heich Clachan
the forenicht faws lichtsum.
Hauf fou, A slounge bi the
houss door. The muin leims in the
gloamin lift. The breeze is that
douce the wattir is haurlie
lippert. A hae wun free frae
lees an mishanter. A im
nae langir o onie importance.
A never want ma brankin naigs
an rummlin chairiots. Here at hame
A hae rowth o pigs an hens.

Leavin the Monastery

In ma sleepin bed, A dream
it seems A im a butterflie.
A crawin cock waukens me
lyke a skelp. The sun cums up
the lest tyme atwein the mukkil bens,
an mist haps the distant craigs.
Ma lang retreat is ower
an ma worries growe again.
Lauchin monks ir getherin
brainches o braw peach blossoms
for a fareweill myndin for me.
But nae stirrup cup wul cheer me
on ma lang traivel back
til the dule o the warld:
intil a warld o truibils.

The Courtesan

Pink an whyte haunds lik roses an rice cake!
Caups fou wi gowden puils o wyne!
The-day the sauchs ir in blossom
bi the Pailace waw. The Spring wund
brings me nae pleisir, an A hate
it nou. Ma intimmers is fair
cruppen wi bitterness. A canna
lowse the cord o the years
that haes bund us thegither.
The Spring is aye the Spring
o ither days, but A im tuim,

wuzzent wi pyne an dule.
Ma rouge is aw begrutten
an ma goun is smirdit wi ma tears.
The peach trees ir in flouer
abuin ma chaumer here, bi the lown
lochan at mirrors the mukkil bens.
A dout A nae langir hae the smeddum
for ti feinish this skreid
an rowe it in the gowden claith.
Whan it is in yeir haund, awthing
wul be by an duin, foraye.

The Herd Loun

In the southlin clachan the herd laddie
grups the bullik's back wi his bare feet.
Throu the teir in his coat the river wund blaws;
throu his brukken hat the hill rain pours.
Frae the lang dyke, he kyths ferr awa;
in the nairrae wynd, we faced him bedein.

The loun is hame wi the bullik in its staw.
A derk reik birls oot the theikit ruif.

Rain on the Wattir

In the blinnd haar we drift here
an thare owre the derk swaws.
At lest oor wee boat finnds
a beild anaith a sauchie bank.
At midnicht A im waukrif,
fair fou wi the wyne. The reikie lentern
is aye smouderin. The smaw rain
is souchin aye in the bamboo
theik o the boat caibin.

Shour at Jianmen Glen

The stour smirds in wi the wyne merks on ma claes.
A traivel on, beglaumert, throu thir lands.
Im A ti be a poet aw ma days?
Throu the smaw rain, A ryde ma cuddie
on intil the shour in the Jianmen Glen.

Standard Language, Rigid Minds

William Neill

Some painters still mix their own colours. I cannot imagine any such artist abandoning a worthwhile process simply because it had been used by Van Eyck, or a pianist refusing to accompany a recorder on the grounds that the concert flute had replaced its orchestral use. It seems, however, that in the great world of literature, there are those who throw out words for even flimsier reasons. There is in fact a kind of critic who objects to the work of poets on the grounds that they use words which are slang, dialect, not standard speech, made-up or otherwise objectionable. There have always been critics who tried to turn the whole flood of literature into the piddling stream of which they, personally, approved. There are even metropolitan reviewers who seem to think that the only valid writing emanates from London, the Home Counties, and Overseas, a kind of imperial preference surviving from the days of the Raj. It is not surprising that writers beyond the Thames Valley Pale should find this irritating: what is surprising is that alleged purveyors of *Scottish* critical opinion should ally themselves to such a narrowly provincial viewpoint. A study of that nation from whom the expression 'beyond the Pale' originated shows quite clearly that posterity considered the poets beyond the Pale the more remarkable. It is worth noting that Henrysoun and Dunbar, despite their northern form of 'Inglis' were considered by G S Fraser to be superior to any English poet of that age. Had they been born in this day, they might well have been ignored on purely geographical grounds.

Parochialism of this kind is not new. Wordsworth read to London audiences who sniggered at his Cumberland accent instead of listening to his poetry, although the Cockney accent of Keats may well have passed muster in an age before Daniel Jones. Burns was continually advised by the Scottish literary cognoscenti to write in English if he wished to gain great repute. Lessons to be drawn from this ought surely to have taught the poets of today that strict orthodoxy (whatever its devotees imagine that to mean) in allophone or lexis should be avoided like the plague. The histories of Herodotus, the poetry of Homer and the Gospels are all written in a Greek not spoken in Athens: all have stayed in print for some considerable time.

Yet it seems that there are still those who have not learned their lesson. Articles appear from time to time which castigate novels and poetry on the ground that they use *archaisms*. Just when does a word become an archaism anyway? The definition on this island might be: as soon as some London reviewer says so. Does this sort of thing all stem from injudicious prattle about 'a man talking to men' and other remarks about bringing 'realism' into poetry? What exactly is meant by 'everyday language in poetry'? Language is a very specialised thing; it has many registers. The conditions on the back of a railway ticket are not written in the language appropriate to poetry, although there are some editors of anthologies who might be tempted to include them were they suitably carved up into lines by a poet of whom they approved. As soon as poetry becomes *genuine* 'everyday' language it ceases to be poetry. This is not to say that poetry cannot be written in colloquial language; it very often is, but if it is recognisably poetry it is not 'real' in the sense that *ordinary* everyday language is real. It is straining the reader's patience to make such an obvious point, but in these days of muddled thinking by reviewers *et al*, it certainly needs to be said. Poetry is *heightened* language. Poetry can also be filled to the brim with archaisms, borrowings, foreign words, new words, made-up words, dialect words, slang words and all sorts of assorted phonemes. Anyone who cannot see this ought to go back and read Shakespeare, or Joyce. One wonders if the critics who carp about which of the few coins in their little purse of words we shall use have in fact taken benefit from any reading at all.

Shakespeare muddles up the English use of 'shall' and 'will'. His pronunciation of English was quite violently different from Chaucer's and divided by the same large gap from the RP accents in which, until a few years ago, it was thought fitting to read him. He uses what were, in his own day, archaisms like 'kneen' for 'knees' and 'eyen' for 'eyes'. (The variant 'een' is still in use all over Scotland where it is certainly NOT an archaism.) He uses forms like 'honester' and 'violentest' which would doubtless gain the Highers student a red underline despite a protest backed by the Shakespearean canon. He invented words, borrowed words from other tongues and made up other phrases unique in his time which have become modern clichés. Joyce's *Finnegan's Wake* is an example of the same desire to play with words and phrases from all quarters. Why then should one attack the late Hugh MacDiarmid, no longer able to defend himself against such snipings, for doing just the same thing in Scots? This seems to me to be simply another example of 'the Scottish cringe'. MacDiarmid is being 'too Scottish' – so we will throw this baby out with the bath water – like almost everything else. Don't let us talk about tartan and bagpipes, not because these have become monotonous stereotypes, but because the Thames Valley Establishment will use them to poke fun at us.

What exactly do we mean by 'English'? I have of late started to call the English language the *lingua franca* for no other reason than that I find the term 'English' obfuscatory. Even in its Old English days it was not merely the tongue of Angles and Saxons. People of Celtic origin spoke it also ... the poet Caedmon, for instance; nor was it then, any more than today, a fixed canon, a fact that naive language 'purists' seem unable to assimilate. Constructions which fifty years ago would have been regarded as solecisms are now accepted by the linguistic 'establishment'. One of the remaining case-endings of English is now in the process of disappearing: the relative pronoun 'whom'. In this century English has become the equivalent of the Greek *koine* or mediaeval Latin. It is used by many different languages for international communication. But there are also many variants of English: Australian, South African, West Indian, East

Indian and – the major voice – American. These are proof against Thames Valley *folie de grandeur* despite anything the media may say or think. Americans are not going to stop putting the word 'gotten' into verses because some ill-educated London reviewer does not like it. If you want royalties galore (a good Gaelic word) aim for America, not London, and write good American soap operas.

Despite the burden of establishment antipathy, Scots and Gaelic poets continue to appear: there are still people who do speak these tongues; monoglot attempts to kill them off in favour of some absolute, fixed, 'standard English' which can only happen when English is as completely fossilised, like classical-period Greek or Latin, have failed under the impact of much excellent poetry in both languages. Poetry is still being written in our indigenous tongues for all the misguided sneers of those who know neither, but seem to gain a media platform on very slim grounds.

Fifty years ago it was regarded as 'common' to speak either Scots or Gaelic. Nowadays there is a kind of snob charisma around Gaelic while Scots continues, at one level or another, to be looked upon as vulgar. One often gets the feeling that alleged critics of Scottish literature who affect to despise the old language are motivated more by snobbery than literary concerns. The accepted pundits say things like ... "of course Scots was already dying in Burns' time" This is arrant nonsense. Scots was far from dead in my own boyhood Ayrshire. Scots is far from dead in the area in which this article is being written. Gaelic and Scots are both excellent media through which to read poetry because they still have a kind of freshness that standard English (I except the English 'dialects') is rapidly losing as far as the poetic voice is concerned. Modern usages of what Garioch called 'hen-hoose noises: uckin-uckin' are back in fashion. Chaucer's 'erses' and 'queynts' have been refurbished for modern use although the excellence of his metrics appears to be despised by our modern verslibrateurs. Even Larkin could not resist it. It is ironic that some appear to see these grand old words as giving a 'modern' flavour to their lines.

The basic feeling behind this extended use of the sexual and scatological word-hoard is not so much a desire in the writers to shock their grannies (who knew the words before they were born) as to give a tired language a short burst of lexical adrenalin. Scots, on the other hand, is so vigorous a tongue that it does not need this intravenous *nostalgie de la boue* though words such as 'aidle' and 'sharn' show the Scottish repertoire to be superior in the cloacal word-chest. That Scots is still robust enough and fresh enough to produce great poetry must be obvious to anyone with an ear. That MacDiarmid's revitalised Scots contains sustained passages of much beauty is obvious to any true poet and those who cannot hear the music should not lay claim to expertise in such matters.

One of the favourite ways of knocking Scots, used a great deal by such as have demonstrated their inability to use it, is to consign all poetry written in that tongue to what they are pleased to call the Kailyard. An expression first invented by Henley to debunk a group of sentimental rural writers is now used in a false context to condemn any rural writing in Scots. Nowadays the best Scots is spoken in rural areas and many writers in Scots live in such areas. Their work is usually a great deal less sentimental than the urban girnings of city poets writing in the establishment language to air their own synthetic *angst.* That good, hard writing in Scots is condemned as 'Kailyard' by writers ignorant of the origin of that term argues more for their obtuseness than their literary awareness. Presumably such critics would describe Hesiod's *Works and Days* or Virgil's *Georgics* as 'Kailyard'.

Much of the splenetic comment anent MacDiarmid (and other symbols of unrelenting Scottishness) seems to me to be rooted in the desire to toady to the London book market. Of course, getting poetry published is difficult enough without compounding the problems by writing in Scots, or Gaelic. But this is not a poetry problem, it is a marketing problem. Anyone who writes for the market ought to abandon the poetry field forthwith. If on the other hand a decision is made that poetry is the target to aim at, then such mercenary ploys should be abandoned. I am not saying that one should welcome the kind of foolish disregard given to Emily Dickinson by her contemporary critics. Most poets want to be read. But surely a run of two hundred (like Eliot's *Waste Land*) has a literary value beyond ten thousand volumes of mediocre maunderings aimed specifically at a lucrative market. The fact that nowadays most good poetry is in the first instance put out by small, brave publishers on a shoe-string budget ought to be a matter of shame to those well-heeled firms too mean to take the chance of losing what to them is, to use American, peanuts.

To write in Scots (or Gaelic) whether synchronic or 'plastic', whether colloquial or 'reconstituted', pure or macaronic, is neither a jingoistic harking-back, nor a bathetic nostalgia for Maclaren's Kailyard, but a genuine desire to find a strong poetic language which has deep relevance for the Scottish psyche. That there are young, forward-looking poets sufficiently aware of this and willing to carry on in the face of criticism by their elders (but not necessarily their betters) says much for the example set by the late MacDiarmid, George Campbell Hay, Robert Garioch and others whose work in native tongues will surely outlast that of their detractors. Notably none of these confined their work solely to indigenous tongues. They were all fine poets in standard English and the much-undervalued George Campbell Hay in all three languages.

A preference for poetry in standard English is not to be decried: to couple this choice with the denial of poetic validity to Scots, whether of MacDiarmid or any other, sounds more like simple malice than fair comment. To make one young Scottish writer lay down his pen because he feels inhibited, not by his own tongue, but by a despair induced by the sneers of those who care nothing for Scots and less for Gaelic (whatever their lip-service) does not make such critics the servants of literature. It indicates a slavery to their own unexamined prejudice.

This essay was first published in Chapman *61-2 (20th anniversary issue) – World Writing: Scottish Writing), September 1990*

Gerry Cambridge

The Light Windmill

The light windmill,
'the smallest sun power plant in the world', taken
out of its space-blue box,
perches today on my windowsill.

In its glass globe the four
squares of black metal
arranged round the central pin
on the small glass cylinder
start to spin

in the light from space –
a miracle!

The simple, lyrical
marriage of ray and mind
whirs with a tiny tinkle
like the masts of yachts in a squally harbour –

the black blades whirring
faster and faster as the sunlight strengthens,
slowing as a cloud
drifts over the sun, to a dead
stop.
            How the rays returning send it
into its circling frenzy –
as if the music powered the conductor's baton,

or as a leashed dog goes
crazy with innocent love
at its owner's return at the day's end.

Two Chirps at the Winter Solstice

I

To think of the crystal of snow: as if
   Hammered in permanent silver, though
Perfectly evanescent:
The blueprint, immortal, of the butterfly's wing:
   The ferned inscriptions of the frost. To think
Of the principles that exist beyond their object,
   Plato's ethereal diamond.
Ark in perpetual rain,
These thoughts that are like lanterns
   Immutably shining in immutable dark.

II

In the white perfection of snow descending
That was simplifying the whole
Intricate landscape back to an un-nibbed page,
I stood with the two great Clydesdales. They blew
Oven-breath through vibrating lips and shook
Their granite heads, grimaced – or smiled –
Displaying their yellow teeth.
When they stamped away disgruntledly,
I saw in that white simplicity
How they had left clear field beneath –
Twin and irregular shadows of green
Where each thrawn frame had been.

The Pluffman

"What is a pluffman?" – question by non-native speaker, on reading the word 'Ploughman'

A pluffman is a man whose pluff
Is not quite sharp enough
To slice the soil like the shining blade
Of the genuine plough, on the winter days.

A pluffman's not a rough man
And certainly not a tough man
Nor (usually) a gruff man.
He fears he may be a duff man,
Poor pluffman,
Even one of a kind.

While on every field bright tractors plough
The pluffman just looks down at his pluff
And shakes his head. He can huff and puff,
It'll make no difference. Who made this pluff,
He asks himself, out of such useless stuff?
He can't get started, even. The hopeless pluff
Sits and gazes at him with one bright eye,
A curious creature with a thick buff ruff
Made out of fluff, and its only sound is – wuff.
And that is why
I made the poor pluffman this poem to live in –
He'd not get far in the actual world.
The pluffman's pluff is not plough enough.

Fairy Story

Belfast

In The Crown she was half-demure,
Though the slipping strap of her bra
Contrived to keep her popular
With men who sniffed like dogs
    Round that allure.

In the street she took his arm.
She liked his face, she liked his height
Beside her in the old moonlight,
She liked the ambience of the night,
    His sleekit charm.

In the guest-room of the guest-house
She liked their mingled whispers, looks
Like covers of exciting books,
And the sense of guests all sleeping round,
    As they could rouse.

In the bed the one she longed to be
Kept on her wedding ring:
His entry was her freeing knife
In the broad back of another life
    Beyond the Irish sea.

The Break Up

Seen in Glasgow

They sit in the bar's loud corner, teatime Friday –
The clenched city loosening its ties,
                                        getting its gladrags on –
She, perhaps mid-twenties, he
Certainly old enough to be her father –
Under electric light.

She's power-dressed
To show her breasts to best
Advantage, rich full mouth waxed red,
Is gesturing flamboyantly
With cigarette for confidence, belying

Her kohl-rimmed eyes' big look –
Sporadically
        A fawn's
                Startled out of cover
To the ring of guns.

And suddenly she's crying,
She stubs the half-smoked cigarette
To ash, her eyes become wet gems,
The careful house of her composure
Clouds of dust and rubble
While he peers down at nothing on the beer-splashed table
And rubs his brow.

What is the old fool thinking of?

Only indifference can help her now.

Christmas Oranges

Clementines
                My dear one
Bought for me –

This pile of orange planets
On the fridge-top, caught in their nylon net.

Some
Baggily-skinned:
Hooking a thumb
                Easily under, then
The whole skin off in a one-er: some
Tighter, more
Reluctant to be separate
From their hearts of juice.
(Danger of making a flesh-sticky mess of those.)

Then breaking each open –
Fragrance of orange on the tips of the fingers –
Peeling away
Segment by segment
Held to this morning light
    that's coloured the juice of an orange, each
Segment veined like the petal of a rose –
To check for the shades of pips
In the cool translucence –
The thrawn wee buggers, the embryos

Lavish with thought of perpetual groves.

Criggie

Matthew Fitt

Senator Calvin Criggie opens his bawkie-bleck een an, for as lang as it taks twa ticks tae go roon, Criggie canna mind whaur he is.

The Senator's hauns jine automatically forenent his face. He canna stap his body tensin intae a foetal baw. There is suddenly swite on his tap lip. He gawks at the hauf-daurk room he finns himsel in but sees nothin throu the anonymous gloam that can reconnect him tae the world as he left it lest nicht.

He fechts tae stey calm but awready the flegs are raivellin throu him, chappin his braith intae wheezlie pechs, garrin him howk his een wi his nieves an kick wi radge-frichtened sturts at the bedclaes taigled aboot his feet. Afore he can think himsel oot, his dream-mogered imagination de-faults, flingin him back temporarily tae the cauld prison cell whaur he tholed fufteen fellie year o captivity on the Asian moontain city o Nanga Parbat.

Time chitters like haar as the roch cell waws, coorse wi damp an rodent kich, close roon aboot him yince mair. He grups his wime as hunger preens stob like dirks throu his gut. An as if the menyie o Ceilidh Rescue troops hadna shoodered in the prison door a twalmonth syne on Hogmanay an shot the loun deid like a radge deleerit dug, Hahn, the Senator's cell maister, lours again as he did for fufteen year in the baillie o the room, his goat an kye bowff claggerin Criggie's throat while he baitchels tae a pouder the banes in the Senator's neb wi his iron-tappit gowk stick.

Paralysed in slow-mo drow, Criggie canna richt breathe as panic threatens tae stap his thrapple. Fae his squatterin consciousness he recaws Doctor Hazelrig's words. "Think wi yir hauns, Senator. Let the air in tae let the pain oot." Gruntlin, he steers his fingirs tae his face an manages tae claw his gab. His mou this time isna stappit wi rags. His heid isnae wabbit fae chloroform. Criggie's no back on Nanga Parbat. Hahn's no here. Hahn is deid.

Criggie snaps on a licht. A lang elegant room wi capercaillie wawpaper jinks ontae his retinae. His siller Intimo briefcase stauns on a persian-ruggit flair. His suit jaiket an troosers hing on a peg at the door while his harrylauder oxter stick leans at a gley angle aside the bed.

His lugs register a fitstep ootside in the lobby, thon o his personal bodyguaird, Sam Boness, taragatin a shooglie board wi his Reidshank captain's tread. He spots his white pre-packit sark an senatorial Hie Hoose grauvit on the airm o a chair. Criggie's pulse resumes its regular dunt. 'Jeelie-knees,' he tells hissel aff wi venom. 'Richt wee jeelie-knees.'

Criggie has waukened in the guest wing o Windyhingin Shaw, a bonnieplenished dryland villa on Tinto Hill abinn the wattery landward o Lanark. The hoose belangs his Election Grieve, Congressman Simon Athelstane, whase Mercedes-Romeo Launlowper flew him here across the Gless Sea late lest nicht fae the sport an recreation glebe o the City's Hietoun district.

Muckillopolis yesterday wis a bobbinquaw o haun-grippin, bairn-kissin an lest minute canglin for votes. A denner for Loch Burgh's five thoosan firefechters follaed a tousie debate wi the weans at Ewan McGregor University in Kirk afore Criggie pit the final steek on his 2105 Presidential Election campaign wi a stoor-stompin speech tae pairty worthies at the Hietoun National Pictur Hoose, cowpin in the foremidnicht ontae his guest bed at Windyhingin Shaw wi three menyies o Reidshank snipers skailed across the law's staney ribs tae bield him in his sleep.

The alarm nock aside the nichtstand reads six-ten am. Criggie hirples tae the bathroom an empties a pish intae the cludge but doesnae flush. Huilin hissel oot o the silk pyjamaes lenned him by the Congressman's wife, he runs the bath tae it's fou wi a brose o almond an thrissle an then dooks his forty-five year auld scaur-scaddit body in tae the craigie. Echty craw-klicks awa across the Gless Sea, the electronic-yetts o Port's pollin hooses hae awready opened. Later the nicht at the ballot-coont in the Jim Baxter Memorial Sports Tron, Criggie's twinty-year ettle tae become the eleeventh Lord President o Port will finally rax its knowe-heid.

He shouldna be alive. Captivity on Nanga Parbat should hae shrivelled him tae a shaup. Thae years there, thrawned in weet, nippit cells, spulyied his youtheid an the yin leal love o his life an wid hae scunnered his appetite for the stushie o politics, tae, if no for learnin on release that his captors had been in the siller-sporran o enemies at hame.

Houstoun Spink, the bygane-Lord President that chored hissel three terms in Argyle Hoose, peyed in 2089 a raggitie punyie o Uighur separatists tae kidnap the twinty-nine year auld presidential candidate Calvin Criggie. Fleyed at the fire-flaucht popularity o the young Senator, Spink had postit his rival hyneawa tae the City's Asian Trade Staple on Bombay Island. When thon failed tae clary Criggie's wallie prospects at the polls, the auld warlock had him warsled awa in the dumb o nicht.

Spink, gollyin crocodile tears at Criggie's reportit deeth, that year bore aff the Presidential gree. Ainlie in 2103 when a glamshachie kidnapper wis deefied by Spink for blackmail siller wis the plot clyped til the meeja on Muckillopolis an Criggie unthirled.

Houstoun Spink nou legislates owre a haurd bink at Inverdisney Penitentiary but Reagan Spink Jnr, brou-skelped intae politics by his faither's gurr, has managed tae styter throu twa terms o office. A shooglie shadda o his faither, he is aw that stauns atween Criggie an the Lord Presidency but, wi Dada Houston's mispauchlins puddlin his son's campaign, the political spaewifes hae consigned the current President tae the bing o history. Gruppin his briefcase an trevel poke, he ootgangs the guest room tae the lobby whuddin the door shut ahint him. Criggie the day has a dynasty tae cowp.

His Reidshank bodyguaird strauchles tae attention fae a weel-upholstered nicht chair an, altho Criggie touers abinn maist o his peers, Captain Sam Boness meisures a heid an spauld-bane taller than him. His premature-lyart hair frames a youthfu face chowed at the edges by a lifetime's cark an care for bodies ither than himsel.

"Mornin, Senator."

"Ay, Boness. How's wir weather?"

The caber-boukit guaird gaithers up his guns. "No joco, sir."

A keek throu the lobby windae advises him o the day's coorseness. Awready, a string o kate-o-shanters has daurkened the Gless Sea atween Tinto an the City while, in the east, the turbulent lift is busy smiddyin thegither bigger, mair girnie altocumuli.

"The Congressman awa yit?"

"Haein breakfast, sir."

Criggie hauns his bodyguaird the briefcase, poke an jaiket. "Let's get tae it then, Sam."

They track their wey doon throu corridors lined wi McVeighs an Vettrianos tae the villa's laich kitchen, a space barely heid-hicht riggit wi bleck steel an reconditioned widd. The flair-tae-ceilin ermoured gless windaes keek sooth owre cushat-gray watter an the din mowdy tummocks o the Soothern Upland Hills.

"Senator. It's yirsel. Park the auld bahookitie. Birgitte's juist waashin the sleep fae her oxters, if ye ken whit ah'm sayin." Simon Athelstane leas aff slaisterin milk intae a joog an flits glegly owre fae a breakfast table o solid birk. The Congressman, wi a tae still in his thirties an a lang kibble body, hurls raither than walks as if he has sma time tae skail atween airts. The Birgitte mentioned is his gudewife, whase sunbed broon legs glistered maist o lest nicht in white cut-aff bermudas at the lanimer o Criggie's vision as he an Athelstane slainte mhath'd brandies on the villa's shadda-deck.

"Muckle day the day, Senator, if ye ken whit ah'm on aboot. Muckle day." The Congressman thrusts his richt loof at him. Three-oorly workoots an a cockapentie personal tailor keeps his figure trig, his appearance swack. The man reeks o new siller an altho three gurlie parliaments has learned him a meisure o sophistication an moyen, tae Criggie's mind an tae a fair few ithers, Athelstane has aye aboot his gait the guff o a used-body-pairts salesman. Walin him aheid o a dozen brawer politicians tae be his Election Grieve wis nae a decision cawed by the Congressman's barra-boy chairm. Criggie prefers no tae wunner hou mony in his pairty an the meeja micht hae guessed the richt reason for the choice, even if Athelstane hasna jaloused it for hissel.

"Nane bigger, Simon." He returns the birkie haunshake an pous oot a lang-backit chair.

Athelstane clatters an ashet, spinn an coggie doon in front o Criggie an scowks at Boness, staunin airms plettit aside the jawbox. "You no hae plenty maitters tae attend tae, Captain?"

The bodyguaird ill-ees Athelstane. He has his sodgers oot on the law tae de-redd an the hoose needs tae be swaibled again for bugs an eemock-cams but Boness is supposed tae tak orders ainlie fae Criggie. The Senator howanever has his gruntle in a spreid o the day's papers. Boness smiles. Considerin hou easy it wid be tae sned Athelstane's thrapple-pipe, the bodyguaird retreats fae the kitchen.

"Richt, know whit ah'm sayin?" The Congressman stobs open the wee-screen o a personal-redder an leets aff tae Criggie the day's programme. "Doc Hazelrig will see ye at eleeven for yir physio. Then a Senate Launlowper will tak ye tae the City for twa o'clock. Wir first TV tryst is at Channel 8. Then we've Shammybraw, Port The Day, Campsie Cooper Wants Tae Ken an the Josie Bryce Shaw aw the wey up tae seeven. We're pairty-hoppin until the votin staps at midnicht an then – ah hope ye winna mind – ah've pinselled ye in for a wee snotter o sleep at wir private suite – the Presidential, allow me, eh? – at the Pyot Knowe Hotel on Hietoun whaur we'll hing on for the result. That's due in juist efter three am the morn's morn."

"Nae time for a quick roond o gowf, then?" Criggie raxes for a daud breid an smeerichs it wi hinnie.

"Ah'm afraid no, Senator." Athelstane pooches the redder. "When ye're no speakin til the meeja, ye'll hae tae be oot haun-creeshin until the pollin hooses shut. We've got three hunner thoosan pilgrimers stowin oot the hotels in Ocean Haven aheid o Max Jaffray's arrival on Wednesday. An fufty thoosan Azeri fitba supporters stottin aboot still tryin tae find their hotels efter lest nicht's gemm."

"Oh ay, whit wis the score?"

"Scotland Wan, Azerbaijan Nil. A fou hoose at Hampden an fowre million watchin at hame."

Criggie tummles ane o the papers owre tae its hin-page."Fine that. Naethin like a Scotland win tae pit the folk in a guid tid, especially on election day. We'll hae tae invite Chae Whitlaw owre tae Argyle Hoose tae git his photie took."

"We'll hing on tae see if they qualify first." Athelstane scarts a note in his diary. "The return leg's mid-week at Alta Tehran. If the General can pauchle us a draw, then we'll think aboot photies."

"The General? Is that whit we're cryin him? Well, ah'll certainly need tae gie Mr Whitlaw a phone afore he leaves."

"An can ah spier aboot yir speech?"

Criggie claps his heid. "In here, ma freend. Dinna you fash. Ah've had fufteen year tae work on it an ah ken it like ah ken masel."

Athelstane nods an pits his pen an redder awa intil a briefcase. "Ah'm shair it's braw. Calvin, ah've a couple o blackdugs nippin ma back, if ye ken whaur ah'm comin fae."

Criggie kens exactly which airt the Congressman's comin fae. Athelstane, the electronics exec that bocht, bullied an whistle-binkied his wey tae a Laich Hoose portfolio, has been guddlin for weeks tae finn oot if he'll be offered a post in the new Lord President's Cabinet.

"Can we no dae this efter, Simon?"

"Weel, see, ah'm fleein tae North Law Burgh in aboot ten minutes. An awfie lot o dinnae-kenners owre there. Need tae mak sure oor chapfolk are at the richt doors. An ah'd raither no talk aboot this in front o the wife, if ye ken whit ah'm..." – Athelstane grups his briefcase ticht til him – "but see the morra when ye wale yir cabinet. Will ye be mentionin ma name?"

The Senator, if he could, widna hae Simon Athelstane in his road. Aneth the ootward nouveau-lairdie exterior, the man is aw geck an grab. Criggie tries but canna ayewis keep his puggie cool. "Sure, ah'll be mentionin it.

Nou is that awthin or have ye ony ither bleck dugs nippin at yir taes?"

Criggie watches the anger staun up an jig in Athelstane's een. "Ah thocht the university wis interestin yesterday, if ken whit ah'm gettin at?"

"No really," he replies, harlt for a moment he micht hae chauved the Congressman tae sair.

"Well, ye'd hae tae be a richt cauld tattie tae no notice the stramash o bonnie lassies up there. When ye're President, ye'll need a wife. Canna hae the Lord President high-kiltit an the claik o the toun. Ken whit ah'm steerin at. Ye'll juist hae tae nip yirsel a bonnie wee postgrad."

"Dinna be daft, Athelstane. Ah've got a face like an auld baffie."

"Are you kiddin? They'll lap ye up. Get them gaun aboot yir trevels, fleg the g-strings aff them wi yir wee stories aboot Nanga Parbat."

Bealin, Criggie scuds the cafetiere back ontae its coaster. He'd been, twa year, tap-bannock wi a staff o three thoosan at the Himalaya mission on Bombay Island when they took him. Heid in a poke, airms in airns, fourteen an a hauf year wi Hahn an his gowk stick, jabbin, clourin, kittlin. The trauma a year efter is still fresh scartit on the circuits o his harns. Ony mention o Nanga Parbat, even in glaikit banter, channers him tae the pock. The body-pairts salesrep should ken better. He taks his coffee tae the kit-chen windae an glowers doon ontae the jabblin expanse o the Gless Sea.

Deef an blinn in his middenie Kasmiri tolbooth, the Senator didna witness the eldritch alterations nature wrocht on the planet an the gleebries o ocean controlled by Muckillopolis. The continent-happin floods, that had drooned the earth tae its tapmaist kips, peaked at the century's hin end, subsequently dwynin, devallin ten meter a year owre the next decade. A gowp at a time, the Atlantic an Pacific returned bittocks o whit they had smoored durin God's Flood in the form o lang thin dry-land whangs that appeared, like the runkled gairters on a pillie-wanton's leg, roon escarpments, alpine-plateaux an on the laicher braes o the Hieland an Lowland hills, cowpin real estate prices tae the bottom o the meal bowie.

Afore, ainlie Port's high-heids an siller-daddies could afford a hoose on the bens whaur men like Athelstane plenished their palaces wi Tuscan foontains, brushbox timmer flairs an gowd-gildit cludgies. But since the watters' retreat, clanjamfries o middle-cless beengers an ledder-spielers hae been fechtin like caterans tae clatch up dream bothies on every spare rig an neb o grund gaun. On the rocky hochbands o Tinto Law, Criggie merks that the auld-empire villas like Windyhingin Shaw are weel on the road tae lossin the gree tae the condos an broon-tiled howfettes that run doon in heeligoleerie order tae the watter's edge.

"Dat's wis oot a Bollinger, Simon. Du should buy some mair. Hit fairly luiks ta me lik we micht be needin hit." Birgitte Athelstane, a watergaw kimono loose owre her lythe hurdies, sclaffs intae the kitchen in licht espadrilles.

"Ay." The Congressman meets her wi a grin that isna returned. "An whit else for ma darlin?"

Birgitte poors a gless o orange an taks a lazy gowp at it. "Naethin else."

"Ah wis juist sayin tae the Senator here that we should see aboot gittin him a bidey-in. Whit dae ye think?"

Birgitte snakes an airm roon her gudeman's waist. Even in hodden hoose sandals, she is taller an brawer than him. Criggie finds her sair tae look at, this twa an thirty year auld beauty wi a lassie's body an howtowdie's smile.

"Göd idee," she snirls. "Lat's reffel him up richt noo wi Frieda Ramsay. Pass du me da phone."

"Frieda Ramsay? Her? Naw, ken whit ah'm sayin. Weeter than the gravedigger's neb, that yin." Athelstane gruggles up his face, then dichtin a dry brou, grins owre at the Senator. "Got ye oot o that, Criggie. You owe me guid style."

Criggie nods his heid. "Oh, ah owe you awricht."

His host glisks theatrically at the gowd watch on his sheckle. "OK. That's me got tae buzzle. Ah'd love tae gab here aw day but ah seriously have tae nash. Somebody's got tae mak sure we win this election, if ye ken whit ah'm on aboot."

While he pinkie-dials a code intae his phone an the rotors o his Alfa Romeo Landlowper croichle intae motion on the heli-plet ootside, Criggie's an Birgitte's een scance at each ither a second.

"Channel 8. Hauf-twa. Dinna be late."

"Mind da champagne." Birgitte's voice tails aff intae the eemock o a whisper while aye at the windae Criggie sweels the coffee roon the bottom o a gless mug. Nane speaks. They listen as the copter's blades tulyie the air an heeze the Congressman intae the weatherie Tinto sky.

"Tinks du dat he kens?" Birgitte flits tae the kitchen's french windae an stares throu the buhlitt-resistant pane.

"Mibbe." Criggie glaiks at Birgitte's back. The mornin sun taigles aboot her silhouette wrappin her in a rosie o licht.

"He tinks du'll gie him a post i dy cabinet. Hit's aa he spaeks aboot."

"Ah'll work him in somewhere." Criggie moves tae staun forenent her.

"Calvin. We hae tae white dis. Hit's jöst gyaain ta hurt wis. I mean, du wis boarn ta steer dis toun." Birgitte spins roon, the strang line o her face blearie wi concern. "Hit's dy life. Hit's whit du kens."

Criggie raxes Mrs Athelstane tae him an, doucely fauldin back her kimono, kissocks her bare shooder. "Ah ken nothin. Juist that ah miss you."

"Du sudna be here, Senator. Du sudna even be here." Birgitte turns awa till she is atween him an the windae but wi his braid bouk, Criggie caws her gently forrit an hauds her. His tongue trevels doon the lang curve o her neck an she closes her een, airchin hersel against the gless o the buhlitt-proof windae. The goun slidders tae the flair. Her breists press at the cauld pane. Criggie haps her completely in his airms an a sab cuts in ablow each short braith she taks. His mooth spiers for hers as he pugs her roon an they kiss.

"Du's no listenin ta me." She says, pushin awa fae his passionate slaichs. "Du'll loss aathin dis wye."

"Wheesht, lassie," Criggie whuspers an, wi a harlie fingir, staps a tear on her cheek an cairries her ben tae hers an her gudeman's bedroom.

George Mackay Brown

Kestrel Roseleaf Chalice

Twelfth Century Norse Lyrics

1: The Accomplishments of an Earl

Chessboard, tiltyard, trout-stream
know my sweet passes.
Old writings are no mystery to me
nor any modern book.
Ski across winterfold flashes.
Deep curves I make with arrow and oar.
I know the twelve notes of a harp.
At the red forge
my clamorous shadow is sometimes rooted.

2: Merchant Ship

Five weeks our keel lay choked
in Grimsby mudflats.
Lugworm and silt, a foul gray honey.
Unfurl, white sail
eastwards, over the loose waves,
a fishing skua
to the hard rock of Bergen.

3: The Westray Monks

Sixteen walkers about the church,
heads bare as stone,
long striders, deep-voiced, rough-handed.
"Brother wind, gentle sister raindrops" –
That's what they call this black whirl of storm.
They haven't a sword between them.
Here they come, in procession,
demure and harmless as girls.

Earl Rognvald Kolson

4: The Burning of a Welsh Village

Brits, did you order cheap kindling?
We poured flame through your walls this morning
till the sun was a cinder.
Stay in the wood, farmers.
We took our pay in advance,
silver coins from a niche here and there.
Sweyn was your coalman.

Cracked hearthstone, charred rooftree.
No flint, bellows, or fireside talk next winter.

Eric the Icelander

5: A Shipwreck in Shetland

Help and *Arrow*, those slender seekers,
scatter to a hundred boards.
Women may weep for that
but the poets
are glad of shipwrecks many a winter night.
The sailors, shamed,
will ravel their sea-skills with a tougher thread.

I've swallowed mouthfuls of sea.
They gladdened me more
than the best wine or mead.
The sea sings like a girl over my half-drowned feet.
With shivering mouth
I draw the hammered snake-ring from my finger.
I pledge myself to Our Lady of the Waves.

In a princely coat, stiff with runes and dragons,
I leapt from the wreck.
Cold now, sea-insulted,
I shiver at a Shetland fire.
With tattered sealskin
the women cancel my nakedness.

Asa the Servant-girl's Song

D-don't d-dare laugh at me,
N-n-norsemen.
I want a s-seat at the f-f-fire.
Ice in my b-bones!
I f-fell in a well in the f-fog.
It was water to sweeten your ale.
M-make way, easterling!
That th-thick arm, if you were to wrap it round me,
might make my teeth quiet.

Einar, laird, though at your board
you give room to no stranger
unless the chief stranger come, the Earl,
yet set out horns
and ring your hearth with benches.
Tonight I am riding
to visit your unpopular house.
The Earl in a fisherman's coat

stumbles on seawet rocks, and
a woman mocks him

"If you fall on land, crab-killer,
how will you fare in a rowdy sea-reel?"
... Cacklings from the crag above.
Fisherman, up with your cowl.
Show that hag
a sea lord, commander of ships.

6: Duel in a Tapestry

Two figures, one a dwarf
burdened with hump and sword,
a sewn glittering toad,
the other a skipper horizon-eyed –
in this lordly web
they dance, fixed and futureless.
Will hunchback pierce hero?
A witch's question.
The swords cross, quiet as fish, in the linen.

7: The Earl Attacked by a Madman

Verse is a golden ring, a gathered silence.
Nobility a cloak, quartered.
Heroism a rune, cold cuttings on stone.
Today in the claw of frenzy
I fluttered, a naked soul.
Masks and songs were no longer a comfort to me.
Earl Rognvald Kolson

8: Crusaders

Storm bends mast like a frantic bowman.
We've salt in our mouths.
To starboard, the loop and curve of the Humber,
and Anglia, a low coast.
Hug the fire, clodhopper.
Ride home, councillor
on measured stone-ringing hooves. *Armod Earlsskald*

9: The Strait of Gibraltar

Three happy days I remember,
the hunt on the mountain,
then ale and talk
beside a fire in the castle
– not those hogsheads of salt
splashing our shields!
The Earl spurs the ship,

a gray stallion
between Europe and Africa. *Oddi Little*

10: Ermengarde of Narbonne

Your hair, lady
is long, a bright waterfall.
You move through the warriors
rich and tall as starlight.
What can I give
for the cup and kisses brought to my mouth?
Nothing.
This red hand, a death-dealer. *Earl Rognvald Kolson*

Farewell to Narbonne

A gale of beauty – like rosepetals
my breath scattered.
Throw, voyagers, now
a last farewell to Ermengarde.
(The cut-throats on the rowing bench
as well as Armod
had one wild dream,
to toss and snore in her bed.)
O heart-broken poet –
that gold-and-ivory forehead! *Armod Earlsskald*

Love Song

The summer mouth of Ermengarde
commands two things –
a sea of saga-stuff, wreckage, gold,
as far as Jordan,
and later, at leaf-fall,
on patched homing wings
a sun-dark hero.

Love and War

White as snow
white as silver
the lady,
a beauty all whiteness,
a kindness
red as wine.
Another redness, fire
about the castle,
a sharp whiteness, swords. *Earl Rognvald Kolson*

11: Instruction to Birds

Between this snow
and the lucent solstice
compel the sunwheel,
seek the balance
of light and winter,
rose and skull
in seeded islands.
Furl, crosswings, there.
Find in a door
a girl with skeins
and a wooden wheel.
Say to the cold one
'Lady, your lover
left the scarred skippers,
eager he entered
the querns of war,
Sigmund's shield
to castle came earliest.'
Sweet throats
at an April threshold.

Sigmund Fish-hook

12: In Praise of Audun, the first warrior to board the African Ship

Audun the Red
was the earliest reaper
in this harvest.
Black sheaves
fell on the dromond.
Flame-bearded Audun
was complete gules.
Erling's Audun
through fire and blood
bound his red harvest.

Earl Rognvald Kolson

13: Poet on Watch

Night. Sheets of salt.
Armod on ship-watch.
A wash and heave of lights from the island.
The lads of Crete
toss in hot tumbled linen.
This skald on watch,
cold, burning, unkissed.

Armod Earlsskald

14: Elegy for Thorbjorn Black, Poet

Lift him, sailors
Thorbjorn with the black beard.
Bear gently, poets,
the harp of Thorbjorn.
Carry with candles
the king's friend
down to the crypt of the kirk.
Requiem aeternam da ei.
Southern stones,
pile over Thorbjorn Black a bright howe.

Oddi Little

15: Jerusalem

We stand here, shriven,
a hundred warmen lustred with penance,
in each hand.
Assoiled from murders, whoredoms, thievings now
a leaf of palm.
Footsteps, free and fated, turn
to the fourteen redemptive lingerings
and the hill marked with this sign.

Earl Rognvald Kolson

16: A Mass at Sea

We left our shares to rust
on a northern hill,
exchanged oxen for green and blue tramplers!
Poet, peasant, priest,
one ark of pilgrims
out of the dragon sea, a seeking
into the lucencies of Christ.
(Salt furrows we make
under your headlands, Byzantium.)
Sin darkens the grain-hoard.
We have branded their coasts with rage and lust,
the old dragon-breath.
No end of sorrow, soultroth, still.
Kyrie, Christe, Kyrie eleison
The Golden Harvester
seeks orient, our swineherd mouths.

Earl Rognvald Kolson

Peter Maxwell Davies *(1991) by John Bellany*

All these poems by George Mackay Brown are previously unpublished. The John Bellany portrait here is to celebrate the extensive collaboration between Mackay Brown and Maxwell Davies.

from *The Voyage of Magnus Quoy*

1: The Guardians

A cradle between a fire and a jar

Chorus of Women

the crying is over
the two cries are over
a child is born.

Let the new child lie
in the small ship
between the fire and the water.

In the silence after birth
we come. We stand
about the cradle, under the morning star.

Soon the women
from the hill and the shore
will come with gifts.

We have more ancient gifts
for the voyager,
for all who proceed from the first to the last bourne.

Courage. I bring the gift of courage.
He will need courage
out there, among the bringers of pain,
wolf-mask and hawk-mask.
Caritas, I bring the gift of kindness.
May he break his bread here and there
among hands glad or thankless.

Laughter. May the child have joy.
In the word and in the world,
not laughter of laceration,
the healing laughter
that holds a people together.
After the city gates
are stones broken and blackened
then there is need of a glad mouth.

Courtesy. Here is that gift.
Where is courtesy to be found,
in high houses?
In high houses are only masks of courtesy.
It is found more often
at hearths and doors of poor people.
A fragrance under the lintel.

Questing. I carry the gift of unquietness.

He should be seeking and finding out
man's blood is vagrant blood
let him unlock far horizons.

Where are our sisters? One
sits at a wheel, she spins a thread.
One gathers the threads in a loom.
The mother sleeps.
The voyager turns in his sleep.
The cloth in the loom is white.
The first neighbour
is on the road with a gift,
a hollow fresh from wheel and kiln.

Light the candle. Out there
is grayness. Even
in a good time, grayness. Often
the tall tower of keeping is red and black.

Cover the child with the white finished cloth.

Pole Star

1
Gentlemen, I propose the ship
be called 'Pole Star',
that heavenly body
having guided many a ship master
past northern reefs and shoals.

2
Now on every headland
stands a white column
crowned by a flame, mirrors, magnifiers.
There, lighthouse by lighthouse
'Pole Star' drops anchor.
The boat goes into the gully
with three keepers of the light,
bakehouse loaves,
letters, papers, eggs, rope, barrels of oil.

3
Now that my fishing boat 'Emily Jane'
is fit only, turned upside down
to be a henhouse
or, broken, to feed the fire
with a thousand sea stars,
they're wanting a deck hand
for this 'Pole Star'.
No more fish guts, bleeding fingers.

4
Sixty miles west of Birsay,
the Sule Skerry
where the selkie prince
suffered the sea change
and came to Lady Odivere's hall.

The teller of tales, Stevenson,
his grandfather, I think
built the lighthouse on Suleskerry.

The prince and the lady
greet sailors and keepers now
through their sea-masks.
Numbers tend the flames now, not men.
'Pole Star' unriveted, sheet and bolt,
a chrysalis of rust.

5
The 'Pole Star'
as familiar to Hamnavoe folk
as the two green islands,
as the granite hill.

6
When we were boys
we saw the old captains
toiling up Hellihole Road
to big houses behind the town.

7
How many ghosts of seamen?
Among the salt shades
I greet Attie Campbell, lover of Burns:
great laugher, mighty beerman.

Midsummer

Teacher: "Children, describe in a simile the sun."
A child with dark hair: "The sun is like a daffodil."
A small thief from the hill: "The sun's a honeycomb in the Laird's garden."
Bright-ringlets wrote, "The sun is like Jimmo the blacksmith's fire."
Number four (Bubble-nose), "The sun's a lion in a cage."
And Jenny who had a black cat: "We are all pieces of the sun. We rise. We dance. We scatter. We lie down at last in the sea – in nests of flames – or under the hill."
The sixth boy was blind: "Could the sun be a fish, or a candle, or a piece of bread?"
The seventh boy meshed dark lashes between six squares of window-gold and a quicksilver glister: "Pirate Ship". He saw blood on the bones of his hand.

Harvey Holton

Ae Wristwatch

circa 1949

Its thon time again   o derkness
an renewal   o empiness an lift
clean white broken teeth   grin
frae   the smertist mooth
In weit deserts   nae finches sing
the yird is wee   nae blae planet
sings   the skull is skelital
an skailt harns   melt plankton
green an bricht as gress shuild be
Times haunds tick   in the nicht
weel seen   banes rot
in leevin flesh   an flesh rots
tae the deein bane   wi practise
time itsell   maks an remaks
the same grin   skin
maks the same form   face
the ain that gomerils   micht wear
asleep tae tell time in the nicht
the lowe o licht   oan the wrist
ticks tear at   flesh an bane
seconds an meenits   rot meat
green grows   ae licht in the derk
the virr o the watch   times cage
catcht   geared teeth tock
click   the next ains past
gone   gaithert
the next ticks kent   noo
then   when
mushrooms mak   the winter
clood

Back tae the Borders (early workings)

bleck moors   heather fuu
sheep shorn   fleece fuu
sheets shewn   airms puu
string breks   oo as new

lanolyn reeks suffolk cross
blackie eats wuids loss
marino bleets Southern Cross
cheviot meats wuids loss

leathers place   mills tak
souters grace   weavers mak
Ridins race   toons mak
their place   fowk tak

mill thirlt   Tweed made
salmon birlt   cleeks played
catch made   Bluidcairt laid
mill thirlt   Tweed made

blue bleck   sitkas staund
hill laund   pleuchs brek
sheeps neck   needles braund
amorphous saund   circuits brek

oval baw   siller brings
gowd anaw   waddin rings
siller brings   gowd anaw
silicon stings   factories faw

weetoons snap   awebodies crack
collies mak   naebodies lap
langheids tap   langsynes sack
bodies hack   memories map

Forest Flooers   wuid brings
bluid rings   honest ooers
watters pooers   saws sing
work comes   short an coorse

yirds tae yoak

Ae Haund

In the sough o the wund
In the swowe o the ocean
whaur gress gies tae rait
whaur bole gies tae leaf
whaur time gies tae yirdpul
whaur space is bent
the stag in deep wuid barks
Ae birk reeshles an its ae breath
gars the hail wuid tae blinter
as leaf efter derk leaf turns tae licht
as licht efter sherp licht turns tae leaf
the fact o the hail wuid grows
Totterin ayewies oan expansion
the thocht gars the veesion
as nicht the day grows

as flooer gies tae fruit
Smell noo the days passin
whaun the rain soaks the yird
an the lift sings sae fer awa
Find the wie bi deid sters licht
an yestereen shines clear the morra
in the wie its been done
in the wie it is done
in the wie it will be done
Nae trinity gars this be
for tae pick ain o the three
pits the fowrth oot o kilter
Its the sters whit mak the nichts bleckness
forge ain in licht an the hail poem blinters
muckle wie its ain daith
Ae hand oan the rock its ain tale tells

B: Goal

A maun screive ma ain goal
licht in the net sees the bars
o a music an cell fertile an catcht
a lane strike glorious in its ain prison
its ain moment a new chord in the licht
a new roped knot wild in the kennin o itsell
burst in the same kennin o time an space
an ainly ain fuit maks the measure, the bend
o gravity, the feel o the final fugue
ayont the iron oan the winnocks o its ain place
lang the veesion the pass tae the empy pairt
that runners yet wull reach in this gemm
in this muckle intensity o the makin o its ain sell
the craft is cracked the file fades intae fileins
the stoor o freedom blaws oan the page
like gies tae like a keepers angles shine
but nae save is safe in this movement
this glaury grund pits mass oot o kilter
nae baw spins strecht intae the net o the sters

A Fragment

sense paitterns sentence structures bind
synaptic structures in the words mind
whar veesion sees wie the senses kind
the days dwams in this nicht anaw

an exercise in rhyme:

Liz Niven

Sang o Bernadette

At ma tenth birthday ma Ma surprisit me,
"A'm takin ye tae the Picters".
Spirits soared, the Picters wis wan thing,
mum tae masel wis anither.

Post-war Pathe News cracklt
lik soor ploom sweetie pokes.
Mum an me lik twa pals.

The Song of Bernadette,
A wee lassie that becomes a saint.
Seein Mary at a grotto she fun
she cuid work miracles.

Her faimilie praised her, neibours flockt,
priests gaithert tae hear her blessin.

That faur fae a Glesca wean's life:
black sannies in summer, black wellies in winter.
Places o worship, the Church, Parkheid.

An noo ye swore ye'd be a nun,
Inhale sweet incense, stroke rosaries,
walk wi a saint's walk, barefit throu convents.

Next, yer Confirmation; bride-white dress,
real shoes. A jowl-slappin Bishop fills ye
wi holy Spirit.

Smeddum ye'd need much later,
tae say ye'd given up that Faith,
the sang lang deid in yer thrapple

This Delicious Attraction

(for Anjum Malik in Manchester)

Exotic,
in your
red embroidered sari
and your tapping, tapping feet
as you read us out your poetry
with its rhythmic, moving beat.

Green parrots, desert sands
cultures and traditions
from some far off Asian lands.

A delicious attraction

of Pakistani music
with its beats of eights and fours
accompanied our efforts
as we stumbled on the floor.

But our heavy Scottish feet
just couldn't find the beat
or the dainty, sultry movements
of your graceful pointed feet.

Such delicious attraction.

Sweeping off to leave us
in a blaze of reds and golds
we watched grey skies return
with their soulful Scottish cold.

It's hard to comprehend
why you left those Asian lands
with their glamour and their climate
for an island less than grand

What delicious attraction?

Two Wanlockhead Poems

1. Touch the Lucky Lead

If only it was so easy
but fate's sealed the future.

No fortune's found
at a forefinger's touch;
the spot rubbed clean,
lead shining silver
on cold cave walls.

Transforming base materials,
it's what we all want;
lives altered to perfection overnight,
when really we work away silently,
long term.

Rubbing till we've fashioned
an existence into
something manageable.

Sometime striking gold.

Note: At Wanlockhead mining village, the miners would rub a patch on the wall at the entrance to the cave, in the hope that they would not be involved in an accident and that they might find precious metals.

2. Fern

Here, deep in a cave dark,
lacking air, a fern grows.

Fed by the smallest drip
seeping from lead slate

it's flourished.
See its glossy leaves shine.

Watch the water caught
in the camera's quick lens,

green fronds outstretched like palms.

That life can spore
and grow in such frail light!

Celebrate the shadows,
for fresh starts can fall out of them.

Around us, unseen,
nothing need be truly lost.

Slowly, much is possible,
even from darkness.

Frontiers

Behind Beijing lay the monastery,
high on a hill at Badachu.
We climbed towards the blue sky,
watched Buddhist monks toil in
saffron robes, tend plants, herbs.
A song drifted,
rhymed with wind chimes,
curled its notes through
pink shrubs, buzzing insects,
fell away into the city smoke below.
We knew that tune,
Auld Lang Syne, now *Old Friends*
in Mandarin.
Our home land seemed so far while abroad,
but we'd glimpsed that harmony, unity,
that knows no frontiers.

Illustration by Shona Dougall

supporting Scotland's written heritage through

The Callum Macdonald Memorial Award

(for poetry pamphlets)
sponsored by the Michael Marks Charitable Trust
and assisted by the Saltire Society

The Robert Louis Stevenson Memorial Award

(for published writers of fiction, poetry,
travel and children's books)
jointly supported by Scottish Arts Council and NLS

The NLS/ Saltire Society Research Book of the Year Award

(for original scholarly research in Scottish subjects)

In addition to these annual awards, the National Library of Scotland acquires manuscripts and archives of Scottish writing by gift and by purchase

For further information contact the Library on
0131 622 4807
or email events@nls.uk

Hamish Whyte

Three Glasgow Haiku

Safeway plastic bag
floats past my first-floor window:
where's the messages?

Green domes and frosty
streets: winter sun on Glasgow
glowing like Florence.

Between tenements
the moon hangs huge and golden:
aura of New Year.

What Can a Poem Say?

what can a poem say
    that a look can't?
what can a poem say
    that a touch can't?
what can a poem say
    that a kiss can't?
what can a poem say
    that sex can't?
what can a poem say
    that words can't?

Oh

The slight hearing loss
we each suffer from
means we sometimes
fail to catch the sense
of ends of sentences
but what we don't fail
to grasp and gasp at are the
vertiginous silent moments
of all this passion stuff –
like the fat magpie
balancing on the phone wire
outside the window:
of course it's going to fall
and of course it doesn't.

Angel, Torridon

Hi there, says the biker girl
in the garden of the last house
in Alligin, as I trudge past
with my new haversack
and silly sun hat. She smiles:
long red hair, big in leathers.
From the seat up the hill
I look back and see her
still standing at the gate
the Harley against the wall.

Prepositions

We walked from Kilchattan Bay
and stopped to picnic
on mutton pies and Blue Ribands
in the ruined inn
at the southern tip of Bute
the place of many a last
Caledonian bite
before the open sea

The Scale of Things

We talk about the scale of things
and weigh our lives against the awfulness
of history on tv, in books –
it's easy to reduce ourselves
to utter insignificance,
the clichés are always at the ready.
But listen to my old Uncle Tom
in Canada who sends money
every year to my mother:
he says, "Have lunch be happy."

Kwik-Unpick

Ruth Thomas

At school, Wendy Bellinger's accident was the main subject of the day. *Wendy got knocked down by a hit and run driver.* Some reports suggested that Wendy was dead, others that she was in a vegetative state. Everyone cleared a respectful little space around her best friend Joanne as she stood by the vending machine, putting 40p in the slot for a cup of hot chocolate.

"Hi, Joanne," Sheena Woodward said in her small, nasal voice. She sidled towards her and put her hand in the crook of Joanne's elbow. Accidents, Joanne had noticed, could generate a whole new crowd of friends.

"How's Wendy?"

"Not great, really. She's all bandaged up."

"Poor Wendy. How awful," Sheena said, and a little cluster of people gathered around them, nodding and mumbling.

"She wasn't knocked out or anything," Joanne replied, spilling some of her drink.

"Yes, but even so. Exactly the same thing happened to my dog."

"Did he get a broken jaw?"

"No, he just got run over."

"But he was OK?"

"No, he died." There was a pause while Joanne stood and drank. She had an image of Wendy in bed with bandages around her face and Mr and Mrs Bellinger sitting beside her, saying positive things. Tears moved down her face and mixed with the taste of hot chocolate. After a while Sheena supplied her with a Handy-Andy. Sheena always had things like Handy-Andies.

School continued to be inconsequential. School was like that. For instance: the skirt she was making. For the best part of a year, she had been making a skirt in Needlework. It was an A-line skirt, which the pattern said was *Very Easy, Très Facile.* Except it wasn't. It was not *très facile*. She had cut it out in September and now it was June. She kept sewing up the wrong seams, and having to take the stitches out again with a Kwik-Unpick. And even the Kwik-Unpick wasn't quick. Needlework was full of lies.

"I can't believe you've done it again, Joanne," Miss Nedley said, the week of Wendy's accident. She sat behind her Bernini sewing machine, held the gingham material taut in both hands and stared at it. This time, Joanne had managed to sew the pocket to the waistband. Over the months, the material had become thin with despair and tiny holes. The models on the pattern seemed to mock her, simpering and swinging their *very easy* skirts around in the breeze. "Look at Michaela," Miss Nedley said, "Michaela is on her third blouson."

Joanne had thought Miss Nedley might be easier on her that week, but she wasn't. Maybe she didn't know about Wendy's accident. But surely she must have. She glared at Miss Nedley, cold-hearted Miss Nedley, as cold as her packets of needles. Then she took her skirt back, returned to her desk and sat looking at it. Everybody hated A-line skirts. That was, no doubt, why Miss Nedley had chosen the pattern.

"Don't let the bastards grind you down," whispered Katie Black across the desk. Katie had recently become a rebel, bleaching her hair and wearing bovver boots. Maybe it was something to do with the fact that her father was a vicar. But even Katie – even Katie! – had managed to finish her skirt and was now onto the *delightful stuffed toy for a child.* As far as the completion of skirts went, Wendy was the only one who'd been just as bad as Joanne. She and Joanne had been The Third Years Who Did Not Complete Their Skirts, just as they had once been The First Years Who Disrupted the Leaver's Ceremony, standing outside the assembly room practising a dance routine. They hadn't known they were disrupting the Leaver's Ceremony until Miss Dock had come wading out of the hall to tell them they were "bringing the school into disrepute". And Joanne and Wendy had looked back at Miss Dock, their little transistor radio still playing *Hey Mickey* on the tarmac. And they had smiled.

Now, without Wendy, there was nothing to talk about. Nobody to dance with. The year was rushing towards the meaningless, dog-end days, when people skived, or did stupid, life-endangering things, or left early to go for family holidays in Weston-Super-Mare. Teachers appeared in class wearing embarrassing summer clothes. Miss Nedley had a hideous cheesecloth smock, through which you could make out a beige bra.

At lunchtime the blackboard announced Shepherd's Pie, Pea's and Carrot's. Somebody should tell the cook about apostrophes, Joanne thought. Pea is what? Carrot is what?

"Are you going to visit Wendy this afternoon?" Sheena Woodward asked, standing behind her with a chipped melamine tray.

"Yeah," she replied, "I go every Wednesday."

"What are you missing?"

"Geography and Music."

"Lucky you."

"Yeah. Laugh a minute." Joanne shuffled up the queue and watched a huge mound of mashed potato being hurled onto someone's plate.

"I wish it was Needlework," she said.

"But Needlework's OK' said Sheena. "It's quite nice."

"No it's not, Sheena. Needlework is not quite nice."

There was something annoying about Sheena, but she couldn't put her finger on it. A kind of innocence. A sweet frumpiness. Joanne was not entirely sure she wanted to be her friend.

"Why do the cooks always chuck a load of potato on your plate, even when you ask them not to?" she asked.

"Because they can," Sheena replied. Joanne looked at her in surprise.

"Good answer," she said.

She left school five minutes before Geography ended, to the annoyance of Mr Grating the Geography teacher. "Manners maketh man," he said dismally as she clattered past him towards the door. "Hmm," she said. She never knew what to say to Mr Grating. She and Wendy had made up a little rhyme about him once, in the second year – something about 'Dating Mr Grating', but she had forgotten how it went.

Wendy was in the Kent and Sussex District Hospital. In the Physiotherapy and Rehabilitation Unit. Joanne arrived at four, just in time to coincide with Wendy's parents. "Hallo, Joanne," Mrs Bellinger said briskly. For some reason, Mrs Bellinger had never seemed to like Joanne. Joanne suspected it was something to do with the fact that Mr Bellinger was a solicitor, while her own father was a bus driver. "Hallo," said Joanne, and together, they sat down at Wendy's bed, an awkward little unit of three. Silently, Wendy looked at them. She still wasn't allowed to speak because it might unravel the huge white bandage stuck to her jaw with tape.

"You look like a mummy," Joanne said. She thought it might be the moment for a little levity. Mrs Bellinger sniffed. She seemed not to have anything to say. She leaned back on her sighing, padded chair and played with the straps of her handbag.

Wendy looked very different now, her face swollen and bruised, like a dropped apple. Not pretty any more. Not heart-shaped. She could have been anyone. Her eyes had become big and dark and she just lay there, against the white pillows, and stared at her parents and her friend as if they were aliens. After a moment Mrs Bellinger got up from her chair and sat carefully on the very edge of the bed. "You'll be out of here in no time," she said, uncurling her right hand and touching Wendy's arm. Joanne smiled at Wendy and felt inadequate. She felt sick and sad and useless.

"Maybe school will postpone *A Streetcar Named Desire*," she suggested. All spring, Wendy had been practising to be Blanche.

"Of course they will," Mrs Bellinger replied, not looking at Joanne. "They couldn't do without their star turn."

Joanne looked out through the window at the big, scary rooks that flapped across the grass. She felt close to tears.

"So how was school today, Joanne?" Mrs Bellinger asked politely. She had pulled on a strange kind of armour, emblazoned with the motto: 'We are Coping'.

"Needlework was pretty bad," Joanne replied. "I still haven't finished my skirt."

Wendy made a noise through her bandages that sounded like a laugh. Mrs Bellinger frowned slightly and looked across the room at a nurse dusting the TV screens. She looked back at her. "Is that the same pattern that Wendy's working on?" she asked.

"Yes," said Joanne. "It's supposed to be Very Easy. But it's not."

Wendy made another noise through her bandages.

"You two obviously weren't destined to be seamstresses then?"

"No." And there was a pause, which stretched from being a pause into being just silence.

At four thirty, a nurse came to wheel Wendy away on a large, metal trolley. The Bellingers went too, Mr Bellinger plodding behind in his big solicitor shoes, Mrs Bellinger clinging on to her handbag as if it could fend off everything bad about the world. With one big whack. "Well," Mr Bellinger said, pausing, "thanks for coming, Joanne." He made it sound as if she'd been invited to a party. "That's OK," she said. Then she stood and watched as they all disappeared behind some grey swing doors. The doors made a kind of sucking sound as they swung back.

By the first week of July she had managed to sew the waistband on the right way round, and was working on the zip. But she'd bought the wrong kind of zip – a clunky, metallic one which was too heavy and dragged the material into a little swathe, like a tiny theatre-curtain. And she was always pricking her fingers with needles, covering her skin in tiny, ruby dots.

Miss Nedley looked at her handiwork. "This zip is meant for jeans," she said. "Were you not listening at the beginning of term?"

Joanne stood in front of her Bernini machine and gazed at the little steel prong that the cotton reel was supposed to sit on. She imagined what Wendy would say. "What the hell kind of zip is that, Jo ...?" she might say. Her lip trembled as she stood there.

Miss Nedley sighed. "Are you listening now?" she asked. "Either you can Kwik-unpick it and sew in the proper zip. Or ..."

Her face seemed to fall a little suddenly, like a cake that had been taken out of the oven too fast. Her eyes became glazed and unfocused, staring beyond Joanne and out through the window, at the blue sky.

"Or you could just leave it at that," she said.

"I think I'll just leave it at that," Joanne replied. She took the skirt back to her desk, which was covered in pins with multi-coloured heads and pieces of tacking chalk. She thought of the day in September when she and Wendy had sat there with their brand new, un-cut material and giggled at the illustration of the hideous A-line skirt. Even the word 'A-line' was enough to set them off. It had become a code for everything that was ridiculous.

At lunchtime she met Sheena Woodward, who had somehow become her new best friend. They sat together on the bench dedicated to the memory of Mr Crumbly, a dear colleague and trusted chemistry teacher.

"I still haven't finished my skirt," Joanne said, getting an enormous Golden Delicious apple out of her bag, contemplating it, and then putting it away again.

"What are you like, Joanne?" Sheena replied in her innocent little voice.

"I'm just not into needlework. I'd rather be swimming. Like some people I could mention."

Sheena's class seemed to be spending the whole of the last fortnight in the school swimming pool. From the Needlework room, Joanne watched Sheena through the window, a tiny figure wading happily in a bright blue rectangle. "I nearly sewed through my finger this morning," she said.

"What are you like?" Sheena said again. She sounded genuinely shocked.

Sheena herself was good at sewing. She was good at tricky, time-consuming things. She even knew how to make lace and turn the heel of a sock. In Needlework classes, she had made the A-line skirt and the mauve blouson with the elasticated waist. She was now working on the child's toy, which involved a lot of panels and Kapok. "So how's Wendy?" she asked.

"She's going to be in hospital for another fortnight. She's got to exercise her leg."

"Still. It could have been a lot worse."

"I know." There was a smell of hot tarmac and paint, and the faint, depressing odour of sulphur from the Chemistry Rooms.

"I did eight lengths of butterfly stroke today," Sheena said after a moment. "It was exhausting."

"Yes, but at least it's fun. At least you're not making a bloody skirt."

"You're doing a lot of swearing these days, Joanne," Sheena replied, unwrapping a powdery grey band of chewing gum and folding it into her mouth. Joanne didn't reply. The bench beneath her legs was splintery and peeling and over-heated by the summer sun. Sighing, she watched Katie Black stomping past, her yellow canvas bag slung over her shoulder. Katie the anarchist. Now her hair was not just bleached: it had been pinched into little spikes. She wore a safety-pin in one ear. And she had taken her school skirt in and cut big splits up each side. She had become the school's official anarchist. Somehow, it did not suit her ability with needle and thread.

"The whole of 1979 has been a disaster," Joanne said, watching her walk away.

"We've had a nice summer though," Sheena yawned and stretched. "Look how brown my arms are."

At home, Joanne sat on the living-room floor and took in the sides of her school skirt with her mother's sewing-machine. Everyone was wearing pencil skirts now. Everyone except Sheena.

"What have you done to your skirt?" her mother asked the next morning as she sat at the breakfast table.

"I've just taken it in a bit."

"A bit? Look, it's all straining at the seams. It looks awful."

"No, it doesn't. Everyone else is wearing pencil skirts."

"Why do you want to look like everyone else?" her father asked, sitting there in his bus driver's uniform.

"When you come home," her mother said, "I want you to unpick all those stitches. You look like a tart."

That evening she sat in the living-room again, cutting all the stitches back out with her mother's big sewing scissors.

Wendy's bruises were greenish now. She still had a bandage around her face but it was in a different position, covering her stitches. She was still not allowed to speak, so her parents made up for it, wading out into the pool of silence like oyster-catchers. Mr Bellinger sang three verses of *Two Lovely Black Eyes*. Mrs Bellinger plucked at positive statements and held them up in the light.

"I've spoken to school," she said, clicking open her handbag and rustling about for pens and scraps of paper, "and they've said they'll postpone *A Streetcar* until next term. Isn't that nice of them?"

Wendy looked at her.

"She's very nice, your drama teacher."

"Is that Miss Burjin?" Joanne asked. Burjin the Virgin, people called her.

"Yes. Miss Burjin," said her mother. "Nice lady. Considerate."

One of Wendy's bruises was shaped like a galloping horse. It galloped across her left cheek-bone and into the cloud of her hair.

"Everyone was asking after you at school," Joanne said. "Sheena Woodward sends her regards." Wendy made a muffled noise that sounded like Who's Sheena Woodward?

"That was nice of her," said Mrs Bellinger, brightly.

"Yes," said Joanne. She tried to echo the Bellingers' up-beat tone, but her voice came out gloomy and flat. She couldn't pretend, the way they did. She couldn't pretend that it was perfectly normal to be sitting in hospital, talking to your silent best friend. She couldn't even pretend that she liked Mr and Mrs Bellinger. She looked up at all the Get Well cards on top of Wendy's bedside cabinet. There were pictures of flowers and cats and baskets of fruit. There were pictures of squirrels with bandages around their heads and cartoons of men in theatre gowns. And then there was one, home-made one, standing out from all the rest. She recognised the picture on it with a little jolt of surprise. It was the picture from the front of their sewing patterns; the picture of the woman wearing the A-line skirt. Very easy, she thought, automatically; *très facile*. The picture was roughly cut out and stuck onto a piece of orange card. She peered at the lettering inside and could just make out the name Katie, followed by a little, unreadable message and three kisses. Katie Black, the anarchist.

Mrs Bellinger was fiddling about with bits of paper, on which she had written little notes. "We spoke to the doctor yesterday afternoon," she was saying, sitting forwards and blocking Joanne's view of Wendy, "and he said your scars will be very faint. They might not even show at all."

Joanne sat completely still on the padded chair. Katie Black had sent Wendy a card. Katie Black was sending her ironic little cards, cynical little soul-mate messages. Messages that said Us v Them. And something about the view of Mrs Bellinger's back made Joanne think 'it's over'. Somewhere, somewhere in these weeks she and Wendy had moved apart, despite all her visits. Perhaps because of all her visits. They had lost something.

"You won't have scars," she said quietly.

Her end-of-term report was not the best she had ever had. In the space for 'Needlework', Miss Nedley had given her a D for effort and an E for attainment. *Joanne continues to struggle with her skirt. Her mind does not seem to be on the task at hand.*

"It's really unfair," Joanne said to Sheena as they sat on the bench. "I've tried bloody hard with that skirt."

"You're swearing again," Sheena said.

"So?"

Wendy had never criticised her for swearing. But maybe she hadn't sworn so much before the accident. She couldn't remember.

"I'll finish your skirt for you," Sheena said, "if you'll help me with my Geography homework. I've got to write about rubber trees in Rio de Janeiro."

"Oh God," Joanne said. She didn't know if she had the strength to write about rubber trees. Or to keep a friendship going with bargains. And anyway, there was something about not finishing her skirt now; some principle to be upheld. She was one of the Third Years Who Had Never Finished Their Skirt. She and Wendy Bellinger. "It's OK," she said, smiling at Sheena. "If that skirt gets unpicked any more it'll fall to bits."

The school bell rang; the beautiful, three forty-five bell. She watched as, after a few seconds, uniformed girls, girls in A-line skirts and pencil skirts, began to plod wearily through doorways, down stairs, along passageways. Then she stood up. "Race you to the gates," she said. An A-line skirt you could at least run in.

Andrew Murray Scott

Nearly Away

The ghost of this man I knew
(Swarming at the window
          climbing out of himself
                    tearing blinds, desperate to live)
wears a heavy disguise.

His eyes roam inwards
in a head bulbously bloated
yet shrunken-in.
Drooling in the morphine madness,
he's wearing only an open shirt, his prick dangles.
He has become an object.

The scene lasted five minutes or less –
the Macmillan nurses were quick,
then I was inside. The smell …
(Does cancer have its own smell?)
Cut to Interior; the devastation – knocked-over TV,
a few of life's family ornaments, a faucet spilled:
adverse reaction.

He stands solemnly, rump to the window,
leaning into his fate, fidgets with a camera.
There is no film; some things are best left unrecorded.
I didn't know him all that well.

He has no tongue; communication is difficult
'Can I trust you' he writes minutely on a pad

in his crabbed, red-fisted hand
among words that are not words –

Until the sedation takes hold
and he agrees to go along with the rituals,
to perform the Quiet Death At Home,
while the nurses mark-up the performance on his chart
and go into the garden for a smoke.

Confronting the disguise and the roar of the greasepaint,
the professional man, pilot, diver, soldier, grandfather
is only 62 – till three months ago –
And I am just a neighbour
warily watching his eyelids droop.

Afterwards, returning home
I meet a neighbour, smiling in the cul de sac,
(the sun filters through cherry blossom)
"Is he nearly away?" she asks quietly, fearful,
like it's a destination – or the title for a poem.

Two Men

Two men with cigarettes stand
in loose colloquy.
They are of different heights.
Their cigarettes and arms
angle upwards
and downwards
hopelessly, semaphoring,
as they cast about
upon the turn of the conversation.

Too far off to hear the subject of their converse
near enough to read their distrust.
In their gestures, the awkwardness,
and futility of nations
in negotiations.

Or signals;
remote-controlled,
on a disused line.

Petaloudes

Chasing flapping yellow butterflies
up the drenched hot ravine
in the midday heat on Rhodes,

suddenly everything is silent,
something or nothing, unheard,
unseen.

Our eyes become suddenly unfocused, confused
– until we come to the stream,
hidden under the wooden bridge.

And then suddenly everything
is a butterfly, or made of butterflies
and even this memory of it,
that special outburst –
is bright and flapping yellow.

At the Uffizi

Armless marble nymphs
with bronze figleaves
bolted on
have been denied the knowledge
that full-frontal porno
is showing
all day.

Next to Boccacio,
Machiavelli ponders the leathergoods sellers
across the *palazzo*
he is slightly stooping,
fingering his chin,
doubtless trying to appear intellectual
to pick up some American girls.

As for Fran Petrarch – his fingers
have been removed – spikes remain.
They have delayed giving him a new hand
till the *frauleins* are out of reach.

The Firth of Lorn

The Sound looked as though it had been photocopied
on a defective machine,
ripples in the ether, Morse code
Doppler-shifting the corpsed sky.

Silhouettes abounding on the tumbled broken cliffs
Mull slumping westwards
Oban switched on behind;
sodium birthday cake,
as we rumble west.

You only have to say you believe in the real,
in the power of the word,
to make a kingdom
by joining the dots of these marginal seas.

Walter Perrie

Desert Notes

I

Where three ways meet the caravanserai
thick-walled, raw desert slaked with water
holds up an overwhelming sky
sagging at centre with its weight of star.

'Everything is water' you declare
but from the democratic air
sand heaps its numerical tyranny
drinking the dumb oasis dry.

Wherever hidden waters are
will be the popular centre, Source
and Way where bull and butterfly
converge, mixing their blood and spoor
to follow the secret watercourse.

At the uncuttable knot of pathways
unsuspecting travellers wait out dry days
and drier nights, weary with dicing and gossip
waiting for the sky to break and how to hope
while far below the caravanserai

answering to moonless tides
great silent seas in darkness ebb
and wait for us to die.

II

Flame quickening the caravanserai
lost in the deep, still spaces of the tale
fearful of lives we might have had, we cry

into frosting spaces. Time is simple:
even so far inland the sea reaches
her sly tongue, salting palmy oases. All

islanders know what water teaches:
shape of the story and the sea are one –
what fattens cattle, almonds, peaches

fattens death. Ellipsis – the unspoken –
civility – is all that keeps us from
the white wind's unintelligible moan.

III

Now there is only one imperative –
to go into the sand alone, leave
all the Promises, the Canaans ripe
with honey, lotteries, libraries, strip
shows, the town shoes and TV, the daily
impedimenta of necessity.
Go at once, tell no-one, leave no
forwarding address nor will and follow
Here-Be-Dragons charts of dune-seas where
only your ghosts will answer.

Take nothing! Body is burden enough. Speed
is everything. What sustenance you need
will flow from rock, locusts and manna – or not –
abandoning us to the bone-white fate
we inherited, weightlessly inert.
Do not believe (it never lies) the desert
deceives with mirages, will-o'-the-wisp
late bargains, promises; here eucharist
is morning cool or cactus shade at noon
or stony voices comforting the moon.

Go without faith, do not even believe
the desert is God but contrive
to go on, persistence will confirm
it all. The desert will not let you harm
it and belief will follow on behind
sorry and weeping in the hot, white wind.

IV

Light here is no longer weightless
but a terrible pressure on eye
on word, on hand, on hope, the incessant susurration of hot blue
so fierce it becomes a colourless
heart-melt, gut-pulse, lung-deny-
ing weight of not yet desiccated flesh.

If you can no longer stand
your own noise, lie face-down
holding tight onto the sand
and listen to the rock-bone
beat out its diurnal
pulse, the differential
tug between earth and heaven.

V

You think from here you can go in any direction
and arrive somewhere different. Different from where?
It is not true. From here every direction, every Where
is the same. At every furious immolation
heart and sun set in the same dark hole and however
many circles you inscribe-descend, alone, together
whether you follow the canyon rim or camel-train
towards the mountains behind you or mountains before
turn, turn and turn again, you never cross the horizon
definitively to arrive but once.

VI

Owl sits motionless waiting for the rocks
to cool and go quiet so She can hear
rustle of Beetle, Snake and Shrew. Silver Fox
waits to hunt stars across a plain scar
shadowed and scythed by the sickle moon.

Dark here is the time for living, space
between amnion and desiccation
listening, looking through the holes in bone
at skies the sun soon tidies into place.

Owl and Fox have hunted here for ever
their bones made of Shrew and starlight, waiting
tasting the dry salt on their mouths where
Scorpion or Fly will fasten kiss or sting.

Sand-trickle, scorpion-scrape, saguaro rose-
burst, spider-scurry; you expect in these signs
from beyond to overhear The Secret, expose
cool springs, green reasonings. But every one here
is a transient, just passing through the lines
even the rock, even the prickly pear.

VII

So much emptiness for heart to people.
Only those self-stripped of purpose
goal, intention, aim can ever become fool
enough to hear how slow the cactus grows.

The owls sit waiting for the sudden dark.
Only in the endless play of direction-less
air is there a silly hope, a desert lark-
trill, grammar of a sudden, sodden *feis*.

VIII

Maybe Desert is only a thought, circle.
When skies melt and the dune tide
is running at full and everywhere the wide
is repeated over and over the individual
grain, dune, even ocean falls into a circle.

Maybe Desert has no size – only position
some Where extending always beyond
hope, like a life we were fond
of – and is nothing but pure duration.

All day I thirst for some familiar star
Arcturus, Antares or Altair
calling each softly name by name
hoping that like shy animals they will come
to drink at my heart, to mate and purr.

And every night I wish for some new sun
certain tomorrow something strange will happen.

IX

Sulphur-pale surfaces, pure curve and plain
skin stretching grain-cells over sky and stone
continual rearrangement of the Same.

Only as surface yourself, sheer plane
stripped of interiority will any Thing begin
all sense intensified, not to happen.

Your life a steady rosary the desert tells
each station equal in the desert scales
dry grain and ash of endless shattered shells.

God, how far from here to some ending?
A mile? A thousand? A year? A wakening?
When dream and scorpion are stripped of sting.

Only where Abiding IS is transformation
possible. Grit in a shoe? Take off your skin.
This, whether it please you or no, this thin

coating of time is where you will stay
where your life, quick streams of red can flow
into endlessly absorbent sand into

a desiccating air, so quickly you will
hardly notice your life ended here a mile
a year, millennia ago.

X

Out of an absolute No Where
thin black scribble scrawls
immaculate dune.

Vivid, intent, the epic column
winds its inky measure
till on a secret sign

scurries of plural chaos
flower and fragment
around the massive corpse.

Reduced from purpose to problem
mechanical calculation
mass, stresses, forces, work and load

concerted jolts and jerkings head
pushing, scrambling, dragging, certain
millimetre by millimetre
the scorpion corpse to its destination.

Legible momentarily
the desert inscribes
singular epic.

Later, with perfect clarity
the sky can look again through holes
in the scorpion shell at itself
recognising a job well done.

XI

The sands are timeless but partake of time.
Their substance shimmers and a black sky hangs
burning above them in pantomime
of transformation while the ancient songs
promising Cactus, Owl and Shrew send roots down
into dying, drinking from speech and bone.

Because I and Adam are a singular man
because all women are Eve, we remember
that, fleeing Paradise, we followed a river
down, down through mountain, hill, savannah, plain
until it steamed and vanished in this dried-up pan.

Hopeless now to try to follow that river
back to its source, a hole into nothing. So
all we can hope to do is drink and swear
by salt and brackish pools that somewhere flow
into the slow dark breakers of the Common Soul.

XII

Sedated death will not undo
decades of distraction.
Nothing now will help you
cope with all you gave up
at the start. No matter how deep
you dig you will not recover
the life you buried –

> with neither prayer nor offering
> without forethought or provision
> neither of wine nor barley wine
> nor wheaten cake nor harp nor coin

– whatever is here
is preserved forever
as over and over
the miser desert counts each grain.

XIII

You always know it is going to happen.
There are warnings, lightnings and green
horizons flicker and a sudden stir
goes ghosting through. Rain here is never
just rain, gradual progress from smirr
through drizzle to a steady downpour
but vomit, utterness, opening
sky heaving stone and frozen water
straight into yawn, distress or need
deconstructing earth, sky, everything
to original mud.

XIV

I had been travelling all day – Oh, and for many days
and night was near and my travel was all blur and haze
a sort of walking half-dream on the edge of sleep
weary, weary so I had nor heart nor energy to weep.
At first I thought: some trick of the failing light
behind the black light and above the burning skies
as though a shadow shape hung just behind my sight
a pale triangle, merest outline: then I realise
that what, below the moon and vast above the glooming earth glows
white and luminous and high beyond the uttermost horizon
is the perfect, endlessly distant, Mother of Snows

who, when all else is darkening, still catches from a sun
invisible to me its glows of warmth and light
pure formal beauty, water-giver, always renewing
itself from frozen form, river and flood-source, lithophyte
amnion, inscribing in snowmelt, watercourse and desert Spring.

XV

Some days it is hard to say
which is You, which is shadow.
Shadow is often solid
Self mere parody. Shadow
is light interrupted
Self broken from the other side.

Courtesy of Walter Perrie

My Son, My Son

Pat Gerber

"Weill, that's him awa." Her brown eyes burn briefly into mine over the edge of her cup. I know perfectly well what she means, but say, "Have another biscuit, before you start?" She shakes her head.

"So, he's off to Ireland?" I turn on Radio One, to keep the mood cheery.

A thorn tree branch rattles on the window like a bony finger. Wind streaks rain across the garden. I am being deliberately dim, to put off the unthinkable thing she's going to tell me. I can't bear to hear it.

"No tae Ireland. Tae Afghanistan."

"But I thought his lot were to do a tour in Ulster?" A tour. Sounds like something from a holiday brochure. Pop music beats into the silence. Jackie takes out another cigarette. Her hand shakes. She frowns, focusing on the lighter flame. She drags smoke into her lungs, as if it were courage. "Plans were changed. They got sent straight tae Kabul."

"When?" There's no escape. I have to hear her through. We have so much in common, Jackie and I, hate ironing, love bright colours, both the mothers of sons. For the time being, my boy sleeps.

"Ah got word on Friday. They just phoned and telt me. Like that. Some weekend Ah hud."

"Did you have a chance to speak to Iain?"

"Ye're jokin? Naw. It wis this wumman. I says tae her, 'Weel, hen, I wouldnae hae *your* job'. That's whit she hus tae dae. She hus tae phone aa the families and tell them their sons is gettin sent aff tae war. Then, if – if somethin happens, you know? She hus tae phone them. Us. And tell us, like. She says, 'I'm your contact with Iain, for *everything*'."

Jackie can think of another woman's feelings at a time like this?

"Louie's her name. She says tae caa her Louie, it's no sae formal and that, she says. She's got this posh voice. She says, 'Iain's a character. The boys were all supposed to pack their effects away and label them in case – but Iain said "I'll be back, you'll see". Nice boy.' Nice boy, eh?"

"She says, 'Iain is very mature. He understands where he's goin and what it's all about.' My God. She should have saw him afore he joined up. Mature? Eighteen and niver done a day's work in his puff. Comin hame aa oors o the nicht and God knows whit he'd been up tae. Ah couldnae control him. Yon day the polis cam roon. 'Time you wis oot, son,' Ah says. 'Time you were oot roughin it a bit, at your age. Ye'r a man noo, no a wean. On yer way,' Ah says. 'And don't come back till ye've made somethin o yersel'."

"You put him out of the house?"

"Ay, that Ah did. A grown man. Time he wis staunin on his ain feet, no trampling aa ower mine." Her voice cracks in the effort to sound harsh.

"So, he went into the army." This is safe, known territory we've been over before. Jackie loves to talk about Iain. He is her only child.

And my son is upstairs. Oh, he's not lazy. No, he's a good student. Has to work late in that bar too many nights. The cistern flushes. He'll be with us any minute, tousled and slow with sleep. He is the light of my life. I obliterate the sounds of his approach with talk. "Remember last year, Jackie – Iain's Passing Out?"

"Ah wis that feart, aa the way tae London on ma ain."

"Have you the photo, still?" I know she keeps it next her heart.

She fishes it out of her overall pocket. A small plastic wallet protecting the picture I've seen before. Iain, tall and stiff beside her, she dressed in her best, self-conscious in the too-frilly outfit, he expressionless under the army hat, anonymous, like any other soldier. She smiles at it with such tenderness. Vulnerable now, she says "It's him. Like, it's his eyes. Ye know?"

I try to keep her on this comfortable track – for her peace of mind? Or mine? To help her forget where he is now? Would anything make me forget? As she talks, TV newsreels flicker through my mind, towers collapsing in showers of debris and dust, bombers and helicopter gun-ships dealing death over Kabul. I'd always thought of helicopters as quaint, kindly, helpful. Helicopters rescued fallen climbers, shipwrecked fishermen, workers off burning oil rigs. Now they spit death from the sky like malevolent insects. Another picture, a young Taliban giving himself up. He's crouched against the base of a wooden post, three young Brits surrounding him, their guns pointed at his heart. His brown spaniel eyes look up at them, expecting death. What if his mother sees him? The last sight of her son, on TV?

Why is he there? Why are any young people there? We still try to solve world problems with human blood, no different from our ancestors who threw young people into bogs or burned them in sacrifices to appease some nameless god. Is the idea of peace an impossible dream, a luxury, like health fads, useful only to fuel endless undergraduate discussions, or to flesh out dinner party chatter among the fat middle classes? I keep talking. "You were so proud of Iain that day." What makes women feel pride when their sons are sent into battle? What on earth is there to be proud of?

Jackie always looks straight at you. Her eyes are goldy-brown with very bright whites, and they normally express a kind of ironic humour. "Ay, Ah wis," She's almost excusing herself for loving her son. "It's his eyes. Disnae maitter whit he's done. He just – luiks at ye. He's that wey – ye cannae help but love him." She shrugs and drags in more smoke, doomed. "I've even wrote him a letter. His pal's mammy – she's writin aa this sob-stuff, aboot missin him and that. Whit good's that gonnae dae the boy? He's no wantin tae hear aa her worries, is he? There's nae good greetin."

"So, what do you write about?"

She grins. "Ah telt him aboot Nancy up the sterr."

"Nancy who's pregnant?"

"Ay, her. Well, Ah telt him, she's got that big on top she canny get a bra tae fit her. Ah says, 'see's a perr o yer helicopters, son, tae haud up each side o Nancy, or she's gonnae trip ower hersel and fa doon the sterr.' Och, Ah jist tell him onythin that comes intae ma heid. He's no wantin tae hear ma worries, is he?" She searches for truth among the tea leaves in her empty

Illustration by Colin Dunbar

cup. "They'd tae mak their wills. Yon Louie telt me. Ye know, in case..."

I think of Iain. What does he believe he is fighting for? He probably has more personal grudge against a boy from the next scheme than against any Afghani. The voice of a Radio One newsreader speaks of the War against Terrorism. How eagerly he describes cluster bombs, explosives that suck all the oxygen from caves, so cleverly suffocating all who hide there. He goes on to threaten nuclear weapons, as though trailing the next episode of some kids' space adventure, not real life. These commentators scoop their livings like vultures from the piles of burned and twisted bodies, cameras lingering almost salaciously on close-ups of the anguished and bereaved. Disgusted, I switch channels to Radio Scotland and Fred Macaulay's inane giggle. But now he's playing Hamish Henderson's *Freedom Come-All-Ye* and for a moment or two my soul is soothed with hope.

When my son was little, I discouraged him from fighting his friends with any sort of implement, gave him no toy guns. Have I made him a freak? Too soft to survive in this brutal world? Have *I* made him anything? For he is an individual, not my plaything, capable of thought and actions that have nothing to do with *me*. My father fought a war yet I am a pacifist. And Jackie. She didn't force her son to be a soldier.

Should I feel shame in the face of her pride and fear? Why do I feel a flush flowing over my face as my son shuffles into the kitchen, his chest bare above his torn jeans, his movements so gentle and easy. He kisses me on the cheek, squeezes my shoulder and smiles sleepily at Jackie. He doesn't speak, brewing coffee, cooking himself a bowl of porridge. I am conscious of his presence, embarrassed as if I'd been caught showing off illicit booty.

Who makes the decision about which boy stays at home and which goes to war? Will it ever be my turn to be in Jackie's position? Maybe, if things get worse, there could be conscription. I fight away the terrible thought with speech. "What made Iain choose the army?"

A long plume of smoke fogs the table. Jackie's voice is tight. "Choose? Whit choice dae ony us huv, where Ah come fae? If they'd only gave us decent hooses. If the weans had hud a place tae play. If there'd been jobs for them when they left the schule." She snorts derisively. "It wis the army or nothin. He gets a trainin, some discipline, his claes and his food. Ah thocht – like – well, Ah couldnae sort him out masel'. Ye've saw the height o him – can ye see me tellin him aff? But I thocht maybe the army could – could dae somethin fur him, make a man o him or somethin, maybe..."

My son looks from one face to the other, and frowns as he throws a jersey over his head and lifts his jacket from the peg. "Wake up, Ma," he says. "You're miles away. I'm off to give blood, before the march. It's for the soldiers. Don't forget to put the peace poster in the window, to show solidarity. Cheers, Jackie," And he swings away out of the back door.

Jackie's brown eyes follow him like a dog's, dull, without expression now, her thoughts battened down again, unreadable. She gets up from the table. "Ah weill. Life goes on, eh? Ah'd better get movin hen."

A cold wind blows through my kitchen.

Alison Prince

Publishers

I hate the publishers
who pick black-beaked
at what they have been given,
cawing in London voices,
clacking in pride at
maggoty ideas
dragged in by salesmen
to their treetop meetings.
MARKET, MARKET.
How they squawk
in their square, glass elms!
MARKET
flickers on their screens
and through their entry phones
as if nobody reads
but only buys.
The sky seen through their windows
is a white page
with no writing.

Christmas

This Christmas morning
while the wind blows from the sea
I'm cutting back the privet
and the grey-limbed hebe
to give the small fir
the space it needs.

Indoors, the red poinsettia that Ramesh brought
recovers, and no longer casts aside
its widowed leaves for suttee in the fire.
Its flushed hearts beat more slowly
now the cellophane is gone
and the cold, shocking car-ride
fades from memory.

Unopened parcels wait, but I delay
the solving of their papered mystery.
The sea
breaks on the wall, scattering spray
like cherry bloom.
The bare trees nurse their buds
until the spring.

Armistice

My parents' wars were always silent ones,
He reading and she knitting in a flame
Of icy rage, an unexploded bomb
That ticked and ticked. For him, the silent guns
Deafened her clicking needles, and his shame
At making her so angry shrank away
Into that white remoteness which had been
His refuge in the nightmare of the Somme.
He could not tell her that his safety lay
In her un-knowledge of the things he'd seen.

Minnows

Minnows. A hopeful jam-jar, a bare arm
deep in the pond. Look, they are venturing
into the round mouth – wonderful to bring
them and their liquid world into the air,
a skin of glass between us. Their alarm
gives me a small pain, but I love to stare
at the fin-fanning balance and round eyes
of minnows in their water, held face-high.

Now, things have changed. It's aeroplanes
I catch these days – or rather, they catch me.
The shining fish looks small in its blue sky
but as it swims down with its wheelfeet spread
and wings tense as a stickleback's bright spines
it's not a fish at all. Immense, grounded,
its jam-jar mouth gapes in a glassy grin
and we, obedient minnows, venture in.

Willow

Willow has always half a mind to fall.
Roots loosen in wet earth, an elbow leans
into the bank with an unbreathing sigh
of comfort and collapse, then it is down,
a branching pile of buds soft-furred
as rabbit paws and silver leaves
thrown sideways. In a month or so
each joint will be new-rooted and fresh growth
shoots upwards. Willow-fall
is not a death, merely a moving on.

Neil mac Neil

Minstrelsies and Noise

Older than thunder, our three vowels, as one breath, one voice.
Nomadic echoes, rural and urban sounds, our uncertain old testimonies
biblical and unbiblical, both visible and invisible.
Our three vowels today unable to hold up every stable
thing from quark to quasar or coiled curves of time and space
liturgies. They huddle together in our less and less ordinary ways.
We lower our gaze on more and more extraordinary follies.

From this ancient sound sensorium of hidden songs
come our poems, operas, hymns, laments, melodies.
Tonight's Shell Bay sky collects eclipses of our dark light fears.
This slack tide whispers echoes of half remembered wrecks.
Back home, friends watch millennium candles gutter, splutter out.
Granny would've read this moment as a sign from old and new stars
about their half coherent histories. Singing out their light biographies.

Today, this year's Easter Monday, gods in grey boil Fife's sky
into thunderclouds. The sound of giant egg stones rolling in a zinc pan.
Hiss. Crackle. Crack! Lightning sizzles open volumes of blue
violent air in arcs under four dolphins leaping eastwards to the North Sea
across what we keep saying is (but not the map) 'Leven Bay'.
On shore we hear wallop after wallop of dolphin cadenzas.
Noise we first took to be a wave bounced run aground boat.

The river's thunder rumbles and rolls away its percussion
over metal coloured water. Horizonless sea beckons the dolphins.
Wallop of water and roll of thunder fade together as they part.
Remember last summer here? And, as it rose above the knoll,
the litany, the slow lift and ascent of the lark's heart,
its song of self radiant in the small cathedral of its soul.
Last summer our bay held in its green arms, this minstrel.

Our memory's rhythms beat along tides and sound scenarios.
Each song of self, sings of all selves. Our three vowels, one voice
haunting psalms, hymns, laments, the lost pibroch before logos.
From clan histories of time, one whisper. An echo prior to galaxies
we now hear as eternal vowels, as flowing waters, as symphonies
of all earth's waters, confluent, separate, gathered again and again
as burns, streams, rivers, torrents, seas, oceans. The flood of floods.

In our dreams water sprites dream us dreaming them.
Fractals of waterfalls ripple purer vowels as gently as a breeze
upon rockpools. Here where seas surge and foam, spume heals
when we breathe in unbiblical invisible ions older than tornadoes
drawing them in from their dervish dance through surf's nearby thunder.
Rain. It seems our continent's rainfall deluges our delta. Soaks our first exodus.
That first of our remembered and half forgotten wonders. Or splinters.

And now? Our drawn out gasps! Whoops of excited ooh-aahs
over each electron's fractional orbits, their black light power.
Who does not long to hear such vowels as may have come before one word
in some lost time? From some lost quantum? Three vowels, wavilinear,
knot into one sound uttered in a single voice at the dawn of the world.
Louder than any thunder, than the sound of blood pumping in my ear,
older even than poetry's ancient pilgrimage are such minstrelsy and noise.

Tides of Light

From this window looking west
I am moved by that cloud sailing past.

It is not all beautiful over there
just soft, white, blue, green.

What does here look like from over there?

Fluctuations of variable stars echo
in me. Who knows how it will show?

Is there an encyclopedia
for high and low tides of light?

Auld Laird Muin

Wan lyart haufmuin
Nae mair than orrals, banes.
Normaist nicht, swastika.

Fower Craws at Ratho

Fower craws curcuddoch on the wa.
Fedders black as Earl o Hell's weskit.

An owre bi yon skinny pailin stob
Yin aesome yowe lamb flisks aboot

Ablow Wast Lothian's grey hert-sair lift.

Thowe wins fuffle
The craws' caw-cannie weengs.

Power craws scoor puir lammie-meh's een.

Eemage o Prayer

Pittin up ane word syllab
Hauden the hoolet's prayer
Neither hishie nor whishie
Nicht wund weengs.

Igloo

Steven Taylor

Late late snow. Pushed down from the north and east and then tumbled, finally, into the sunken dockyards that have always lined this jigsaw coast.

The snow interrupts the baleful progress of the cold afternoon and Kevin blinks, responsively, harnessed into a high cradle, steadying himself uneasily with his left hand and tipsy from the beer taken with the noon break. He flexes his shoulders at another layer of damp, a pale seagull churning beyond him, high above the dockyards to the south, towards the distant traffic. Speaks.

We are blurred Turk, blurred by this split pillowcase of sky, blurred out. The Turk gestures back to him across the weathered hull, pointing with exaggeration towards the uneven ropes above the cradle. They have grown closer since Helmut fell, setting their tin shaving mugs on the window ledge, no longer competing for space, but half-comrades, almost familiar, certainly less brittle than before. Warmer. Their alliance, intimacy, it might even survive the tulips, their contracts, the renewal of the Turk's permit.

Kevin acknowledges the warning with a tired salute, captive, taking out the extra pair of gloves, less slick with paint. A primer, turning the hull into the texture of wet meat, spreading upwards in thickening abstracts as they work from bottom to top. The cradle will rock, precariously, if he winches himself towards a better view of the city, creaking towards the welcome dots of yellow windows and spires, flecks of neon already present against the air. Kevin believes that the sight of the clock tower is worth the momentary swirl of vertigo, time blending and unblending in a second flurry.

We spider up, Turk. Spider up. The Turk, who now delights in Helmut's bunk, dipping his fingers directly into sugar for a suck, but what the hell. The sea claws at his nostrils, purple and salt.

Kevin once told Helmut that his father had been a Jew. Inventing it again last month, telling the woman that his family had spent the war huddled as versions of Anne Frank, but surviving her, travelling afterwards to see the birth of Israel. A stark landscape greeted them, Helmut. They were starved as a carrion. Did I say that my cousins were Romany? Inventing further. But he owned honestly to a sister who lived with his mother's people, still in Dublin. We used to visit, but you can't contrive a family from imaginings.

Kevin admitted this in the parlour where the most brightly embroidered cushion sat, where the wood was heavy with varnish, and there was a green smell of peppermint from somewhere. But where?

Don't you see? It's a given thing, identity. Given. The bottle waving in front of him, the Turk preparing for an evening out, washing, lathering himself with soap. And then what did you tell her?

Kevin sits back onto the couch, his face too ruddy, and she moves into position beside him, his buttons undone so quickly. The angles of the room actually resemble a church. He wants to tell her this. Show her. It has taken him two months to find this woman and it was Helmut who introduced them, translating generously in the worker's bar, organizing their liaison in halting Slovak. Helmut, her skin tasted of lemons, and then that thicker scent coming from underneath, a different type of vertigo. She kept her table decorated with plastic yellow flowers and a stitched mat that has been printed to resemble a phoenix rising.

The moon seen from the corner of her street was hooked like Islam. Another night, raining, she sniffed at his wet jacket like a dog. Kevin thinks of her too much. In late October, gin-riddled, he explains to her that his brother is in Canada. But I was the younger, he says, always the younger, digging for oil in the Arctic. We haven't spoken for years.

The Turk reading and rereading Kevin's passport, the Irish harp embossed on each corner in the dim light of the room when he returned from her. It's all disguises, Turk. All of it. The Turk peeling another orange on the edge of his cradle in the falling snow. Grinning. Turk, do all you heathens carry gold in your teeth? His final words to Helmut, Helmut, she keeps a warm house, fruit in a bowl from the Chinese quarter and it is always fresh.

It's not that I want her for anything unnatural, he says to Helmut, I just need to explain myself. To unburden. The Turk listening to them, adamantly sober, refusing to share the bottle as it passed between them. You tell her that, next time Helmut. Explain it for me. Say to her that it's what I need. She'll understand then, not think me so foolish. And it was true.

She looked at him as Helmut told, eventually nodding her assent, picking up her bag and beckoning for Kevin to follow. Kevin adjusting his long stride to take her into account. She clutched at his arm as they approached the edge of the city, claiming him, squeezing him tightly, pushing her head into his shoulder, the first neon beginning to fizz into the canals. They surrounded themselves in a soft web of alleyways, hurrying, hunched, cupped cigarettes in bad weather.

He thinks of the Turk later, undressing shyly in the corner of the room. Helmut flicking a lit match at his dark backside. The Turk glaring for one brief moment in response.

Gin? She fetches glasses from the kitchen and slips his coat onto the back of a chair. It was earlier than he had expected. Was it definite that Helmut had arranged for an entire night? Helmut had said so. Sure, no problem. She understands. She likes you. Grinning at the Turk's sudden flare of anger, turning over in the soft bed. Stars will come out everywhere, Kevin.

Your happy igloo will sparkle. He married and then remarried, made his mother dead and then alive again. She had brought us to Dublin, furious at our daft father, her husband, who she claimed had gone ahead. I watched her turn into porcelain beside the fire. The flames looked like Hell. Her death exploded us. Left nothing but fragments.

Helmut tells me that you live alone? Yes, Helmut. Perhaps we might love each other eventually? And she crawled onto him, felt the beginnings of him against her. I have never killed anyone by hand. My hands have been used only for making. And he tries to reassure her with his touch, absently curling her dark hair between his fingers, her eyes closed, somewhere else entirely. I never even thanked Helmut for introducing us. Do you think I should? Swallow me up.

Helmut's body has not even cracked the ice and Kevin and the Turk stare down at him until the ambulance arrives, the two of them waiting, watching the careful blue figures edge gradually towards him. A crowd gathering on the wharf and someone official, important, adjusting his tie before stepping down onto the ice, looking up at them for a brief moment.

Kevin and the Turk, the Turk quietly unpeeling his third orange, the cradle rocking and their metal boots clanging against the hull.

Opium

Before you
I pined for love like a left dog
Outside the Argos at Craigleith

But now. On my divan. I watch wild
Oriental dragons stalk the soured
Veins along the back of my fist &
Permit the light from their ruby eyes
To caress my own fey imagination
in such

A delicate manner, darling
I know everything
Like modern Israel & my breath

Is as sweet as your touch

Ever was. I am even more certain.
More beautiful. More needed. Occupied.

Almost Afghani.

Mexico

It is not necessary for you to believe anything
you are my children and I have men with guns
to protect you from such nonsense. The price

of bread is the price of bread. A disaster
at one end of the country will most often
be balanced by something delightful down
in Mexico.

Women will do whatever is required of them.
Trust me. People are generally quite musical.
The truth is like forecasting the weather.

Tomorrow will be followed by tomorrow and
Today will commence with the final parts of
Yesterday. Remember to breathe.

Chapman

Even before you were one hundred
Few of you died
For want of a quick description.

Look yourselves up under land mammals
Or something similar
In a dictionary with pictures

Of a dog performing tricks
Alongside words like sit. Sit
Or fetch or freedom. Roll over.

Roll with me
For a moment in this dark ink. Listen.

You Chapmans are rare and different.

Jim C Wilson

Still Life

(Giorgio Morandi Speaks)

1964, and I'm here still,
painting my portraits of bottles and jars,
in umbers, creams and *eau de Nil.*

What, though, is time? 50 years
are as five minutes, with countless
receptacles to rearrange, then paint,

in here, in my mother's apartment.
I'll edge the moon-coloured one to the right:
a change is as good as a holiday.

My sisters say I'm in *need* of a break:
Giorgio, they ask, why not step out
and paint the vibrant streets, the teeming people

of Bologna? Go, now, to the hills;
capture the colour of wind in the pines,
follow the flight of the mountain eagle.

I say, no need. And those who see
no evidence of progress in my work
don't know this ochre jar is nearly perfect.

perspectives eternally changing.
I pour my life into these bottles
but my art, like love, cannot be measured.

Come Close and Listen

(For David Hart)

It seems at times I am sentenced
to echo endlessly
inside this skull,

sifting through a cairn
of inadequate words,
ambiguous phrases.

Visitors peer inside my eyes
yet fail to distinguish
a hint of presence,

while I rehearse responses,
try out perfect arguments,
prepare my case yet again.

The specialist thinks I am silent
but he can't hear the hiss of blood,
the thudding of each second.

And he doesn't detect me, from midnight
till noon, as I stack and restack
my words of gold

to build another absolute poem.
Sometimes ideas just fall away
like soft old cobwebs;

and images will suddenly crack
like dull broken moons.
But poetry is possible

and often I will sing out loud
in here, to myself,
in this hall of bone.

Will you please come close now?
Listen. Syllables are almost
on my tongue.

The Sea's Message

I am the sea; my fingers explore you,
flow across your smooth white sand until deep
down I stroke you, silently, yet again –
and then forever. Now my currents swirl
in each salt pool, every shifting hollow
of your shore. My shape mutates with the moon

but always I'm close, as you move and shine
through incessant hours and times and seasons.
My waves retreat, seem to abandon you,
allow you to drift in the east's raw wind.
But I'll return and return and return.
My tide is turning now; is coming in.

Love

She says that love is like a paper bag
(a brown one). What, I ask, of stars and hugs,
the whole hot paraphernalia and rag-
nerved chaos of the thing? Love cuts and tugs;
but a bag? (Isn't it destined for the bin?)
Eternal summer, fever, wine-sweet lips
and waning moons seem relevant. And sin
can be there too. But a bag! Then she slips
in a couple of afterthoughts: notions
that grow and begin to appeal. She tells
how the bag is mine to open; oceans
of images surge through my mind. All gels,
makes sense. And when she adds the bag is mine
to rummage in, her simile's just fine.

Ending

I hear you saying what you said to me
when we made this trip a year ago, when,
after eight hours of our lives and times, we
agreed to read each other's poems. Back then
the roads led anywhere: Ayrshire, oceans
and the moon. You'd telephone at 9 am,
just to ask me how I was. Devotion's
what I felt – and feel. Don't, please, condemn
me as immoderate. (I know you had
your doubts the day I said you were my Muse.)
I drive alone; I hear your voice. And, sad
to say, I'm listening desperately for clues.
There's a poem in this; somehow, I need it,
but can't face the ending; will you read it?

Liz Lochhead

Clothes

There are dresses – good dresses,
dresses you always loved –
that are suddenly so clean gone
they never become a duster or
leave so much as a square of themselves
rubbing around decades later in the ragbag.
This was what I learned listening
to my mother and my aunts
when on one of the good days in the long Summer holidays
they sat out on backdoor steps
or – skirts spread out – on a tartan rug
on the back green under the white sheets
hung high. "What *happened*
to that wee dress?" one of my aunts
would ask my mother or she'd ask them
coming out of one of the fridgeless kitchenettes
of the fifties with a jug of Boston cream
saying "Johnnie aye liked me in that costume ..."
Maybe it was my grandmother saying
"That was a good coat that"
with all the reverence and gravity
remembrance of such a garment
was rightly due. You knew how true it was
she liked *good things*. When someone said
"That was something I always felt right in ..."
what you heard was the real regret, the yearning.
If something could be explained away
as having been worn till it was well and truly *done*
this would dismiss it from discussion.
But the mystery of that *wonderful swagger-coat* –
a *great* coat – left on a train in the nineteen thirties
that *disappeared before it was gone back for*
only minutes later
was enough to make it mythical to me
as Joseph's Coat of Many Colours,
as the one dream dress every one of them had danced in
and no one was sure who it actually belonged to or
whatever happened ...
You learned that everything was in the detail,
that their mouths made rosebuds
to recall *rows of toty-wee covered buttons.*
Their knowledgeable eyes narrowed at *darts*

or *edge-to-edge, bugle-beading, Peter Pan collar,*
gleamed when they as much as said *sateen.*
Something had never been 'blue' but
saxe or *duck-egg* or "a shade somewhere
between *peacock* and a *light royal*
almost an *electric blue* – but no as gaudy"...
Talk was of *barathea, grosgrain, watered taffeta*
organza, covered coating.
When it came to this stuff *stuff*
every one of them was her mother's daughter.
I'd say every sister had three sisters
who were women after their own hearts
if I didn't remember my youngest aunt, the looker –
the one who later divorced and remarried,
with the perfect eyebrows
and who never had a bad perm or a tint that
went metallic, harsh, who never had fireside tartan
or visible veins measling her legs in their glassy nylons –
smoothing down the glazed cotton over net
splashed with huge impossible blue roses,
admiring the *this-year* almond toes
of her gorgeous gunmetal shoes
and saying nothing
while her mother and her sisters argued enjoyably
over a past no one could quite agree the colour of
and that might or might not have been
sprigged with tiny flowers.

Illustration by Colin Dunbar

The Predicament of the Scottish Writer

Joyce McMillan

(first published in Chapman *35-6)*

It is an unoriginal observation, but nevertheless a true one, that the predicament of the Scottish writer is inseparable from the predicament of Scotland itself. In *Scott and Scotland,* Edwin Muir describes the place as "... a hiatus, neither a nation nor a province..."; in his introduction to the same book, Allan Massie calls it "a country which has become a sham". That the political absorption of Scotland into the United Kingdom and the British Empire has been accompanied by a relentless suppression and trivialisation of Scottish literature and Scottish history is beyond doubt; the pressure on every talented and ambitious UK citizen to ape as closely as possible the speech, manners and life-style of the English upper middle class has taken its inevitable toll on the richness, the continuity and the self-sufficiency of Scottish culture; and looking back even over my own relatively short life-span, it is clear that there has been a tragic loss, a kind of theft.

I was born into a well-doing, respectable, upwardly-mobile-artisan kind of family, with a pedigree of almost perfect Scottishness for generations back on either side, and brought up in a stoutly Presbyterian village in the west of Scotland; between them my aunts and uncles and grandparents possessed a tremendously rich – if slightly bowdlerised and Lauderised – fund of Scottish language and manners, songs and stories. Yet one of my most powerful memories of childhood is of my mother's concern to train us away from the Scottish speech of the children in the streets round about, and to insist a that we speak 'properly' – that is, with Standard English grammar and syntax, English intonation, and only a tasteful smattering of Scottish vocabulary; although, interestingly, there were limits to our admiration for Standard English speech. We drew the line at saying 'little' instead of 'wee', or affecting a really posh accent.

At Primary School, we did history that was shapeless and colourful, and full of Bonny Prince Charlie and Robert the Bruce; we also learned long Scottish poems (with no dates at the bottom) about dead sailors and battles. But in Secondary School, all that vanished in favour of serious, important, shapely history which fitted together like a jigsaw and actually helped me to understand significant modern things like the Labour Party and the Welfare State – and most of that history seemed to have taken place in England. In literature, the same thing happened; the odds and ends of colourful Scottish poetry disappeared when we begun our certificate courses, and we studied real literature that started from Chaucer and finished with Yeats and Eliot; and it was only much later that some little Scottish pieces reappeared – Scott, Burns – neatly slotted into the big English pattern. I don't think I have quite rid myself, yet, of the feeling that Scottish literature and history are somehow for children, whereas the English equivalents are for grown-ups.

Later on, at St. Andrews University, I ran full tilt into what is possibly the most anglicised of all Scottish institutions, and often found myself in classes and coffee-rooms where mine was the only Scottish voice. The Honours English exam demanded *one* paper out of *nine* on Scottish literature, and that was regarded as something of an imposition by the two-thirds of arts undergraduates who were, in fact, English. But I remember the shock of delight at my first encounter with Henryson and Dunbar, and the sudden realisation that Scots had once been a living, confident, flourishing branch of mediaeval English speech instead of the couthy, whining political plaything into which it had latterly dwindled; and I remember too the moment when I suddenly understood – well into my 20's – that the working-class speech I had been carefully trained away from in my infancy was not just a cheap, scruffy and inaccurate version of modern English but some kind of surviving remnant of real Lowland Scots, the language of Dunbar and David Lindsay. It is because of this kind of 'Scottish' education that I sit here in Edinburgh today, having lived more than 28 of my 30 years in Scotland, looking Scottish, sounding Scottish, and knowing myself to be Scottish; and yet surrounded by bookshelves full of Shakespeare and Milton, John Donne and Bryon, Jane Austen and Evelyn Waugh, and as ignorant, when it comes to Scottish literature, as the day is long. All I ever had to do, in order to complete my Scottish literary education, was to scribble four short, hasty exam answers on Dunbar and Hogg, Scott and Burns.

Under this sort of disgraceful circumstance, it's hardly surprising that the Scots tend to see themselves – whenever and wherever a slightly raised level of cultural consciousness breaks out – as an oppressed group. Like women, or blacks, or the economically exploited, Scots came together in organisations – the Scottish National Party itself, groups like the Saltire Society, the persistent Scottish republican tendency within the Labour Movement – to share their grievances and try to win back some control over their political and cultural lives. Many Scottish writers, naturally enough, belong to such groups or at least feel some sense of common cause with them, and they begin, inevitably, to judge themselves by the standards of –through the eyes of – those groups. This is the process Allan Massie describes in his New Edinburgh Review article on James Kennaway, when he says of Scottish writers: "We are always being tested – perhaps test ourselves – against our Scottishness...anything not insistently Scottish is *ipso facto* un-Scottish ..." The Scottish cultural establishment itself cherishes its hard-won consciousness of the ways in which Scottish culture has been discriminated against, and tends to demand that that consciousness never be let slip; and it is at this point that the artistic rot set in. Because a creative writer cannot play to that the kind of ideological gallery; cannot – if he or she is to progress, break new ground, find new ways of looking at the world – cater for the preconceived opinions and prejudices of any group, however sympathetic and supportive. When I read modern feminist novels, I can often sense, breathing down the writer's neck, a kind of internal group of prefects of cheer-leaders from the women's movement, whose predictable and insistent cries of 'right on' or 'sexist bullshit' can be seen influencing the progress of the novel at every turn. Likewise, a great many Scottish writers seem to be accompanied by a mental band of Scotland supporters, an internal Ally's army who are liable to shout 'English poof', 'snob', 'traitor' or 'we wuz robbed' if any incorrect, English-looking or (god forbid) middle-class sentiments creep into the prose; and this situation is intensified by the fact that the west-of-Scotland working-class has come, in some circles, to be seen as the main repository of genuine Scottish language and culture, so that the self-righteousness of the oppressed working classes and the culturally-robbed Scot comes into play simultaneously.

Of course, writers have as much right as anyone to be feminists, socialists, Scottish Nationalists or Scots and Gaelic language activists. But at the moment when they sit down to write creatively, they must turn themselves from campaigners into explorers, discard their existing mental maps, their fixed ideologies and aspirations, accept themselves as and where they are, and work freely from there. Given the choice, few Scots would have wanted to start from here; I, for instance, might have preferred an education that made a big, seamless, meaningful Scottish pattern of my history and culture, stretching all the way from the broad Scots songs my granny sang to the devolution referendum. But if I've lost a great deal, I've also gained something, in my early training in and continuous access to one of the richest literatures in the world (I mean English Literature); and I am content, in my work as a journalist and critic, to begin from where I am.

There's no doubt, though, that the fear of betraying either their Scottishness, or their working-class origins, or both at once, has a very limiting effect on some Scottish writers. As Massie has observed, it can lead to a kind of infantile quality in style and subject-matter; writers who feel guilt-stricken about the middle-class literary milieu in which they live their adult lives tend to avoid writing about it, and there is a curious tension in Scottish writing between those who actually try to work out of their middle-class experience (Stewart Conn is a good example among playwrights) and are accused of producing material which is not 'really Scottish' – although one might point to a dozen thematic concerns, habits of thought, aspects of atmosphere that mark the thing as anything but English; and those, on the other hand, who worry away obsessively at the 'matter of Clydeside', long after they're capable of producing something more modern, than sentimentalised memories and quasi-realistic chunks of nostalgia about their tenement childhoods. The worst recent example of this kind of writing in the Scottish theatre was undoubtedly Bill Bryden's *Civilians;* but almost every play which deals with working-class life carries some trace of this guilt-ridden, sentimentalising tendency. The temptation to 'edit out' those aspects of personal experience which don't fit in with some preconceived political or cultural ideology is simply fatal to a creative writer; before artists can move anywhere they have to see the truth of their own cultural situation steadily, and see it whole.

The destructive obsession with the need to emphasise and preserve the 'Scottishness' of our writing far beyond what comes naturally and truthfully to writers will persist for as long as Scotland remains in a political limbo; in other words, it will last until Scotland either becomes a full nation-state, or loses its sense of nationhood altogether. That is not to say, however, that no good writing can come out of Scotland until that political millennium arrives, and indeed there are several grounds for hope. Certain gifted individuals have always been able to transcend the cultural limitations with which fate presents them. There are those with a natural self-confidence that enables them to relish and use *all* their cultural experience no matter what their circumstances, and those whose internal compulsion to write truthfully out of their experience is so strong that it completely drowns out the chanting of the mental supporters' club; in Scotland, there are those – still Scots in their way – whose privileged education has spared them the distorting experience of cultural oppression, and those who live out their lives in small rural or working-class communities, never sallying forth to be corrupted by middle-class affluence or Edinburgh ideologies. Such writers will escape the prevailing obsessions of the Scottish literary scene.

Secondly, there are vast cultural movements afoot today which make the internal problems of Scottish literature look relatively insignificant. The Scottish working class may still be the main repository of un-anglicised Scottish language and culture, but over the past 50 years – without much reference to the Scottish literary establishment or, for that matter, to the dominant Oxbridge culture of the British arts and media – their cultural experience, like that of the mass of people everywhere in the West, has become overwhelmingly international. The generation of Scottish playwrights now in their early 40's is remarkable for the fact that they don't care one way or the other about English culture; their ideas on narrative, dramatic structure and style were all formed by American films of the 40's and 50's, their greatest musical influences have been black American jazz and rock and roll. These days, working people in Glasgow are much more concerned about the next episode of *Dallas* than about the survival of Scottish culture in any form, and the persistent preoccupation with Scottish forms of cultural expression and Scottish writing is one factor which, in itself, alienates many Scottish writers from the Scottish working class, who are fully as sophisticated, as up-to-date, as well-travelled and as internationally-connected as any modern Western proletariat. Part of the brilliance of John Byrne's *Slab Boys* trilogy is that it not only sets itself firmly in the west of Scotland in the 50's, and conjures up that society perfectly; it also places it in its context of James Dean and Radio Luxembourg, and the post-war economic boom that swept the whole of the Western world up in a wave of consumption and prosperity. "You're nineteen wi' a wardrobe full of clothes – you've got everything to live for ..." as the catch-phrase goes. Unimpeachably Scottish, written in the rhythms and vocabulary of a perfect Paisley demotic, *The Slab Boys* has absolutely nothing to do with the self-conscious preservation of Scots language and culture. It is just a brilliantly theatrical and truthful play about the lives of ordinary Scots in the boom years of the 50's and 60's, and because that truth has far-reaching implications it has proved itself infinitely exportable. A tough, modern, well-made and clear-eyed reflection of Scottish life like *The Slab Boys* will do more, in fact, to affirm and reinforce the vitality of our culture than a thousand carefully-crafted Lallans columns in *The Weekend Scotsman*.

Finally, the part played by women writers in Scottish literary life is increasing, at the moment, by leaps and bounds, and with that development there must come a change in old psychological patterns and tensions. It is a curious thing that women never have been so obsessed with the questions of Scottishness as men; men have always been far more inclined to support the SNP, to get hot under the collar about English arrogance, and to feel the whole business of Scotland's colonial status as a personal insult and threat. Why this should be is hard to say. It's tempting to speculate about some kind of Bannockburn complex or Flodden factor, the connection between national military prowess and personal virility. It is also a fact that women in any working-class culture in Britain will tend to speak less broadly than their men, to adapt their language more easily and flexibly towards received vocabulary and pronunciation. Perhaps it has traditionally been more important for men to be seen not to kow-tow to cultural and class domination. But the simplest explanation is probably something to do with football; women far less than men are brought up to attach a profound emotional and personal significance to the hysterical fortunes of the Scottish football team, the very existence of which must be seen as something of a socio-historical anomaly (although I will never forget the look of utter contempt which I once received from one of my uncles when I suggested, in my innocence, that we might do better in the World Cup if we just had a British team), and Paul Pender's fine play *The Game* thoroughly exposes the morass of political, personal and sexual neuroses aroused by Scotland's World Cup disaster of 1978.

At any rate, most Scottish women writers seem relatively free from the little-brother complex, the chip on the shoulder, the need to assert and re-assert Scottishness. In writers like Liz Lochhead and Marcella Evaristi, Alma Cullen and Joan Lingard, the Scottishness of theme and manner and often of languages is indisputably there; the need to prove it – the mental team of Scotland supporters distorting and disturbing their personal vision – is not; and their increasing prominence in our literary life can only have a positive and liberating effect.

All writers have predicaments, difficulties, personal limitations of character and experience which cause them problems; but insofar as the Scottish writer has a special dilemma, I think it lies in the particular difficulty, for a culturally colonised people, of developing a strong and uncensorious confidence in the validity of one's own experience – as a man or a woman, as a Scot, a European, and what is called 'a citizen of the world'.

Maureen Sangster

Anatomy Lesson

(inspired by The Anatomy of Nicolaes Tulp *by Rembrandt van Rijn)*

These are the veins, gentlemen, along which
The blood returns to the heart. Remarkable
That, below this skin of ours, our life blood flows
In such intricate ways for next, but from the deeper region
Of this hand and lower arm – Bear with me
Till I snip and peel these veins back – the arteries:
Here, fairly thin but, in the rest of the body,
Thicker walled than the veins, conveying the blood
To the furthest part of the body, to the very finger-tips.
Circulation gentlemen, as Harvey explained.

The Way through the Woods

(after 'The Way Through The Woods' by Rudyard Kipling)

Is there a way through the woods
for those with no cars? I don't think so.
The woods are so far away. And no
bus passes along the road
except Wednesday. And there's no stop
by the woods. The woods whose natural decay
falls in showers of gold
are only reached by those who can drive,
are only lived in by those who have cars.

And those whose need for the gold
of the woods with their reds
and their browns and the sharp
green returning life
is far greater
than that of professionals
who glide up to the woods
day or night
taking into *their* imagination's lap
the now curled up
leaves, coloured pale pink like a bridesmaid's dress,

Those who need the woods
to survive their lives
– like the push-chair mother from the estate –
the way through the woods is not theirs:

Pinched lives must inhale stale air,
not the green breath of the woods.

No path through magic for the poor,
no depth of peace into which they can go –
the breath of the wind.
The way through the woods
is as far away as the stars.

The way through the woods
can only be loved
by those who have cars.

The Shop Assistant's Feet

The shop assistant's feet crave water water
does not grip the feet
water is of the feet plapa plapa lap
the feet go into the basin of water.

A sea-faring tribe in the Basin Delta
know the dangers of the submerged
feet. Expert sea-men with neat beards navigate
their craft and never hit the sharp toe-nails.
Sore feet – too tired to move – to make waves.
Are they the drowned dead?
Below water the flesh is swollen
like the dead become ballooning up with gases.

The shop assistant's feet, they walk
to Timbuktu "I feel fine," says Timbuktu
"I've been flooded by a turquoise sea.
Marry me – I can give you
the dazzle of the sea-horse
long snout of a face to kiss and love
silken dolphin to ride
armpit armpit armpit
of octopus."

Nimble, the shop assistant in a turquoise
dress of the sea – loose – (what can be
is the sea) – forgets her feet – dances –
moves the heavy veined monuments of legs –
weight of injustice, low paid hours – what
is the sea? – it is mean and merciless.

Bread beds down upon the sea-bed.
Wholemeal loaves lodged malicious.
Rough rocks seed barnacled.

Chug chug chug across the Basin Delta
comes the sound of the freezer cabinet.

And the cries of the insatiable customers
"Buy the shop assistant's soul!"

The feet come out of the basin of water
two items related to the body
Bring them back home now,
a sister, a brother
both little orphans from the water.

Splish splash blubber blubber
splish splash blubber blubber.
They must go to work tomorrow.

The Almond Tree

Ootby, far the gless wis het
wi the burnin bricht mou o the sun, Grandad.
A wee mannie mair suited tae
bidin unner a stane bit here thrivin
a Livingstone in Africa!

"Liars who say there canna be
a Scottish branch o the almond tree."
An His thunderin words proved richt.
His fingers, lang as the Nile,
coaxin first the riggin o the plant
an then its sails an then hoistin me up:
"You quine, bein a maiden,
breathe het summers on it
an find the weak crack,
the wee tinkle o growth
as the sheath aroon the unseen fruit
is peeled awa by the almond
rivin oot."

Inside, in a bed got up for the deid
wi the curtains shut an the only din
the clatter o distant tea cups, Grandad.
Only his heid stickin oot o the fite sheet
like a fibrous fattened tusk.
He wis up fur the kissin noo, an she,
Granny, who'd hardly said ane word
tae the mannie aa the time he lived
bent ower him, an pit her ugsome mou
up agin his. He'd tellt me some tales
ootby – o snakes, buggers o craiturs,
gripy an greedy wha had swallowed
ae moose fur breakfast an anither fur dinner
an then gaed slippity baPPITY

ower the flechy sands. Fat targets aa o them.
But if carressed, aye that wis the word he eesed,
fan injured – oot wid pop
the twa swallowed prey, nae a morsel taen
oot frae flesh or bane!

I wis feart then tae look at
the wye Granny wis feedin on Grandad's lips.
Made me think o a wee wriggling moosie
in by her mou or his
bit naethin came o that except
a muckle big funeral wi a lot o sponges
an a lot o tears,
Granny saying she widna manage wioot him.
Gweed God, she spent a her time wioot him
shut awa in the derk front room.
He'd only penetrated that shrine fan deid.

Inby, there wis a wee table
wi a green velvet skin
an ower it her ebony elephants trauchled
wi their freen, a plastic goose wi a nodding heid,
a bit like Grandad wis wi Granny
an a wee yealla cat –
didna seem tae belong tae the ithers:
seemed tae rin alane, unner a fierce gormless moon.

I thocht she'd gang back tae this:
Clutter o ornaments; curtains drawn;
fatality in the atmosphere bit
she wis oot in that greenhoose
the morn aifter the funeral
an there wis something green aboot her:

As Mum said
That coat, flapping, lang an keich coloured
shud hae been at last year's kirk jumble.
Bit she wis cryin as she touched
the lang leaves o the almond tree.

Ower late I thocht
tae love
her love a dry husk bereaved
an lacking Grandad's hands

bit it wis like the almond
her hert wrenching love that hid matured
an come oot
o the concealing skin o years.

Rediscover Scotland's finest...

Today Tomorrow
The Collected Poems of George Bruce 1933 – 2000
Edited by Lucina Prestige

A celebration of the life and work of the great Scottish poet George Bruce.
'The life,work and sheer energy of Bruce is a result of a dedication to the art of poetry few can sustain or hope to match.'
£14.99 Pbk

Dream State (2nd Edition)
The New Scottish Poets
Edited by Donny O'Rourke

An indispensable sampling of recent Scottish poetry.
'It marks a coming of age and does so in style.' – Independent on Sunday
£15.00 Pbk

An Aghaidh Na Sìorraid-heachd / In The Face of Eternity
Edited by Christopher Whyte

A bilingual anthology bringing together Aonghas MacNeacail, Myles Campbell, Catriona and Mairi Montgomery, Fearghas MacFhionnlaigh, Christopher Whyte, Meg Bateman and Anne Frater.
£9.99 Pbk

An Tuil
Anthology of 20th century Scottish Gaelic verse
Ronald Black (ed)

A unique bilingual anthology providing a much-needed and impressive overview of the high achievement and dramtic development of Gaelic verse in the twentieth century.
£19.99 pbk

ORDER FORM

NAME (Block capitals) ....

DELIVERY ADDRESS ....

....

POST CODE .... DATE ....

Title	*Price*	*Qty*	*Total*
Today Tomorrow	£14.99 pbk		
Dream State	£15.00 hbk		
In the Face of Eternity	£9.99 pbk		
An Tuil	£19.99 pbk		
P&P (Free in the UK for overseas add 30% of total)			
	TOTAL NOW DUE		

☐ I enclose a cheque (sterling) made payable to Birlinn Ltd

Post your completed order form and cheque to:
**Birlinn Ltd,
West Newington House,
10 Newington Road,
Edinburgh EH9 1QS**

**OR call us on
0131 667 7799
to order by phone.**

Tel: 0131 668 4371 Fax: 0131 668 4466 www.birlinn.co.uk

Looking for My Father

Carl MacDougall

He went for a pint and never came back.

He's late tonight, my mother said. There must've been an argument.

We knew what he was like.

Next day he wasn't around when I came in from school and still wasn't back when my mother got home.

We watched television, neither of us talking. Every now and then she'd go to the window, peel back the curtain, look outside, sigh and sit back down beside me. At ten o'clock, watching the News, she held my hand.

Two days later the doorbell rang. CID.

They kept asking questions. One did the talking, writing the answers into his notebook, while the other, the one with the skinny face and a turn in the left eye, stared at us, moving his eye from my mother to me and back to my mother. They left with a photograph of my father and told us to get in touch with the Salvation Army.

A cheery looking man with bright eyes and a red face came round with his wife. She nodded her head while he spoke about the strains of modern living. They promised to help and said a wee prayer, asking God to give us strength in our hour of need.

Nothing happened.

Then my mother said she'd seen him. I'm sure it was him, she said. The bus was past before I could turn, so I only got a glimpse, and it was raining; but I'd know your father anywhere.

Maybe once every four or five weeks she'd come in and say, I saw him again today, crossing the road by Marks and Spencers. He'd a Tesco bag, but I recognised his jacket.

When the Salvation Army man came round to say God had called him to work in Sheffield, I knew I'd never see my father again. If anyone asked, I said he was dead. If they asked how he died I told them his heart stopped beating, and when that happens there not a lot of hope, you're pretty well finished.

I thought I saw him at my mother's funeral. The undertakers wheeled the coffin out on a wee trolley and we followed behind. It was like following a pram. Three or four pews from the front I scanned the church.

Nothing. He must have gone, I thought.

But I kept looking, on the way to the cemetery, at the graveside and in the hotel afterwards with the sandwiches and tea. I looked in the bar and even out the window to see if he'd turn up. I half expected to see him get out a taxi and argue with the driver over the fare.

With my mother gone, I knew I didn't want to be married. I'd stayed married to keep my mother happy. She liked my wife and treated her like the daughter she never had, and I know my wife and her family were fond of my mother. They turned out for her funeral and shook my hand at the church door. She was a fine woman, your mother, my father-in-law said, a very fine woman who did not have her sorrows to seek.

I thought at first he meant my father, then I thought he meant me. And other things fell into place, little things I had never considered, remarks, innuendoes, comments, glances, all of that.

When I told my wife I wanted to leave, she said I was mad.

How could you manage on your own? she said in the same tone of voice my mother used when my father started on about ideas he had for this and that. I knew she couldn't keep me, that all I had to do was pack a few things, say I was going for a pint and disappear.

I looked at bedsits. The man always asked if I was DSS, told me I could move in straight away and did I want the milk and rolls delivered.

But when I was home, sitting in the house with my wife, watching TV or reading the paper, doing a crossword, I knew I wanted my things around me, wanted the house to be as it was, except I wanted to be on my own.

So I started driving round at night, looking for my father. I'd sometimes see him in the street, stop the car and run down the road, but he'd disappeared by the time I got to wherever I thought he should be waiting.

Is that you off? my wife says every night at the back of nine. Are you away for a pint?

Spitting it Out

She thought the coughing would kill him. It came in the night and left him clawing air in the dark. His chest let out dollops of noise when he seemed to be taking nothing into his body.

And she lay there, invisible, letting him cough and wheeze and splutter till he was done, or nearly done, when he'd lie back onto the pillows and mutter; No more. No more cigarettes. I swear it, God. No more cigarettes.

She never tried to help him, not since the time he hit her and said he'd manage and she'd to mind her own business. And he never spoke. One morning she said, You were bad last night. And he pressed the button that turned up the sound on the television.

She watched him move round the house like a ghost and knew he was going to die. Everything was an effort. He sat on the bed and waited for breath to let him to stand. He didn't wash properly and took more than an hour to get dressed. She'd put the socks on his feet and tie his laces; sometimes she'd button his shirt and tie his tie. His clothes looked baggy.

He touched the furniture as he passed, and stopped at the bottom of the stairs, looked to the top and tried to take a breath before going up, one stair at a time, stopping every now and then to hold onto the railing or wave his arm to find a support he knew wasn't there. When she followed him into the lavatory the water was still pink with his blood after he'd flushed the bowl. She stopped looking at his underwear.

What's the use? he said when she mentioned the doctor.

And he'd stopped eating. He'd have tea and a smoke for breakfast, drink tea throughout the morning and maybe take a piece or a roll at dinner time, but he usually settled for a couple of slices of toast. He looked at his food as if it was an effort. She bought things she knew he liked, a wee chop or a nice bit of ham, and he'd pick away at the meat, then leave the rest, even when she'd cut the meat and roasted the tatties. He'd take a drop soup now and then, but stopped eating when he started to sweat.

Every afternoon he went to the bookies. He'd put his line on and climb back up the stairs. The journey took between three and four hours.

He never lingered. She'd watched him. He moved along the wall, stopping every now and then to take in air, or just stand still. He couldn't take the atmosphere in the betting shop: Too smoky, he said.

And so he went on for most of the summer. Then, near the end of September, after he'd eaten half a poached egg for his tea he told his wife, I need to see her. Maybe a Sunday'd be best.

She ordered the taxi, laid out his clothes and spent the morning dressing him. The taxi came at one o'clock.

Did you tell her? he asked when they came off the motorway. And when they pulled into Margaret's street he asked again if she knew he was coming. The taxi waited while he shuffled on the pavement in the broken glass and litter watching weans play. A group of girls, quiet and aloof, stood at a corner. When the taxi pulled away, he shook his head. A minute, he said. Give me a minute. And he stood, taking the air.

Half an hour later, they were two storeys up. A wee boy opened the door and shouted, Mammy. It's a man and a woman. He walked past the child into the house.

A man in his semmitt lay in bed, reading the paper. He looked up when they came in. A couple of weans were watching a video and a woman stood up from turning on a bar of the electric fire. She'd a can of superlager in her hand and threw it at the man who came in.

Not here, she said. I don't want to see you here. Get out. You've no right coming here. This is my house. I can do what I like. Get out.

The man jumped out of the bed and the weans cooried in behind the sofa, their eyes shut tight and their hands at their ears. The man from the bed pulled on his shirt and trousers.

Just see him, the older woman said. Just see him this time.

No.

He's your father. You have to see him. Margaret. Please.

I'm dying, he said. I know I'm dying and I need to speak to you.

The man from the bed turned him to the door and pushed him out. He fell in the lobby and as his wife tried to pull him to his feet, the younger woman fell on her knees and started punching his body. Her mother tried to stop her and the two women pulled at each other on the floor.

Look at him, the older woman screamed. Look at him. He's dying.

I hope he dies. I hope he dies soon and I'll spit on his grave.

Don't, Margaret. Please. Don't say that.

You knew. You're as bad as him. You must've known, but you let it happen.

The children turned up the volume on the TV as the man on the lobby floor shouted, Help me. Help me stand. For God's sake, help me stand.

His wife got him to his knees. The other couple went back in the kitchen and shut the door. He tried to grab the lobby walls and eventually crawled to the door, where he gripped the handles as his wife helped him rise.

They waited for more than an hour in the rain. When the taxi came, he slumped in the back. The driver had to help her up the stairs with him, where she stripped and washed him with a flannel while the bed warmed with three hot water bottles. In a pair of crisp, new pyjamas he lay staring at the ceiling and coughed again in the middle of the night, grasping air.

Do you want to tell me? she asked, when the coughing subsided. Do you want to tell me what happened, with you and Margaret?

The only sound was the wheeze of his chest.

You know what I'm going to think, don't you. Tell me what happened. For God's sake, tell me.

Nothing happened, he said. Nothing. It's her. She's off her head, always was and always will be.

He died three days later. She'd to go to the mortuary to identify the body. Nobody in the betting shop knew where he stayed and he'd no identification. They'd to wait till somebody who knew him came in three hours after he'd collapsed. By which time the ambulance had taken him to the mortuary.

Maurice Lindsay

Mr Oddevens

Punctually he arrived every morning
at his office, on the exact stroke of nine;
to those less punctual he gave only one warning –
they thought him impossible to know or define!

He left the office precisely at five o'clock
with rolled umbrella even when it was fine
and brisked the station at a fast-paced walk.
As seven o'clock chimed, he sat down to dine

With his routine wife, whose patience habitually listened
to the eagerless trivialities of his day,
then faced the TV screen, till his eye glistened
and up the stairs they both made their bedding way.

He made average love according to the book
his climax a matter of timed routine;
the animal, on which he preferred not to look,
with blankets drawn, so that nudity wouldn't be seen.

On the right side always of some invisible line
that couldn't be crossed if life were to stay as it should,
eschewing passions, the wiles of food and wine;
an even manner that neither praised nor was rude.

Until, on the road from which he never strayed,
his heart gave out and he dropped to a public scene,
his final thought as he fell, how he'd been betrayed
by death attracting all he had never been.

Sunday Morning

One English Sunday morning, in a village
slept deep in countryness, dark-coated men
and best-dressed women, summoned by the pillage
of silence – the *again, again, again*
the bell retolled, to symbolise God's love
for all creation – made their pious way
to kneel in cushioned privacy and pray;
for fancied sins that conscience couldn't prove,
or sins no moral rinsing could unsay.

Meanwhile, mere speck in the blue-circled sky
a keen-eyed goshawk swooped, then hoisted back
a rabbit in its claws, ordained to die
to keep the preying chain of life intact
surpassing what their supplications lacked.

Not Arriving

On the rough field that was the island airport
flying from Stronsay to the Orkney mainland,
the pilot held one wetted finger up
to test the wind's direction. We took off
and landed on another field, near Kirkwall,
sophisticated by a wooden shed
for waiting passengers.

That was my first
flight, now almost eighty years ago;
for the first time briefly entering
the cerulean blue which lies around
the rim of cloud that harnesses our earth …

Over the years I've flown from many *heres*
to *theres* and back again, stretching vast continents
beneath the engine's drone.

This, I suppose,
is just about the last time that I'll find
myself, as it were, outside looking in

Henceforth, I'll stay terrestrial, until I
am taken off, a silent tannoy call
for an unnumbered flight that has no <u>there</u>
to aim for, nor the thrill of nearly landing
at some roof-sheltered destination – absent
since superstitions can't be landed on.
According to the Stevensonian adage
they say the pleasure's travelling, not arriving.

Pray, They Say ...

Where does it come from? How so freely spread?,
the man asked as the foot-and-mouth disease
resulted in the hundred thousands dead –
sheep, pigs and cattle – slaughtered to appease
an epidemic, like the human plague
that blighted mediaeval villages,
borne by the wind; strange retribution, vague
as the supposing sins it pillages.
Pray!, the religious cry, although it's odd,
seeing burnt carcasses they still assume
disease is not as much the work of God
as bodies falling victim to its doom,
unwilling, as they are, to realise
how lonely the unhearing empty skies!

Wakeful

Wakeful in bed at night, sometimes the moon –
or Jupiter, or Saturn? – stares clean through
my bare uncurtained window; but, restless, soon
they roll themselves across the darkened blue-
absorbing sky, and I sink back to sleep,
half-wondering how the planets hold their place;
what silent and invisible forces keep
the universe intact in edgeless space,
and us upon a mite of man-made time,
tracing the lines upon a loved-one's face,
or fashioning our wonderment in rhyme
as, pulsing through our brittleness, we pace
the passaging of what we call 'the years',
mocking the prick of all our human fears.

Some Observations on how the Scots Define Themselves with a View of the Native Philosophy

J Maxwell Hastie

The ensuing remarks are not intended to trespass upon the domain of such specialist publications as *The Scottish National Dictionary,* Dwelly's *Gaelic-English Dictionary,* Johnnie Gibb's *Gushetneuk* or Baxter's *Parliamo Glasgow.* I merely wish to inform our English or foreign visitors of certain usages which are common throughout the Lowlands, Borders and most tracts of English-speaking Highlands and Islands.

How Scotsmen Define Each Other

A Braw Bugger[1] One who can shite[2] with the best of them.

[1]The term 'bugger' when applied by one Scots man to another has no sexual significance, even in sheep rearing parishes. Since to the Scot a man is the highest form of created life, to call a man 'a man' is to over-praise him.

[2]The male Scot prefers excretion to sexuality because although both are equally inevitable, the first is less expensive.

A Dour Bugger One who can't shite yet refuses to take the medicine.

A Thrawn Bugger One who can't shite, takes the medicine yet still refuses to shite.

A Canny Bugger One who can't shite, takes the medicine, still can't shite, returns the medicine and his money is refunded.

An Uncanny Bugger One who can't shite, takes the medicine, won't shite, returns the medicine, has his money refunded – then shites!

Note that the Braw Bugger and the Uncanny Bugger, the alpha and omega of this spectrum, have a common characteristic – their bodily functions are unimpeded by moral imperatives.

The Scots and their Property

The Scots, like many deprived races, have a passionate attachment to the basic essentials of food, drink and slumber, which they underline by their frequent deployment of the personal pronoun:

eg *Do you want a bit of my fish?*

You'll have had your tea?

I'm going home to my bed.

However, the male Scot's lack of all proprietorial instinct towards the female will gladden the hearts of the most ardent feminists. It is shown in his preference of the indefinite article over the personal pronoun when identifying his spouse, actual or intended.

eg *No thanks, I'm going home to the wife.*
No thanks, I'm going out with the bird.

Contrariwise, the acquisitive and rapacious attitude of the average Scots woman towards the male counterpart is nowhere more evident than in her heavy-handed insistence of the personal pronoun:

eg *My man kicked hell out of me last night.*
It's aff his Da my boy gets his nae brains frae.
My fiancé's done a bunk again.

Scottish Positivism, the Perennial Philosophy

Scratch a Scot and you will find a philosopher. Scottish philosophical thought is so deeply engrained in the national psyche that the works of Hume, Hamilton, Carlyle and Horatio McTeague must be regarded as mere outcroppings of the native bedrock, whose quality is best revealed in the following dicta, which may be heard in any laundrette, turf accountant's office or football changing room:

What's for ye will no go past ye – The world is all that is the case. (Is-ness is all; is replaces if.)

It'll aa be the same a hunner years frae noo – In that the past is irremediable, any finite point in the future will display the same charateristics.

It'll no be this in the mornin – Since the present is tolerable, it is highly unlikely that a finite point in the future will display the same characteristics.

This by no means comprehends the extant. Further observation may well yield fruits.

Editorial note: *this contribution arose in a strange and amusing way. Carl MacDougall wrote to me, saying that this mad friend had taken possession of his garden shed and his typewriter. I wrote back, accepting it, asking him to continue to act as contact-person and saying that I especially liked the first of the three-part piece and would like more of anything similar. By return, I received a diatribe from Mr Hastie, who had blown a gasket at the merest thought of any questioning of his deathless works, and who was I, a mere editor, even to comment. Through Carl, I immediately did one of my editorial grovelling apologies (which one has to learn to do in this business), withdrew my comments and said I'd use every word, word for word, and hasten no further importunate editorial comments.*

Needless to say, we knew all along it was a huge joke, and that Maxwell Hastie was in fact Carl, inhabiting his own garden shed and doing whatever he happened to be doing to his own typewriter. The correspondence is in the Chapman archive in the NLS. Carl and I enjoyed ourselves hugely over the whole matter!

Carl MacDougall writes: *Maxwell Hastie eventually appeared in my first novel,* Stone over Water, *though not as Maxwell Hastie but as a piece of work by the protagonist's father. Mr Hastie tells me he's appalled by the way the national fondness for drink and its place in our culture has been overtaken by chemical alternatives. He blames the younger generation and has written something, which he says he can't find; when he passes it on, you'll be the first to know!*

Association for Scottish Literary Studies

Join the ASLS and receive:

- **Two issues of *Scottish Studies Review*** – this journal is essential reading for any serious student of Scottish culture
- **One issue of *Scottish Language*** – in-depth studies of Scottish languages
- **An *Annual Volume*** – each year a different work of major importance. Previous Annual Volumes have included *Scotland's Ruine*, *Flemington* and the award-winning *Poems of William Dunbar*.
- **Two issues of *ScotLit*** – a newsletter packed with relevant articles
- ***New Writing Scotland*** – previously unpublished poetry and prose from both emerging and established writers
- **ASLS members** also receive a 20% discount on *all* other ASLS publications

2003 Subscription Rates
Individual: £34/year
Institutional: £63/year
(EU subscribers outside UK: add £3.50 p&p. All other non-UK subscribers: add £6.00 p&p)

To join, contact:

ASLS, Scottish History Dept.,
University of Glasgow
Glasgow G12 8QH, Scotland

Tel/Fax: +44 (0)141 330 5309
www.asls.org.uk

Sorley MacLean

Dàin do Eimhir
Poems to Eimhir

Edited by Christopher Whyte

0 948877 50 2	*£12.50*	*Paperback*
0 948877 49 9	*£25.00*	*Hardback*

Though it is widely regarded as his greatest achievement, Sorley MacLean's cycle of love lyrics *Dàin do Eimhir* (*Poems to Eimhir*) was only published in part during his lifetime. Drawing on manuscript and published sources, this new edition brings together all but one of the poems, including six which have never before appeared in print.

With facing English translations throughout, an authoritative introduction and extensive commentaries on all fifty-nine poems, this new edition makes a major masterpiece of 20th century Scottish literature fully available to the general public for the first time.

"This is one of the most moving books you will ever read, a towering work of obsessive love, enduring humanity and uniquely elegant insight. Scotland — and Europe — should be proud." *The Scotsman*

ASLS
c/o Scottish History
University of Glasgow
Glasgow
G12 8QH

Reviews

Collected Poems, Burns Singer, ed James Keery, Carcanet, £14.95, 242pp; *Caledonian Cramboclink: Verses ... and in Conversation,* William Neill, Luath, £8.99, 176pp; *Dream State: 2nd Edn*, ed Donny O'Rourke, Polygon, £15, 320pp

The canon of 20th century Scottish poetry is always a debateable territory, a quagmire of quicksands where reputations struggle and sink, studded by a few flinty promontories. For all MacDiarmid's greatness, he can seem an oppressive rhododendron, stifling any sapling unfortunate enough to try to grow in his shadow. Hidden beside the 'Poet's Pub' is the 'Outsider's Oasis', frequented by figures like Hamish Henderson, Ian Hamilton Finlay, Tom Scott, George Campbell Hay, Kenneth White and Gael Turnbull. Reviewing these three volumes – which, I should say at the outset, should all be owned by anyone serious about poetry, Scottish or not – I was struck again by the thinness of the 'traditional' literary history of the 20th century.

Burns Singer (born James Hyman Singer, 1928, New York; raised Glasgow) received only 2 pages in a recent 1000 page anthology of 20th century Scottish literature edited by David McCordick. Moreover, he does not appear at all in the new Penguin book of Scottish Verse. This is a grievous under-estimation, and barely indicates his range or his talent. After his death, his reputation was not properly established, due both to the lack of appreciation of his own work, and also of other poets he admired, like the Apocalyptics and W S Graham; and he was vociferous in attacking the Movement poets. Moreover, as a regular writer of the *Times Literary Supplement* leader column, he occupied an odd position as an Establishment figure espousing a*vant-garde* writers. His one collection (*Still and All*, 1957) is a meticulously organised and still challenging volume: one quibble with this edition is that, as with the Carcanet edition of Sorley MacLean, the chronological sequencing means that the intact collection is scattered throughout the book like an elephant's skeleton. Without even notes to indicate which poems were in *Still and All*, an important part of his poetic identity is lost. But the poems *are* here; and they shine.

Although Burns Singer's imagery can, like that of his early mentor Dylan Thomas, misfire on occasion, when he hits, he hits bull's-eye: 'An Elegy', for example, has the exquisite line 'Hot panting seas and the lightning-antlered storm'. It is, however, in his radical approach to syntax that Burns Singer reads most like a contemporary. Although he does not take this approach as far as Berryman – let alone J H Prynne – he does seem to originate from the same point as Berryman: the 17th century Metaphysical poets (an interesting piece could be written on Burns Singer and Andrew Marvell, and their mutual obsession with the colour green). In the *Sonnets for a Dying Man*, whilst staying true to all the demands of the form, he interpolates a struggling grammar: the opening octet from No. XXIV is worth quoting in its entirety.

Weigh anchor into windfall and lurch at last
Up the ribbed ocean, green swell
                    and unruly foam
Combed back in curls beneath you as you climb
On keels of wool and what you're
                    drenched in dressed.
Its purl or plain, its odd or even twist,
Takes your blood nevertheless
                    away towards home
From a heart weighed up more heavy
                    against its doom
Than ever that sailor in a hornpipe lost.

Burns Singer's great theme was the proximity of death and the idea of immortality; and, although he died of heart failure at the age of 36, the work at least approaches the latter.

William Neill's new collection will do nothing to dispel his reputation for tetchiness; it should, however, introduce new readers to a deeply committed poet with an enviable formal fluency. And I don't mean that as faint praise – the rhyming couplets and Byronic stanzas are carried off with true aplomb, and fit perfectly to their subject matter. To my mind, the best works in the collection are the satires; the 'Canto Macaronach', 'Sawney's Complaint', 'An-other Letter to Lord Byron' and 'The Jolly Trimmers'. Neill's attacks on 'pan-loaf' English – and RP are gloriously scurrilous, thoroughly splenetic and worthy of Pope himself in their indignation. Neill can deploy his considerable linguistic skills to the gloriously expressive Anglo-Saxon as well, attacking he metropolitan arrogance that so often accompanies it. These works sizzle and spit, a shower of linguistic sparks from the deep insistence of a point being hammered on the anvil.

My caveat on the collection is not the manner; but the frequency of the matter. In the satirical work, Neill's beliefs are integrated into their form. When, however, he grafts yet another attack on free-verse and London O'Centric pseudo-Scottish modern poets into a Lallans piece, I wish he would just get on and write in the style he claims they despise, rather than hijack the form for another torrent of intemperance. MacDiarmid's 'Empty Vessel' would be a slighter work if it had a third stanza stating that Scots was the 'bairnie ... nae langer there'.

Neill is right to assert that poets working in Gaelic, Scots and English are less highly regarded that those specialising in one language: no-one slights Brodsky for writing in Russian and American. The 'three languages of Scotland' phrase, however, has surely outlived its appropriateness. Urdu, Cantonese and Romany are also three of the languages of Scotland. So, for that matter, might be Klingon and BASIC: and if we restrict it to origins, we'd expel everyone except the extinct Cymric speakers.

The interview that concludes this volume gives an insight into the 'maverick sensibility' of Neill, as well as some further palpable hits against poetasters, pretension and pomposity. Gerry Cambridge, who conducts the interview, clearly brings out the best in his subject, with only a minor lapse into special pleading in the case of American neo-Formalism. More thrawn than sonsie, Neill is nonetheless a consummate and unfalteringly exact writer: I only wish he would write more about his enthusiasms and less about his *bêtes noires*.

It would be interesting to know what Neill makes of the revised edition of the *Dream State* anthology; especially a poem as formally, linguistically and imaginatively precocious as W N Herbert's 'Cabaret MacGonagall', which manages (unless I'm totally off-beam) even to include a nod at Ronnie Hazelhurst. Very few anthologies are so influential to warrant a reconsideration in less than ten years, and to Donny O'Rourke's credit, he has not only re-edited, but re-imagined the whole volume. The subtitle, *The New Scottish Poets*, drew some flak before; and even now, I'm unsure where to find New Scotland on a map: mid-way between New York, Nova Scotia and Caledonia Prime, I suspect.

The two poets who launch the collection, John Burnside and Carol Ann Duffy, embody an antisyzygy that runs through the whole volume. Burnside's work is in a constant, sophisticated and almost self-consciously poetic voice, with an under-murmuring cadence reminiscent of Matthew Arnold. Duffy, on the other hand, is ventriloquistic, integrating 'non-poetic' material such as tabloid headlines and often flagrantly syncopated. The meat of the book is still the loose grouping once known as the 'Scottish Informationists' – Price, Kinloch, Herbert, Crawford, McCarey and Riach. Any good anthology works in part as a primer, which will send the reader off to investigate further the work of the included poets: certainly in the case of Peter McCarey it is to be hoped that interest in a major collection might be whetted by *Dream State.*

While the Informationists deconstructed and reconstructed the myths of Scottish identity, placing it in global contexts that alternately highlighted and jarred, the work of many female poets in the anthology seems to move towards a self-conscious mythologisation of identity. This can sometimes be slightly cloyingly confessional: and I am glad that Angela McSeveney's much starker, unswervingly honest work is there as a counterpoint. The idea of a canon of female writing in Scotland is perhaps even more fraught with difficulty (who, for example, is taking up the mantle of the late, great Veronica Forrest-Thomson's work?).

It is good, if somewhat melancholy, to read again these now-influential writers, to see them, again, with a fresh eye and renewed enthusiasm. Many of the poets' entries represent work from an earlier, and in some ways more interesting, stage in their career. To look at some of the collections published more recently, there is a distinct sense of poets impersonating themselves: one can now speak of a 'Burnsidian' voice; the new volume by Carol Ann Duffy looks suspiciously like the same old same old Duff.

Dream State succeeds in that it does not propose a new 'canon' or 'mainstream' – such ventures are precarious at best, as the Poetry Society's 'New Generation' so amply demonstrated. Rather, *Dream State* offers a plethora of potential ways in which Scottish poetry might develop, the parallel and divergent trajectories which could be taken. It is not a manifesto, but a smorgasbord. I cannot resist quoting part of one of the real gems of the collection; Rob McKenzie's wonderful 'A Home For the Words Lost By 'Contemporary' Poets':

> The the and the a and the and and
> because bu and of the way if that
> to be in or on or at or besides
> in which is and are and can and
> do perhaps of course it seems am

That Scottish poetry is, at present, diverse, exciting and confident is nothing new; nor is the fact that our heritage contains a great many under-appreciated and radical writers. If only there were more publishers ready to meet their challenges.

Stuart B Kelly

Edinburgh International Book Festival 2002

Taking Words to Market

This was the year quality control and Market Forces came to the Edinburgh Book Festival. At the programme launch, it became evident that the commerce of culture and the business of books was to be promoted often at the expense of discussion or literary evaluation. Previous press launches have been short, simple and informative. This was an overcrowded and manipulated circus, self-referential anecdotes boosted by sycophantic laughter and later false acclaim – with no question time – irritating on this first chance to discuss the use of Lottery money awarded in 2001 (well spent on welcome improvements on the site in Charlotte Square).

This was one of several points I made when I wrote to *The Herald* (29 Aug. 2002) sponsor paper for EIBF. First I praised their coverage, especially literary editor Rosemary Goring's. I then lamented that such incisive coverage was not available to all correspondents. "Due to last year's record number of ticket requests" the new Press Administration put a limit of ten tickets to correspondents such as I – to ten events from 650 over 17 days. *The Scottish Book Collector* was offered a limit of four and its editor was rightly affronted considering her comprehensive coverage the year before. As writer for *Chapman* and a Dublin paper, such limitations were unrealistic and I came to an amiable compromise with press staff. But it was personal kindness from authors and publishers, and mischievous championship from author-agent Giles Gordon, that enabled me to record a number of 'big-name' events.

A second issue was programming. Despite the quantitative leap in authors attending many were so timed as to effectively deny access to others. The most obvious was the overlap of Kathleen Jamie's TLS Centenary talk with the Heaney lecture. While Ms Jamie was in the large Consignia tent, Heaney was given the smaller Studio Theatre. And one had to could choose between the important Herald Debate: *What Next for The Middle East?* and Irish novelist John McGahern on his first Edinburgh visit. This programme was most distracting and audience-unfriendly. Alarming numbers of cancellations 'disappeared' from the final statistics. The marketing people did try to notify ticket holders but again and again I heard "too late". Visitors arriving on spec had also to work around some very erratic cash-registers.

My final point was the failure of the Scottish media to report these issues. Daily I heard press colleagues complain. It has become an honourable trait not to criticise the Book Festival, not even in 1997 when fulminating hacks, goaded beyond tolerance, included a vociferous Catherine Lockerbie for *The Scotsman.* Justified praise was abundant for the many successes this year. But there comes a time when public silence is complicity with errors that once aired and examined can be rectified. My letter was not published.

The Festival itself: notably rewarding was 71 year old Egyptian Nawal El Saadwi (directly competing with Arnold Bennett). With ambitions to be a dancer she instead "found patriotism" and became a medical doctor. She was appointed Director General of Public Health. Then patriotism became political feminism and she wrote *Women and Sex* (1972). She was dismissed from her job and later imprisoned by the West's favourite Egyptian Anwar Sadat. At times she flared and we felt the heat of her contempt for "fundamentalism" and "George Bush the son" who "inherited stupidity from his father". We would be stupid to ignore the experience moulding the wisdom of this woman. The crass cry of profiteering war-drums could not silence her and should awaken us now.

Former Radio Scotland presenter Brian Morton was in Chair for Paul Muldoon's Festival debut. The Armagh-born poet visibly relaxed as the knowledgeable, admiring and informed Morton led him into the new poems in *Moy Sand and Gravel.* "I once said you could rhyme knife with fork," purred Morton. "Did you?" asked Muldoon with Ulster earnestness. He then allowed the rhymes of childhood succumb to the rhythms of adulthood. I have attended many Muldoon readings, but this, by far, was the most rewarding and revealing. Morton appeared frequently. Could he be the first male Director of EIBF?

Fables rather than parables were central to the dialogue between novelist Phillip Pullman and Episcopalian Richard Holloway. Pullman, a clergyman's grandson, killed God in his novel *The Amber Spyglass*. Holloway was sanguine about his aversion to the Church of England, comparing it to being "angry at a lemon meringue". Then they began to talk about creativity and Genesis (both Bible and pop group). Bring them back.

Cancellations accumulated on opening day causing gatherings of book lovers in the nearby Oxford Bar. Three mountaineers from "north of Inverness" retired there late morning when they discovered Joe Simpson was not to appear. Soon they were joined by two Londoners who had hoped to enjoy American Walter Mosley. By late afternoon several locals were hissing at the absence of Ted Hughes biographer Elaine Feinstein.

At the opening party, *The Herald*'s editor spoke of the "devotion" of Ms Lockerbie. She introduced herself as a "Bibliobibuli", (one drunk on books). Another sponsor told us she was a "phenomenon"; her staff concurred loudly. Of course she is and realised it enough to joke about the "mud moat" surrounding the "Press Pod" from which "would emerge creatures, centuries later, perfectly preserved". I returned to other cultures in the Oxford.

Next morning I started with Don Paterson and Edwin Morgan. Dundonian Paterson told us "Britney Speirs" is an anagram for "Presbyterian" and read a long poem with echoes of MacNeice. Then there was a moving half hour with the seriously-ill but defiant Morgan: "I'm not talking of death/ I'm talking of life". Reading from *Planet Earth* (1997) he affirmed: "Forgiveness that's the thing. It's like a second life". As the audience went silent in appreciation, he concluded: "My friends, do you want to know what you should feel?/ I can't tell you, but feel you must. My story's real." We were touched by his reality. In the subjugated cultural hinterland of the sound-byte this emotional arrest was almost heretical. We were all the better for that.

That opening Sunday ended with "Reflection on America", subtitled '11th on the 11th'. It focused on murders and suicides in New York and elsewhere on 11 September, 2001. What should have been a reflective session became an expression of egos. Ruth Wishart chaired and writers Joyce Carol Oates, Kathryn Harrison and Claire Messaud were to respond. Oates opened with a firm rejection of "the virus of patriotism", but even she became embroiled into nostalgic sentimentality. Maybe it was the lead-off question "So where were you when ..." All on the platform became reporting ciphers. Most guilty, in her monopoly of the talk, was novelist Harrison, who three times repeated, almost as mantra, a line from *The Seal Wife* about "a predatory black column" which obsessed her.

Next day Israeli novelist Amos Oz demonstrated the benefits of brevity. Reading, at times in Hebrew, from his novel *The Same Sea*, he introduced details, then elaborated on their importance. Born in Jerusalem (1939) he has chosen to live with his family in Arad. He is conscious of the self-censorship some use when "dressing-up" their writing in allegorical format. Parables on politics today. He wittily recognises this and rejects it: "If ever I write a story about a father, a mother, a daughter and her pocket money, it will be said that the father is the government, mother is religion, the new generation is represented by the daughter and the money refers to the inflation rate. That is the lot of any writer who comes from a troubled part of the world."

One of the great pleasures of "covering" the Book Festival since its inception in 1983 has been the ability to meet much admired visiting writers, like André Brink (1985 and later), Yehuda Amichai (1995) and the Portuguese novelist Mario De Carvalho (1998). So it was the New Zealander C K Stead this year. He is, as Alan Taylor of *The Sunday Herald* said, "a real writer". Paul Muldoon had earlier commented that his ground-breaking *New Poetic* had "probably set us all up on writing and understanding at the start".

This tall man, poet, novelist and academic, spoke of "a long career, a gradual transition from literary criticism to literary nationalism in the earlier novels and now ... that the themes cross continents ... literary regionalism". Listening to him was a pleasure and his gentle but wise veneer distracted me from the more bombastic South African Etienne van Heerden who shared the platform.

I emphasise a sense of emerging schism. Celebrity, not eminence ruled. Visitors like Bennett, Weldon and Keillor were given star status far above their literary content or contribution. Headlines were blazed for Germaine Greer, blustering and bullying instead of replying to Sheena Macdonald's probing questions. Apparently, "she felt a tart" in the "company of the simple lives of aboriginals". She pleaded for privacy and understanding for public figures, then showed mock indignation at the religious beliefs of the Blairs. A revealing throwaway: "A lot of what I do is not done well because it is done in too much of a hurry ... and I have no social life".

One day I sauntered with Ian Rankin into the Authors' tent (the 'Yurt'), in mid-conversation;. the rain was ever-present. Almost immediately we were accosted by a clip-board-hugging member of the EIBF team. Press was forbidden entry to the Yurt, we were shrilly told. Since the instigation of this space for authors in 1996, I've carefully complied with the intention which had not yet become a rule. But I bridled this time since this was a personal encounter between friends.

One event blossomed unexpectedly, sending me words-reeling across the gardens: – the dialogue between Aonghas Macneacail and Tom Leonard. Both poets focused on familial matters and it was good to hear Leonard read early pieces like 'The Good Thief' (1969). Then sparks flew. Language and the imperative of communication were emphasised as Gaelic- (Macneacail) and conscience- (Leonard) driven. The latter emphasised the need to "learn to speak yourself". A first-time visitor beside me filled pages of enthusiastic notation long after the event. A haunting, and telling image.

Over the years, a number of moments have redefined the importance of the Book Festival. Visits by James Baldwin, Gore Vidal and Joyce Carol Oates, have created a true "special relationship" between American ideas and attendees in Charlotte Square. The much-missed 'Bigger Picture' slot often introduced English-speaking audiences to the thinking of fellow Europeans. This year writers from the Middle East war-zone honed our sensibilities away from the bombastic rhetoric of politicians. In an Irish-Scottish context there was a day of singular literary significance when Nobel Laureate Seamus Heaney spoke of Sorley MacLean, annotating his new translation ("an interpretation") of the Scot's poem 'Hallaig', then later more generally of Scottish-Irish cultural matters.

Through erudition and generous empathy, he drew the Scot into the forefront of 20th century literature in a way the pundits of Stockholm failed to do during MacLean's lifetime. His address, *The Trance and the Translation,* opened by citing both William Blake and Karl Marx as inspirations for MacLean's poem. It is in 14 four-line stanzas that move from iconic images of the Clearances to a near fatalism for the future of "the deer" whose "blood will not be traced while I live" (MacLean's own translation). The Irishman's closing lines tell of "the light headed deer ... Will freeze while I live, /His blood won't be traced in the woods".

This more gentle linguistic emphasis on continuity is there in the new text. It is both an illumination of the original and a singularly complementary poem in English. MacLean, echoing Rilke, introduced his poem: "Tha tim, am fiadh, an coille Hallaig" *(Time, the deer, is in the woods of Hallaig).* Heaney telescopes the moment: "Time, the deer, is in Hallaig Wood". Then he elides the line into the first stanza

There's a board nailed across the window
I looked through to see the west
And my love is a birch forever
By Hallaig Stream,

MacLean, blandly, has this as "The window is nailed and boarded/ through which I saw the West". Again and again the Irishman's Hiberno-Anglo cadences give flight to the Gaelic original in a fusion of linguistic faiths. Articulated beliefs coalesce. Heaney continued to communicate, "as if embracing the ebb and flow" between the Gaelic and his "new poem". Deliberate concealment of personal emotions became cogent revelations of shared vulnerabilities. There lay the depth and beauty of this collaborative moment. Before "rendering" his final draft, Heaney placed and connected his affinities by emphasising a common awareness: "MacLean's sense of belonging to a culture that is doomed but one that he will never deny".

It was an important Gaelic and Celtic literary occasion but not a single Gaelic speaker was among the seven allocated Press tickets. I was there courtesy of Catherine Lockerbie herself for one of my most rewarding and enriching experiences of the Book Festival.

The preservation of optimism was central to *The Herald* Debate: *What Next for the Middle East?* Chaired by David Pratt (*Sunday Herald*) this event brought together Israelis David Grossman and Amos Oz and the Palestinian lawyer and author Raja Shehadeh. The latter had been a revelation earlier, reading from his memoir *Stranger in the House.* It recorded the intellectual journey from a privileged, disjointed childhood to a "coming of age" in his 50s as a defence lawyer in "occupied Palestine". This quiet-spoken Joyce-lover was painfully intense and informative. Oz was reflective and curiously pacified in his responses. Grossman seemed most influenced by recent killings and incursions becoming almost muted. There was no posturing in this dignified gathering. The audience left silenced by the ongoing fratricide in the 'Holy Land'. Pratt was a good and knowledgeable chair but this event would have benefited from the presence of his colleague Trevor Royle. Royle writes widely on the Middle East and is author of a well-received biography of *Glubb Pasha* (1992) who worked with the difficult father of Raja Shehadeh as Commander of the Arab Legion.

In his solo spot Grossman was equally meditative, even melancholic but always eloquent. He felt events had moulded him as "an armoured suit without a person inside. I need to be able to write about the person inside". Then in one of the bleakest moments, he talked of imminent conflict. "Because we are fighting another nation we deprive ourselves of understanding the other side and if we continue to cut ourselves off from an understanding there can be no peace, no knowledge of peace." Then, as if remembering his designated role as author, "In fiction we must understand the other totally".

The second Sunday opened with a sedate stroll into the past with Allan Massie and George Rosie. Excavation was their common theme. Massie has departed from the Romans to explore the Dark Ages. His matrix is Michael Scott, magician and Borders balladeer. As ever he makes the conjuring tricks of myth become a practical tale for the present. Rosie went abroad to tell of the 19th century Cherokee Indian John Ross. It was a great start to a Sunday without sermons.

My responses to the celebratory commemoration for John McGrath were mixed. My anger at the way he was side-lined during his lifetime was diluted by the genuine affection he engendered among this audience. Still I do remember (ref. *Chapman* 97) how his articulate attack on the Scottish media was ignored by many who were now exhorting his worth.

The final week got off splendidly with poets Stewart Conn, Allan Riach and Tom Pow under the consistently good chairmanship of Diane Hope. She joined the poets not only in a tribute to David Daiches who was in the audience but also led spontaneous applause in memory of George Bruce who had spoken memorably here the previous year.

Then came another of those moments, or more literally hours, that reinforce the value of Book Festival. Baroness Mary Warnock spoke of her 20 year championship of IVF. More pertinently, she charted the knowledge she had gained from over thirty years in clinical practise in a central London hospital. Individuals, couples and families touched by her humane approach to *Making Babies* (her most recent publication) are indeed fortunate. Clearly and concisely she focused on problems such as embryo experimentation, its 14 day legal limitation, and the moral dilemmas surrounding abortion. She dismissed, with just a hint of impatience, tabloid hysteria and the pomp of religious dictates that hinder rational debate. She demanded open screening and sensible financing for investigation into genetic diseases and AIDS. Artificial insemination for Lesbians was given a moral dimension in quietly witty fashion: "It won't affect the general pattern if we have a few eccentric families". Though uneasy about human cloning, and anxious that further research be first assimilated, she concluded that "there is nothing outrageous about discussing its morality in the present or as a fertility aid in the future".

My day had begun with a splendid reading by Matthew Fitt, Ron Butlin and John Herdman (with an appreciative Irvine Welsh in the audience). Then came Ian Rankin's reading from the new novel to be launched during Festival 2003. The opening sentences are: "There is no mystery. Herdman's lost his marbles". Ian himself almost lost his when, after his morning slot and signing session, he interrupted his well-deserved lunch to attend an alleged interview set up by those in the Pod. No BBC interviewer emerged. A justifiably-irate author had choice things to say about "organisers", "breweries" and "piss-ups" in the Oxford later on. It is not wise to antagonise and fail to apologise to Mr Rankin in such circumstances.

More unfortunate programming meant missing Blake Morrison to listen to the incomparable Jim Crace whose undimmed

Socialism motivates his every appearance. Ostensibly he was reading from his bitter-sweet novel on avarice *The Devil's Larder*. In reality he gave a moral lecture punctuated by acerbic humour on the failure of political nerve when conscience dictates against greed. Powerful and necessary stuff.

Briefly I heard Colm Toibin read from *The Master,* a novel concerning Henry James and the opening night (and failure) of his play *Guy Dormville*. An added quixotic touch was to learn that the great prose-minimalist was an early user of the term "blockbuster". In the audience for Toibin (and a disappointing Zoe Strachen) was Canadian Alistair MacLeod. He later read from a new novel set in a lighthouse. This most charming of men remarked "writing is a solitary profession. Sending things out is like messages in bottles, hoping they'll wash up somewhere ... it's nice when people pick them up".

I yield to few in my admiration for Harold Pinter as a playwright. He is a long-time hero since 1956 when I first saw him as a spear-carrier in *Julius Caesar* at the Savoy Theatre Limerick. I was 11. However, while Arthur Miller is still around he is not "the world's greatest living dramatist". With writers like Churchill and Wesker still writing, he is not "the only English playwright of worth". In his much publicised and recorded Edinburgh appearance, he did not say anything new or unexpected. Both organisers and bemused Scottish press should cut the hyperbole and listen to what he had to say a few weeks later when he spoke with Michael Billington at the London Film Festival. There, thanks to intelligent and probing questions, he was at his revelatory best. Not in Edinburgh, where mere presence can be elevated to ridiculous pitch. Two years ago the same excitable Australian who faced Pinter sent the ebullient Norman Mailer into a Pinteresque pause when she questioned him on his "manliness". Pinter himself may have raised an eyebrow when similarly challenged before going on to deliver an obviously prepared text.

On the final day I contacted 25 people who, since 1997, have filled in a simple questionnaire dealing with that year's Book Festival – writers, publishers and members of audiences. With some of them I had enjoyed James Robertson, Des Dillon and Donny O'Rourke at the last Celtic Writers for Breakfast slot. They were not so sanguine about a similar all-Scots occasion earlier. One comment read "After a morning of Scots writers, where the dour became a grumble, I remembered Alan Sharp's line on the Scots collectively. It was after the World Cup in Argentina in 1978. 'Eleven is clearly too many Scots in one place. Three should be about the limit. Any more you're asking for trouble' (from a Scot in exile)". My favourite press line came from Ninian Dunnett in *The Scotsman* enthusing (I think) of "poets and novelists of understated demeanour".

If the Book Festival is to reclaim qualitative merit rather than offer quantitative statistics, it must recognise areas to be improved. Eighteen of my correspondents wrote about the "divisive" and "clumsy" programming. Nine found the same "too fussy". Eleven complained of being "pushed around", "hassled", "bloody well primped up for photographers" and as one somewhat overwrought poet said "fed up of being whored about". Among the public there was an ominous consistent criticism of Chairs and misinformation. In the end all, without exception, spoke warmly of at least one highlight and the overall impression I got from them, as opposed to the press commentators, was of a deeply flawed but immensely enjoyable experience.

My own conclusion. Gratitude to *Chapman* for allowing me this opportunity both to question and praise at this length. The sublime moments far outnumbered the fractious occasions. Moments of irritation became nonsensical blips when one focused on the great moments mentioned here. The intellectual challenge that is Book Festival sustains it for me as *the* event of the Summer. Pace it better, Ms Lockerbie, and you will ease the heart to where the mind is biddable.

Hayden Murphy

Theatre Roundup

It's not only *Chapman* that's celebrating milestones. In 2002-3 Scottish theatre has several. It's 60 years since Bridie's Citizen's opened its doors in Glasgow's Gorbals. 40 years since the Traverse set up in the Lawnmarket and 30 years since 7:84 Scotland started taking theatre to halls and improvised stages, large and small all over Scotland.

It's not been easy for any Scottish companies to continue to survive and create. The financial climate has been variable and sometimes harsh, with frequent numbing dark days where nothing shines out. Sudden unexpected weeks of settled sun, where optimism and feeling all is possible, too soon suffer high winds of change and adversity.

It is hard to grow a crop of full blooded culture when the winds keep changing and the accountants and measurers are always in the fields. The consumers of the crop can find the fare they like replaced by the synthetically engineered product. Raised for the funders' table who wants them extraordinary enough to catch the media's eye.

In the Citz for over 30 years we have had three outstanding directors Giles Havergal, Robert David MacDonald and Philip Prowse. Directors who have in translating, staging and designing for productions, often classical and European plays, kept reminding Scotland that it is part of the world. They have been criticised for drawing from abroad, even England, not using Scottish actors or doing enough Scottish material. But a nation which looks only at itself is in danger of endlessly self-parodying. It's not enough acknowledged by funders that creative people do their best work when they do what stimulates them rather than respond to a political correctness.

With the Citizen's looking for a new directive team this theatre will change but I hope they will continue to use all three spaces. In autumn 2002 Robert David MacDonald's version of Racine's *Britannicus* took verse and strong themes and recreated them using the English language in passionate formal verse, we have been well served over the years by MacDonald, a translator of intellectual and instinctive heart.

Also at the Citizens Mark Thomson, director apparent for the Royal Lyceum, used the smallest space, the Stall Studio, to direct his new 3-hander play *Pleasure and Pain*, a dramatisation of Guy de Maupassant's life and writings. In the tight space John Kazac was intense and rousing. While Thomson's script brought together real and imagined life and achieved making dramatic the largely invisible life of a writer. Maupassant's struggles are much the same as ours, the trials of being overlooked or dismissed or the perils of being feted as society's cultural darling.

Meanwhile upstairs in the Circle studio Mary McCluskey, Artistic Director of Scottish Youth Theatre, directed a professional adult cast in Stuart Thomas's new play, *Damned Jacobite Bitches*. Charlie's perhaps significant women gathered for a dinner and snarl and scrap like feral cats over their part in Charles's uprising and protracted departure. Cut between these scenes we got the Bonny Prince back in France entertaining the French King at Versailles with rather a different slant on his and their past.

Apart from Flora, who "would have done the same for any man", these women behave like bitches as they snipe with insults. The Charlie of the shortbread tin and romantic memory has been replaced by the weakling young pretender, for some the bastard version. Thomas's play is a useful, entertaining examination of a historical myth and worth publishing. It echoes with modern resonances as the women struggle to understand their changing Scotland – as we do now.

7:84 Scotland are a company who try to keep a challenging, often political brief. In the days of Thatcher's scything attacks on society the company nearly disappeared (as 7:84 England did). Nicola McCartney's *Cavedwellers* was premiered and toured by them in Spring 2002. Three people wait on an unnamed shore for a boat to freedom, the scenes between them intercut by monologues from another man who seems to have escaped with them. Played by Liam Brennan, this character fascinates as he responds to questions from unseen questioners. Who he is, a refugee, survivor or trafficker in human cargo, is never clear. But the dire situation of needing and seeking asylum comes through in him so strongly that the others stories become irritating diversions from his and Brennan's powerful presence. In 2003 7:84 will be one of many theatres and companies which will be welcoming new artistic teams. So Scottish theatre is in artistic change as well as the ongoing flux of stop-go funding.

Even without a formal Scottish National Theatre, companies do take work South and abroad. There is an increasing number of productions from touring and building-based theatres touring Scotland, including islands. The challenge of our geography and transport means that's no easy or cheap undertaking.

The Traverse continue to have notable success in getting their Festival plays and productions seen elsewhere. Sometimes these are co-productions with other UK companies. Co-production was also the case with *Helmet* by Douglas Maxwell early in 2002. Directed by John Tiffany, ex-Traverse Literary Director then with Helmet's co-producers, Plaines Plough. Set in a video shop, weedy Roddy aka Helmet, played by Tommy Mullins, plagues shop owner Sal, Ameet Chana. In the video games they play, and in their conversations the modern powerlessness of two young males is explored. The technical set had power bars framing the shop setting, the bars displaying who is winning not just the game but the power struggle between them. Created to appeal to a young audience, dealing with our lost males trapped in a world too constraining to escape from, it never got free of its technical, expensive production despite the two fine actors.

The next new play from the Traverse was *Green Field*, set in a new housing estate near Glasgow where the house-styles bear English names like The Derby. It deals with the dislocation of modern Scots. Jo's a woman who never now goes out except to the local hypermarket but loves Europe, her successful businessman husband Bill has no time for old things. Like them, guests Chris and Viv don't know how to live in the new Scotland.

There's some well-observed dialogue and interest as they try to relate to Bob, the guest who didn't escape his working class life. But it never develops a dramatic heart, or its TV play feel. The set changed from sitting room to bedroom to dining room and back, using huge sliding sections. But is there any real need for these concrete and expensive designs at the Traverse? They trap the writing more than release it.

Lastly at the Traverse, Ian F MacLeod's *Homers* directed by Philip Howard fulfilled the promise MacLeod showed in his Gaelic Highland Short *Alexander Salmandar* (1999 Traverse). It took place on a blissfully simple set. In 1967, two Glasgow orphans, the homers of the title, Mary and Alex are sent to live with a new family on an island. Until the late 1960s this happened to some Central Belt orphans. With a mix of Scots, Gaelic and Island English MacLeod's play is linguistically rich, showing how varied are our indigenous Scottish cultures. The children's uprooting and the different life of the islands revealed as they encounter the Gaelic speaking School mistress, the wise minister who loves Elvis and Andrena with her enthusiasms for Highland delicacies.

Mary fits into the island life but Ian finally pushes foster-father Calum too far and is dispatched back to Glasgow. There with Calum apprenticed to a brutish pork butcher, the production has a wonderful sequence when pigs run amok in the slaughter house. Played in fast-moving, generous and funny style, MacLeod's text is full of lively light touches and makes one eager for his next play and distinctive approach to Scottish diversity.

At Edinburgh's Royal Lyceum premiered Liz Lochhead's *Miseryguts*, a Scots version of Molière's *Le Misanthrope* – a really gutsy verse play set in today's Scotland, stuffed with recognisable contemporary references. The audience revelled in her puncturing the puffed-up New Scot and his attempts to be a big Haddie in the North. The cast was headed up by Jimmy Chisholm as the disenchanted presenter Alex Frew and John Kielty as the most accurate portrait of young Oscar Scougall, Scottish poet on the make. As a media cultural reviewer Janette Foggo's Zoe Arnott was a wonderful mixter-maxter of several prominent female critics. The only shame of this play is that in 50 years the text, now published with her *Tartuffe*, will need footnotes.

Premiered by Lyceum Youth Theatre and directed by Steve Small, *Big Country* by Tim Primrose, also a member of this group, was staged at the Traverse. Set on a hill above a small Scottish town, young people gather to while away their leisure hours. All but one are Scots, the drama developing through its very recognisable characters. One is a recently arrived English girl who encounters that racialism we try to pretend we don't have. Sometimes comic, sometimes troubling Primrose's third play for this talented group shows he can handle a full length play with a variety of themes.

In the Old Fruitmarket in Glasgow Gerry Mulgrew devised and directed *Brave*, a co-production between Communicado and Sounds of Progress. It took the story of the Cherokee, a settled Indian tribe who had a half-Scottish tribal chief, and their 1000 miles trek. With an unspoken strong echo of our own Scottish diasporas, chilling songs, extraordinary images (and occasional lecturing moments), its promenade took us into a terrible past where cultures and peoples clung to the wreckage of their displacement.

Suspect Culture tried to give us *Lament*. In contrast to *Brave* it looks at our here and now and the lost thirty-somethings who mourn for their youth and their lost direction. Some in that age group it visibly moved and spoke to. But for others, and especially for people of an older age-group, this devised work with text by David Greig, directed by Graham Eatough, speaks of that generation's vacuous inability to get really stuck into life and grow up. Lament is too powerful a word for their small dilemmas.

Running Girl from Boilerhouse was an extraordinary promenade production with Kate Dickie running and acting throughout. Her character trying to discover why she was running through the night streets encountering a traffic accident, a preacher and a man about to jump. Using huge moveable video screens with preshot scenes and a running machine, it merged video with theatre and produced a near-exhilarating effect.

Up in Pitlochry John Clifford's *Queen of Spades* was a rare chance to see a play by this internationally appreciated playwright. Directed by Patrick Sandford and staged using *periaktoi* to change the settings it richly took us to Russia as revolution rose. Based on Puskin's story, it has Tchaikovsky's real life patron Nadezhda von Meck as the Countess while the composer finds himself looking on in her opulent rooms able only to talk to us. Speaking through Tchaikovsky, her Scots speaking Russian servants and several members of Russian society and army, Clifford's play lights not only those times but the Scottish present and the role of the artist. Containing these layers with flair and inventiveness the play is very theatrical and dramatic, though the first production was marred by one actor who lacked its 'out-there' style.

I've concentrated on new work, but 2002 had many other productions of note. Particularly Howard Barkers' *Victory* at the Lyceum, the most outstanding production of the year, directed by Kenny Ireland. My concern remains though that companies large and small find it still hard to plan ahead with certainty, and that too many playwrights find few opportunities to create. Some insecurity can be a spur to creativity, too much and innovation and spirit go into decline.

Thelma Good

Published Texts

Britannicus trs Robert David MacDonald, Oberon Books 2002; *Helmet* by Douglas Maxwell, Oberon Books 2002; *Highland Shorts*, Traverse Theatre 1999; *Homers*, Ian F MacLeod, *Miseryguts* and *Tartuffe*, Liz Lochhead, Nick Hern Books 2002.

Pamphleteer

Pamphlet publishing continually seems to be as fertile in quantity as in quality – there is definitely a lot to choose from out there. Shoestring Press brings us four passionate poetry issues, somewhat different in their nature and inspiration (19 Devonshire Avenue, Beeston, Nottingham, £4.00 each). In *Imagining Dr Minor,* John Gohorry explores the three-verse stanza formula, providing the reader with an account of an imprisoned man's fictional impressions. There is a continuous investigation of the relationship between the enclosed space where the character (addressed by means of a very powerful 'you') is trapped, and the outside world to which the titles of the poems refer. Despite the historical and veridical nature of Dr Minor (presented to us in a small introduction), the pamphlet's title is underlined by the poet's belief that "each text/ is a doorway through which we pass into its author's thought". *Imagining Dr Minor* is undoubtedly enriched by Jone Delahaye's impressive linocuts of haunted and distorted faces – when combined with the compelling text, this is a striking work which will linger long in the mind.

In *No Age*, a somewhat more introspective pamphlet, Peter Carpenter certainly shows how one can come to terms with one's existence (past and present) through verse. Without being confessional, Carpenter's poems are violent and disturbing in each image. Inspired by day-to-day occurrences, they display the abruptness and the uncanny side of life itself. After reading this, Sunday afternoons will never be the same again. Shoestring Press also gives us the opportunity to discover two female voices of unusual sensitivity. Sheila Smith's *Chalk and Cheese* is a very personal exploration of one's own sentimentality and the legacy left by previous years on one's perception of the present. This enquiry into the influence of days past on current events is a predominant element in this collection of poems. At one stage Smith uses the expression 'foretell the past', suggesting the unknown repercussions of the episodes she tries to come to terms with. The diverse motifs are interwoven by an equal diversity of bodies, faces and 'languages'. And fortunately for us the poet is constantly trying to make sense of it all. Despite (or perhaps because of) all the swirling phenomena, readers are almost certain to greatly enjoy the end product. *Saltings* collects poems from Annabel Luery or, better said, it assembles strange evocations whose subjective origins remain deeply secret to the reader. But it is precisely because no names or identities are given to the female subjects that the language has room to express the crucial human relations involved. Beyond the illusionary use of first and third person, Luery builds the foundations of some very intense (auto?)biography, deeply affected by seawater and the weight of death. An admirable collection of verse deserving of a thorough exploration.

Mariscat Press takes us on a journey with *On a Roll: A Jena Notebook* by Donny O'Rourke (3 Mariscat Road, Glasgow, £5.00). Scottish poet, editor and translator, O'Rourke acknowledges here the extremely inspiring effect of the small East German town of Jena. The collection's inner structure somehow resembles that of an intimate diary, in which, although drawn from a common experience, the poems are as diverse in form as they are in mood and expression. Overall a very personal, not to mention affecting, journey through the birth city of German Romanticism. *In India* (Selkirk Lapwing Press, 1 The Glebe, Selkirk, £3.00) is the title of Robert Leach's poem in seven parts. Joy Parker's admirable linocuts all throughout the pamphlet make it a very pleasant illustrated trip through a land of myth and solemnity. Despite the variety of language adopted (descriptive, purely lyrical and sometimes almost mystic), one might feel the poem is overpopulated with references that only someone perfectly informed of "the colliding montage that is/ India" can fully grasp. Yet it leaves the reader wondering what more you can ask from poetry.

Moving on to a different level, you don't have to be a cat lover in order to enjoy Douglas Clark's poetry pamphlets *Cat Poems* and *Kitten Poems*(The Benjamin Press, 69 Hillcrest Drive, Bath, £5.00 each). Beyond the animal as both object of detailed observation and source of amazement, Clark lets another voice be heard: the voice of anguish when faced with his disease, sometimes even the voice of sorrow: "All I can say is/ Thank God you only live once". *Cat Poems* is the story of Fritz Cat's existence, told in a series of episode-poems until his sad death. Language becomes a strange sort of permanent tribute to that furry companion: "He was a famous cat,/ Known throughout the world due to the poems". *Kitten Poems,* besides a vivid account of Marty's (the kitten) first adventures, has in 'Biotext', 'Discharged' and 'Old' the most striking compositions of the lot. The title and the cover photograph would never suggest the presence of such violent texts as these.

Winner in the Poetry Business Book & Pamphlet Competition 2000, Robert Hamberger's *The Rule of the Earth* (Smith/ Doorstop Books, The Poetry Business, The Studio, Byram Arcade, Westgate, Huddersfield, £3.00) is no ordinary collection of love poems. Without reflecting abstractly on the condition of love and of being in love, these one strophe poems seek to understand it with the help of life's unique and overwhelming moments: the gestures, the words/ confessions, the weight of adversity, the time spent together. In Hamberger, the reader finds a continuous awareness of the crucial elements in the bond between the two beings: "The pressure of your fingers can insist/ This is what matters: us. Here. Today." One of the best poetry pamphlets in recent times – a steal for three quid. From the same publishers and for the same price, it is worth spending a quiet hour exploring both Tim Dooley's *The Secret Ministry* and Bob Cooper's *Pinocchio's Long Neb*. There is a certain vagueness in Dooley's words, supported by quite a variety of structures and a very insightful contact with reality. On the other hand, Cooper's verse contains someone's observations (his own?) of the way life's trivialities work in one's inner life. It is the kind of work that poeticises common life and people, rather than vulgarising poetry's content. Cooper's compositions are filled with human characters that somehow appear to us to be more than motifs in a poetry book. Although about everyday events, this is far from an everyday book. Warning: contains explicit and disturbing language.

Numbers 20 (*The Familiar*) and 21 (*Godhead*) of the Peppercanister series by the Irish Thomas Kinsella (distributed by Carcanet Press, 4th Floor Conavon Court, 12-16 Blackfriars Street, Manchester) are purely for the enjoyment of intimate poetry. The title poem in *Godhead*, for example, is an impressive account of a personally experienced Holy Trinity. In *The Familiar,* Kinsella's words do not simply relate to emotions or recall a given instant. The juxtaposition of words as imprecise concepts, and some of the short verse used, reflect timid yet courageous attempts to handle what seems to be bigger than language itself. The size of the pamphlets is not at all in proportion to the dimension of the poet's awareness.

Akros Publications (33 Lady Nairn Avenue, Kirkcaldy, Fife) have selected and republished some of Tessa Ransford's poetic work and the result is three pamphlets entitled *Scottish Selection, Indian Selection* and *Natural Selection*. Founding director of the Scottish Poetry Library, Ransford is the sort of author whose biography may contribute to a clearer reading of her work. The first two titles refer to the two geographical, cultural and emotional territories essential to Ransford's identity: "India and Scotland are entwined like a Kashmir shawl round my life", reveals the poet in a small introductory statement to *Indian Selection*". The *Scottish Selection* is much more descriptive than the *Indian Selection*, the latter containing intense reflections on one's (torn?) identity. There is somehow a need to belong or at least to recognise some place of origin: "Let me reclaim/ myself. I cannot/ be curtailed." *Indian Selection* also includes excerpts from Ransford's letters to her parents during more than eight years' stay in Pakistan. *Natural Selection* is, as the title suggests, a tribute to nature and its calling. These poems embody a profound effort of unification with the natural world which cannot but affect the reader.

Two good contributions to the proliferation of Scots are to be found in from pamphlets by John Mason, both brought to us by Markings (1 Longacres Road, Kirkcudbright, £2.00). *Malevitch in Edinburgh* is Volume 9 in the Galloway Poets series and *Frae Glesca til Manila* is an admirable work of translation into Scots (as we are informed, the translations "reflect the language of the north coast of Caithness"). Mason, who in 1995 was the first recipient of a Scottish Arts Council bursary for translation, handles 20th century European and Latin-American poets such as Cernuda, Montale, Manuel Bandeira, Henri Michaux and Vallejo (whose caricature fills the cover of the pamphlet).

In another moment of remarkable inspiration, Robert Belcher has himself published *Out with the Tide.* It is certainly not easy to describe this poetry pamphlet, mostly due to the multiple sides of the poet's perception of things and people. There are landscapes with and without humanity and people's eyes filled with landscape; there is the "horizontal spell" (neutrality of feeling) of those 'Flat Days' whether it is a 'Sunday Afternoon Walk' or a 'Saturday Afternoon in the Light Room'; and there is plenty of body contact disguised in words. However, remarkably enough, Belcher's diversity of paths finds its consistency in that one tireless voice: "I imagine an end to feeling", though the reader experiences a great deal of emotion and we should all be glad for it.

Readers who are in the habit of climbing or 'bagging' Scotland's most demanding mountains will surely identify with Gordon Jarvie's intense landscapes in his *Climber's Calendar* (Hapercroft Books, 81 Comiston Drive, Edinburgh, £2.50). The poems reveal an overwhelming perspective of the relationship between nature's magnitude and man's reverence toward it. Jarvie composes his short verse in extremely honest emotional language often as raw and challenging as the mountains themselves. The *Climber's Calendar* contains one year of unique impressions, acknowledging the weight of the mountain's Gaelic names in a similar fashion to Tessa Ransford's 'Viewpoint' (in the aforementioned *Scottish Selection*).

The final two pamphlets considered differ, at least in genre, from the ones mentioned above. *St Andrews Citizen: Homage to Dr Jean Paul Marat* (Aura, £4.00), is a surprising and varied collection of texts and illustrations in memory of one of the most controversial and mythical figures of the French Revolution. The book gathers texts from the editor Gavin Bowd, from the historian and philosopher Thomas Carlyle and also from *l'ami du peuple* Marat on himself. Rose Birrell's 'Death Scenes' bring the pamphlet to a dramatic and fitting conclusion. Also worth mentioning is *Seduction* by Frederick Lightfoot (Northern Lights, Cumbria City Council Cultural Services, Arroyo Block, The Castle, Carlisle). The pamphlet includes two short stories from a writer who proves to be just as gifted an observer of human behaviour as he is a storyteller. The first story is a flashback account of the days of clandestine activity in Salazarist Portugal prior to the democratic Revolution of 1974. Told in the first person, the 'subversive' plans of the forbidden Communist Party serve as the background to one man's self-discovery and self-affirmation. The second story, less attached to an identifiable context, is the 'seductive' depiction of the love and speech strategies between a man and a woman. Congratulations are more than due to Mr Lightfoot who has produced a diverse and diverting collection of work.

Joao Henriques

Catalogue

Edinburgh University Press continues the mighty task of reprinting James Hogg's complete works with *The Jacobite Relics of Scotland (First Series)* (EUP, £60.00). Reprinting the 1819 edition beautifully, this contains Hogg's notes and transcriptions of the Jacobite cause, along with additional editorial notes. Song titles such as 'Perfidious Britain' have gained a modern relevance – perfect for an SNP singalong. However, given that the price is as weighty as the tome, readers would have to think before buying it.

For those whose pockets are less deep, EUP also publishes a paperback version of the complete works. In the latest batch: *The Private Memoirs and Confessions of a Justified Sinner* (£8.99), *Three Perils of Woman* (£9.99), *The Shepherd's Calendar* and *Tales of the Wars of Montrose* (both £8.99). The last is especially worth mentioning since it corrects the many errors in the first edition – one unrelated tale was included, for example, to bulk out the set to fit the then three-volume norm. Thanks must go to Dr Gillian Hughes, James Hogg Research Fellow at the Department of English at Stirling University, who went back to Hogg's manuscripts and restored the five-tale set to its original finery. However, every edition contains an extensive introduction and editorial notes with practically no stone left unturned. If you want to read Hogg, this is the place to start.

Talking of literary stars, Canongate seems on a mission to publish as many 'big' Scottish works as it can in its Canongate Classics series – Alasdair Gray's *Lanark* (£8.99); *Smeddum: A Lewis Grassic Gibbon Anthology* (ed Valentina Bold, £11.99); *The Canongate Burns* (eds Andrew Noble and Patrick Scott Hogg, £14.99) and *Sartor Resartus* by Thomas Carlyle (£7.99). *The Canongate Burns* enters with a fanfare, grandly declaring itself to be "the most comprehensive and challenging edition … ever published". The book is huge – 6 centimetres wide on the spine and over 850 grams in weight. It clearly fancies itself as the definitive Burns for the 21st century. All Rabbie's surviving jottings have been corralled into chronological order – you're surprised that his shopping lists aren't in there. Complete with a huge introduction and explanatory notes, this really provides everything you need (and some things you don't) about Mr Burns. But size can be intimidating as well as impressive – many readers who might enjoy his works in a new context could be put off.

Sartor Resartus jumps less wildly off the hyperbole meter, but has definite slow-burning pleasures. Through the veil of an academic spoof, Carlyle gleefully challenges and knocks down systems of beliefs, morals and symbols. Added to this destructive festival are the wonderfully dark and evocative drawings of Edmund Sullivan, which appeared in the 1898 edition. In a world obsessed with symbols (£, ©, Coca Cola etc.), his work is more relevant than ever.

As well as providing the introduction to *Sartor Resartus*, Gray's *Lanark* appears in its own right. Probably the most important late 20th century Scottish novel, this free-wheeling adventure tumbles through time, imagination and Glasgow. It simply demands to be read – as does *Smeddum: A Grassic Gibbon Anthology*. Collecting together Grassic Gibbon's short stories, poems and *The Speak of the Mearns*, his last novel never published during his lifetime. While many pieces are well-known, like the 'Scottish Scene' section, others will be new to many readers. A book to be read if all you know of Gibbon is *A Scots Quair*.

Almost a companion volume is the *Encyclopedia of Postmodernism* (eds Victor E Taylor and Charles E Winquist; Routledge; £75.00). With essays, critical terms and biographies spread over 466 pages, this is definitely something to be dipped into when in decontructionist mood. A sample entry – 'sublime' is defined as "the negative pleasure resulting from the mind's unsuccessful attempt to represent the infinite". A mind-expanding read for a mind-blowing price.

If you're feeling that postmodernism is a little expensive, philosophy, in the form of the *Concise Routledge Encyclopedia of Philosophy* (Routledge, £25.00), is a soothing alternative. With clear and accessible entries such as 'Indian and Tibetan Philosophy' filling in your knowledge outside of Socrates and Plato, this book is to be dined on in small morsels rather than guzzled in one sitting. Amaze your family with your knowledge of Luis de Molina ("a leading figure in 16th century Iberian scholasticism", do try and keep up), wow your work colleagues with aggressive deployment of Kierkegaard and confuse the hell out of bus drivers with epistemology.

Former star of *Chapman* 99 Rabindranath Tagore pops up in *Geddes Tagore: Correspondence* (Bashabi Fraser, ed); (Edinburgh Review, £5.99). Chronicling the letters that flew between Tagore and Patrick Geddes, this is a fascinating read. Geddes, previously best known for his work in ecology and town planning, reveals himself to be a keen cultural activist who strikes up an active (if unlikely) friendship with one of India's most eminent writers and thinkers. Writing about his plans for an International University for India, which would involve both academics and poets(!), Geddes revels in the planning and organisation, which would be set up on distinctly unorthodox lines. Bashabi Fraser, as a Bengali living in Scotland, was uniquely qualified for taking on such a project and carries it through with aplomb. Her illuminating introduction shows how she approached the task and sets out the background of this unusual cross-cultural interchange.

Also from Edinburgh Review is *Scotland 1802-2002: figures, ideas, formations* (£5.99). Celebrating 200 years of the *Edinburgh Review* (and quietly glossing over the fact that the first *Edinburgh Review* was in 1755), it is apparent that this is not really meant as an overview. Although there are the near-obligatory pieces from Macaulay, Hazlitt and Walter Scott, it sells its past a little short by not mentioning any early political material – its anti-slavery campaign, for example. To be fair, though, the pieces here ruminate usefully on the development of Scottish writing – Trevor Royle on the myth of the Scottish soldier, Ronald Turnbull on Tom Nairn's contribution to political philosophy and Donald Ross on the practicality of being a working writer in Scotland today. Due to editorial distance, we cannot analyse Ross's story fairly as there is a starring role for *Chapman* as he tries to convince his Jobcentre that he has been working by showing his contribution to the latest issue!

Scottish Literature (eds Douglas Gifford, Sarah Dunnigan and Alan MacGillivray; EUP; £24.99) is reassuringly broad-brushed – at over 1000 pages, there is much to take issue with. While Burns and Scott are given entire chapters to roam around in, Hamish Henderson is dispatched in passing mentions and women novelists from 1911-1947 are lumped together in 24 pages to mention a few contentious decisions. Part of the problem must stem from the fact that it is neither fish nor fowl: "his volume tries to … steer between a thorough-going literary history and itemised companion", as the introduction has it. It goes into detail, but cherry-picks names – often leaving writers devoid of the context in which they were writing. An interesting read, if only because you'll want to pick a fight with the editors afterwards.

A Companion to Twentieth-Century Poetry (ed Neil Roberts; Blackwells; £80.00) truly has a price to make your eyes water – for the money, the reader needs something quite spectacular. A bit of a misnomer from the start – only English allowed, so goodbye Neruda, MacLean and co – the book solidly covers the bases: themes, movements, international poetry in English, readings of various notables and so on. Although the writing is often resoundingly academic – a dictionary will be handy for non-professors – it at least begins to address the problem of how to tackle 20th century poetry, if only on a fairly narrow front. One major flaw though: too few women!

Edmund O'Connor

Chapman

4 Broughton Place, Edinburgh EH1 3RX, Scotland
Tel 0131–557 2207 Fax 0131–556 9565
E-mail: chapman-pub@blueyonder.co.uk
Website: www.chapman-pub.co.uk

Editor: Joy Hendry
Assistant Editor: Edmund O'Connor
Volunteers: Shona Adam, Kristina Goetz,
Joao Henriques, Mike Stocks, M Jane Taylor
Special thanks: Angus Calder, Stuart Kelly, Colin Mackay, Heather Scott

Information about the contributors is available on request

ISBN 1-903700-06-X ISSN 0308-2695 © Chapman 2003

Chapman

Subscription Rates

	Personal		Institutional	
	1 year	2 years	1 year	2 years
UK	£18 (£13 conc*)	£34	£24 (£18 conc**)	£45
Overseas	£24/ $38	£45/ $70	£30/ $45	£52/ $84

Single issues £6 inc P&P
* Applies to students, DSS, etc
** Applies to writers' groups and similar artistic organisations
US Dollar cheques, and Donations to help the work of Chapman welcome.

Submissions:

Chapman welcomes submissions of poetry, fiction and articles which ***must*** *be accompanied by SAE or International Reply Coupons*

Production: Scotprint, Gateside Commerce Park, Haddington, East Lothian